Links to the Past

The Hidden History on Texas Golf Courses

Dan K. Utley

With Stanley O. Graves

TEXAS A&M UNIVERSITY PRESS College Station

This paper meets the requirements
of ANSI/NISO Z39.48-1992
(Permanence of Paper).
Binding materials have been chosen for durability.
Manufactured in the United States of America.

Library of Congress Cataloging-in-Publication Data

Names: Utley, Dan K., author. | Graves, Stanley O., author.
Title: Links to the past: the hidden history on Texas golf courses / Dan K.
    Utley with Stanley O. Graves.
Description: First edition. | College Station: Texas A&M University Press,
    [2018] | Series: Swaim-Paup sports series | Includes bibliographical
    references and index. |
Identifiers: LCCN 2018016696 (print) | LCCN 2018022436 (ebook) | ISBN
    9781623496432 (ebook) | ISBN 9781623496425 | ISBN
    9781623496425q (hardcover: qalk. paper)
Subjects: LCSH: Golf courses—Texas—History. | Historic sites—Texas. |
    Texas—History, Local. | Texa—Environmental conditions.
Classification: LCC GV975 (ebook) | LCC GV975 .U95 2018 (print) | DDC
    796.35206/8764—dc23
LC record available at https://lccn.loc.gov/2018016696

To Festus John Utley Jr.,
who loved sports and good stories,
and to Rufus John Graves,
who instilled in his son an appreciation
for the game of golf and for
history where it happened.

Publication of *Links to the Past* is generously supported by Mark Philpy '77 and Sarah Philpy '84, who wish to dedicate this book to all golfers, especially small-town Texas players who have a keen sense of their surroundings while attempting to play a rewarding yet humbling game. Such small local courses provide not only recreation but also social interaction, leading to lifelong friendships and the understanding that "it's not about the score."

These courses honed the skills of many who play the "barbecue tour," who, though in position for victory, invariably "spit the bit" at a most inopportune time, only to move on down the road and do it all over again the next weekend. Thus, this book is also dedicated to these tourists in the "Royal Union of the Choking Dogs." May the ever-elusive victory eventually cross their paths.

CONTENTS

PREFACE

his is a book about golf and about history, but it is not a golf history book per se. Instead, it is an exploration of eighteen sites that collectively represent a continuum of the Texas past, from prehistoric times to World War II, with a common modern element being that all are now overlain by golf courses. This is primarily a site-based interpretation of history where it happened prior to more recent recreational development. Stories are brought up to date to include the courses and their designs and evolution, but the emphasis is always on the past. The general concept is that history has occurred all around us and not just in historic districts, state parks, house museums, or even where official state markers might be found. Some of the places where notable events played out now serve other functions, and a few of those are now the domain of golfers, many of whom have no idea of the hidden heritage of the grounds they walk.

The idea for this book grew out of the association of two colleagues—one a historian and the other an architect—for many years as staffers with the Texas Historical Commission. While golf was regrettably not part of our official duties, we occasionally found time to play a few rounds across the state, though never frequently enough to move us out of the duffer category. As we traveled, partnering on myriad preservation projects and occasionally golfing far away from our homes in the Austin area, we frequently heard interesting stories—some of them true, it turned out—about the local history associated with the courses we played. As a result, we sometimes joked about how our divots, which we created with special long-handled trowels commonly known as woods, irons, and wedges, could potentially prove damaging, not only to buried features but also to our reputations as preservationists.

We have not played all the courses included in this book, although that was our initial intent. New professional endeavors for each of us got in the way and took us in different directions, but we maintained our mutual interest in golf and the possibility of a book collaboration someday. Sadly, some of the courses we originally envisioned for this guide are no longer in operation, having faded away just as many others have across the nation in recent years due to outdated layouts, increased maintenance costs, rising land values, and changing social trends in outdoor recreation. The first course we played together in 2000, at Aquarena Springs in San Marcos, falls into that category, as do about a half-dozen others we considered. As some dropped off the list, others came to our attention, and we kept moving forward to the point where we had eighteen sites that fit our criteria.

Our overarching goal is to talk about Texas history in a new way, one that we hope will be fun and enlightening. We have endeavored to cover a lot of ground, both historically and geographically. Our book is not designed to be comprehensive, but rather representative; there are still many similar stories out there waiting for others to explore—and maybe also to commemorate and interpret for future generations. To that purpose, we hope this will serve as a call for preservation and for the promotion of heritage education. Reminding others that "history happened here" and "this site matters" are fundamental tenets of how Texans pass along our collective story. If we can have a little fun along the way, so much the better.

Fore!

ACKNOWLEDGMENTS

There are likely many parallels between golf and writing, but one that comes quickly to mind is the adage that once a golfer steps up to address a ball, no matter the lie, there are only a few hundred things to remember between the start of the backswing and the final contact. In microcosm it is what makes the game challenging, frustrating, exhilarating, perplexing, and sometimes enjoyable. As a friend of ours notes, though, if you enjoy the game, you are probably not doing it right. Still, countless numbers of people venture out every day to take on the links and try to overcome the odds. In that vein we embarked on this project with the understanding that, despite the odds and everything we had to remember as we got started, we had a unique and untested game plan that might get us all the way through the research and writing and allow us to have a good adventure as well. As our game plan unfolded, we encountered scores of individuals who provided encouragement and support, and without that gallery urging us on, we could not have prevailed. We herewith endeavor to remember and recognize some of those who were particularly helpful, recognizing that there are no doubt many others whose names and contributions along the way have been lost in the fog of the fairways.

The first individuals who are due recognition include those who helped direct us to resources regarding the specific courses and historic sites included in the book. At San Felipe Springs in Val Verde County, for example, we appreciated the solid research of Del Rio historian Doug Braudaway and Austin archeologist Douglas K. Boyd. Farther up the Rio Grande Valley at El Paso, we relied on the work and recommendations of our friends historian Glen Sample Ely, chronicler of the Butterfield Trail, and preservationists Bernie Sargent and Gary Williams, who have set high standards for recording and commemorating local history. At San Felipe de

Austin there was the longstanding historical interpretive team of Superintendent Bryan McAuley, Texas Historical Commission, and researcher Michael R. Moore, and at College Station there was Mark J. Haven, associate director of Recreational Sports at Texas A&M University. T. Lindsay Baker, recently retired from Tarleton State University, and Sally Abbe of Lubbock provided important leads for the story of historic Yellow House Canyon. We also received important leads from golf professionals Jerry Busby in Hondo, Jimmy Metlen in Diboll, and Van Berry in Lampasas. Berry in turn directed us to longtime golfer Harold Harton, who had a wealth of knowledge about the local course. In San Antonio Harold Henk provided similar information about the Riverside course.

It was good to work again with Sylvia Stanford Smith, distinguished leader of the Ellis County Historical Commission, and we thank her for all the leads on the Ferris mules. Another valued friend we encountered along the way was Jonathan Gerland, director of The History Center in Diboll, and through him we enjoyed working with Emily Hyatt and Louis Landers of his team. In Lockhart we worked with still other friends, Texas Parks and Wildlife Department historian Cynthia Brandimarte and Caldwell County historian and archivist Donaly Brice. They in turn put us in touch with staff members of Lockhart State Park: Superintendent Austin Vieh, Assistant Superintendent Chris Dooley, and Office Manager Joanie Buch. We are also indebted to Steve Davis and Jimmy McWilliams, colleagues at Texas State University, for their advice. Importantly, Davis put us in touch with the celebrated playwright Celeste B. Walker, who graciously allowed us to quote passages from her play *Camp Logan*.

One of the smallest courses noted in the book, that at Menard, involved the largest number of research aides, in part because of the complexity of the underlying historical story. Not all were from the local area, but each helped uncover important pieces of the past. They included Jan P. Wilkinson, Dan Feather, Mark Wolf, Ray Rickard, and Terrell Kelley as well as City of San Antonio archeologist Kay Hindes and Texas Tech archeologist Tamra Walter.

Beyond the courses, we relied heavily on the kind assistance of staff from the Texas Historical Commission, where we worked for many years. On matters related to archeology and historic sites, we appreciated the aid and advice of Pat Mercado-Allinger, Jenny McWilliams, and Brett Cruse. Regarding historical markers and designations, we valued the help provided by Bob Brinkman, Sarah McCleskey, and Judy George-Garza.

In addition to all the research assistance, we relied heavily on a behind-the-scenes network of professionals who helped us diligently move the project forward to completion. Foremost for author Dan Utley were Lynn Denton and Mary Brennan, valued colleagues and supervisors at Texas State University. Their steady encouragement, research-time support, and wise counsel were vital and always appreciated. A second collegiate team worthy of recognition is the Texas A&M University Press. The authors, proud graduates of the University of Texas at Austin, offer the highest praise for the Aggie team, whose members have provided note-worthy, professional partnership. The press staff was with us each step of the way, from the initial concept to the final publication. We are indebted to all members of the team for their consummate work, but of particular note are Shannon Davies, press director; Jay Dew, editor in chief; and Thom Lemmons, senior editor. Of those we must single out Lemmons, who directly oversaw this project and gave an initial green light over cups of coffee in downtown Buda. We thank him for his unwavering support and encourage-ment each step of the way, even when the wheels occasionally wobbled on the authors' side of the equation. He worked with us as deadlines came and went, only to be replaced with new goals and solutions that moved us ever forward. We are truly grateful for the team of Lemmons and Dew for their positive thoughts and patience, their friendship, and all their great humor that tempered the toils and doubts. And finally, but not least, we acknowledge an adjunct member of the TAMU Press team, copyeditor extraor-dinaire Kevin Brock. It was truly enlightening working with him, and we appreciate all he did to make this a presentable text.

In Austin we once again relied on two tried-and-tested indi-viduals who stepped up to help with the illustrations. The first was the outstanding cartographer Molly O'Halloran, whose colorful maps grace the pages of this book to provide important locational information for readers. The second was longtime friend Cynthia Beeman, a consummate historian who stepped in near the end of the project to oversee the identification, collection, and captioning of photographs. Working with a wide variety of media, photographers, and collections, she provided significant focus on the task at a critical time, and we greatly valued her guidance, organizational skills, and good humor under pressure.

Aside from all the research, collecting, writing, and analyzing has been the solid support represented by our families. For their unquestioned love and uplifting spirit, we thank, above all, Debby Davis Utley and Diana and Owen Graves. We also remember a great woman, Rachel Owen Graves, who inspired both her son and her friend by leading an exemplary life rich in the preservation of Texas history where it happened.

These then are the individuals we cherish as our partners in this endeavor. While their names may appear only in this section, their influence is evident to us throughout the book. Thanks for being there in the gallery as we made our way down the courses. See you all at the nineteenth hole.

Links to the Past

THE FRONT NINE

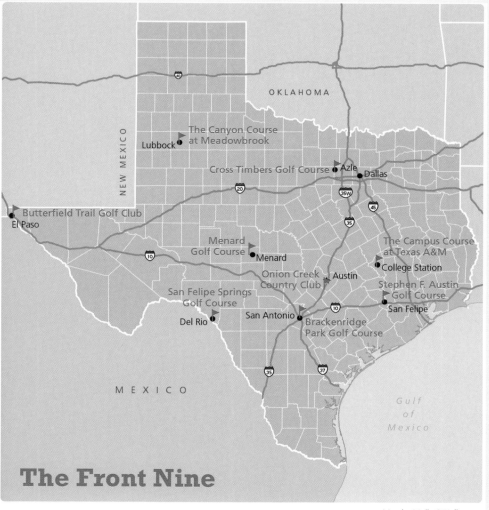

OKLAHOMA

NEW MEXICO

Lubbock

The Canyon Course
at Meadowbrook

Cross Timbers Golf Course • Azle
Dallas

Butterfield Trail Golf Club
El Paso

Menard
Golf Course
Menard

The Campus Course
at Texas A&M
College Station

Onion Creek
Country Club
Austin

Stephen F. Austin
Golf Course
San Felipe

San Felipe Springs
Golf Course
Del Rio

San Antonio

Brackenridge
Park Golf Course

MEXICO

Gulf
of
Mexico

The Front Nine

Map by Molly O'Halloran

1

LIZARDS TO LONGHORNS

ONION CREEK COUNTRY CLUB, AUSTIN

SCORECARD FROM THE PAST

Currently: Onion Creek Country Club

Historic Name: The prairies of Onion Creek

DETAILS: Private eighteen-hole golf course, redesigned in the 1980s, with an additional nine added in the 1990s; distance is 6,530 yards from the back tees

Location: 2510 Onion Creek Parkway, Austin

Historical Context: Geological landmark from prehistoric era to early Texas statehood

Historical Type: Stream crossing

Period of Significance: Seventy to sixty-five million years B.P. to the 1880s

Signature Hole of History: Number two, aligned on a north–south axis roughly following the historic route of El Camino Real and the Chisholm Trail, is a deceptive 131-yard downhill par-three hole with a bunker to the east of the green.

THE COURSE *OF* HISTORY

The natural setting of a region quite often influences the evolution of a cultural-landscape overlay, but the visual reminders of that transition during the period of significance can be transitory and problematic at best for those tasked with interpreting history. There are the encroachments of urban development, as with the Alamo in San Antonio and the San Jacinto battlefield at La Porte, which have obscured or even destroyed important historical fea-

A view of the third hole, the signature hole of history, with Onion Creek beyond. Photograph by Stanley O. Graves.

tures. The change can also be natural, though, as evident at the submerged battleground at Sabine Pass, where a state historic site now conveys a cultural horizon several feet above that of the Civil War–era event it commemorates. Some locations have been archeologically "ground-truthed," as in the case of Fort Saint Louis in Lavaca County, while others, such as the location of Thornton's Skirmish in Cameron County, which served as the flashpoint for the US–Mexico War of the 1840s, have yet to yield definitive, location-specific data. Still other historically significant landscapes are broader in scope and often traversed as part of larger events like westward migration or frontier lines of defense. Such is the case with a tributary south of Austin known as Onion Creek. Rising in eastern Blanco County, it flows through the counties of Hays and Travis before draining into the Colorado River in Bastrop County. Along the way, the creek cuts through blackland prairies and myriad stone outcroppings, forming steep-walled canyons and exposing fossil remains from the late Cretaceous period.

Geological and paleontological remains along Onion Creek provide evidence of ancient flora and fauna associated with a coastal environment from more than sixty million years ago. As noted paleontologist and University of Texas professor Wann Langston Jr. described it: "With what is now North America largely under water, the low-lying coastal regions from Texas to New Jersey were flooded, Florida did not exist, and water reached up the Mississippi Valley as far as southern Illinois. A wide seaway stretched from the Gulf of Mexico to the Arctic Ocean over what are now the plains and Rocky Mountain states and provinces of Canada." Further noting that there were no great mountain ranges or Great Lakes at the time, he added: "The seas were shallow, rarely more than 600 feet deep, and great quantities of fine mud entered them from the rivers. Thick deposits of limey mud and chalk formed in many places around the world. The chalk that forms the famed White Cliffs of Dover, as well as some of the white chalky rocks of Central Texas, were deposited at this time." The mud deposits and tidal pools ensnared coastal sea creatures of the era for posterity, providing rich deposits of ancient aquatic marine life that now provide textural character to local limestone. As dinosaurs roamed the land, life in the sea along the Texas shore of the era included, as Langston noted, "plesiosaurs, great fish-catching reptiles with broad flat bodies, short tails, long, almost snake-like necks, tiny heads, and huge flippers. There were giant sea turtles with shells five feet across. . . . Fishes were of more familiar appearance, but some were much larger than their surviving relatives. A kind of herring grew to a length of almost 15 feet. Skeletons of this Texas-sized 'kipper' have been found near Dallas, and one is on display in the Texas Memorial Museum [at the University of Texas at Austin]." Also displayed at the museum are the remains of another sea creature, one linked historically in name to the site of its discovery—the Onion Creek mosasaur.[1]

Related to monitor lizards found today in Asia and Africa, the Onion Creek mosasaur (*Mosasaurus maximus*) had a flattened tail and fins along with flippers that served as stabilizers as the animal swam in a "snake-like motion" through the sea. Langston, who studied this specimen carefully as he worked to assemble its intricate remains for display during the 1960s, provided a detailed account of the complex nature of these beasts' eating mechanism:

> Their heads were large, the jaws usually long, the teeth strong, pointed, and backwardly-curved, like rows of opposing hooks. In addition to this lethal pattern, some of the bones in the roof of the mouth also had teeth. The lower jaw was hinged loosely to the skull and there was a movable joint on each side just behind the teeth. The two halves of the jaw were only loosely connected, leading some paleontologists to believe that the mouth could be enlarged to permit the animal to swallow large, struggling prey. A means of 'walking' the food into the throat in the fashion of some present-day snakes may have been possible. Thus, while the hook-shaped teeth of one side held the prey firmly, the other half of the jaw moved forward, anchored its teeth, and then pulled back as the other side moved forward to repeat the process.

Understandably, early newspaper accounts of the Onion Creek mosasaur discovery referred to the creature's ferocity and portrayed it as a sea serpent or monster.[2]

In the millions of years that spanned the time from the mosasaur's miring in the coastal muds to its fossilized skeleton's eventual discovery in the early twentieth century, the land changed dramatically. The seas receded to the southeast and nearby uplifts reshaped the terrain, resulting in deeply eroded channels and exposed fault lines along the Balcones Escarpment. Records at the Texas Memorial Museum indicate that a crew on a weekend field trip with UT geologist Dr. Hal Bybee first came across evidence of fossil remains in the winter of 1923–24 but made no onsite collections. Among those assisting Bybee at the time was instructor Leonidas Theodore "Slim" Barrow, who would later become chairman of the board for the Humble Oil and Refining Company. It was not until 1935, though, that a more formal discovery occurred when two UT geology students, W. Clyde Ikins of Weatherford and John Peter Smith of Dallas, found fossil remains, including teeth, in the bed of Onion Creek. While this site is several miles down-

The Onion Creek mosasaur as displayed at the Texas Memorial Museum,
Austin. This animal once plied the waters above what is now the Onion Creek
Country Club. Photograph by Cynthia J. Beeman.

stream from Onion Creek Country Club, the abundance of fossil
evidence along the tributary is a strong indicator that mosasaurs
and similar creatures plied the coastal waters of the area during
the Cretaceous era.[3]

Ikins and Smith donated their findings to the Texas Memorial
Museum, which under the field leadership of Dr. H. B. Stenzel and
a team of professional paleontologists, conducted an extensive
excavation the following summer with assistance from the Public
Works Administration, part of Pres. Franklin Roosevelt's New Deal.
The work, both at the site and at the reassembly point in Gregory
Gymnasium on the UT campus, was tedious and time consuming
but continued at a steady pace to allow for public viewing during
the Texas Centennial in 1936. Unfortunately, as crews attempted
to move the massive skeleton and heavy pipe frame that fall, they
dropped it, resulting in extensive damage beyond immediate

DOBIE'S WHITE MUSTANG

In various publications, the noted Texas folklorist J. Frank Dobie chronicled early stories of a legendary and elusive wild white mustang that roamed the area south of Austin during the republic era. The following excerpt is from his essay "The Deathless White Stallion," originally published in 1954 as part of a collection compiled for the Texas Folklore Society:

While mustangs were still plentiful in all the prairie country, there appeared among them in the vicinity of what is now called McKinney Falls, on Onion Creek in Travis County, an extraordinary stallion. This was in the early 1840's. The animal had the markings of a pure-bred Arabian. His form was perfect; his alertness and vitality were superb. He was pure white. His tail brushed the tall mesquite grass that carpeted the earth, and his tossing mane swept to his knees. His only gait out of a walk was a pace, and it was soon found that he never, no matter how hard pressed, broke that pace. His *manada* or bunch of mares, normally numbered from fifty to sixty head—double the size of the ordinary mustang *manada*.

His favorite water place was on Onion Creek near the McKinney Falls, but he led his *manada* over a wide range, southwest across the Blanco, the San Marcos, and to the Guadalupe. It was known that he even at times ranged down as far as the Nueces, though this was not on his accustomed round. He kept clear of the timbers, never crossed the Colorado to the east, and did not range into the rocky cedar hills to the west; he seemed to like the rich mesquite grass of rolling country edging the blacklands themselves. His habits were closely studied. He was the most magnificent horse known between the Colorado and the Rio Grande, and many men, alone and in parties, tried to trap or walk down or otherwise catch him. . . . .

The White Stallion, no matter how chased, always in
time came back to the water of, and the mesquite grass
along Onion Creek.

Source: J. Frank Dobie, "The Deathless White Stallion," in *The Best of Texas Folk and Folklore*, 1916–1954, ed. Moady C. Boatright, William M. Hudson, and Allen Maxwell, Publications of the Texas Folklore Society 26 (Denton: University of North Texas Press, 1988), 107–8.

repair. The pieces went into long-term storage at UT's Vertebrate Paleontology Laboratory at the Balcones Research Center in north Austin, with only the mosasaur's skull on regular display in the museum, until funding in the 1960s led to the skeleton's restoration under the direction of Langston and his team. In the spring of 1965, the local newspaper reported that workers successfully transported the thirty-five-foot specimen, this time in "dismountable sections," to its new home in the museum, where finishing exhibit work on the more than three hundred bones took place in the great hall.[4]

Moving forward millions of years from prehistoric times to the historic era, the Onion Creek area south of present Austin once again served as a backdrop for the movement of beasts, although this time it was with the aid of humans who, geologically speaking, had only been on the land a relatively short time. Native Americans traversed the watershed and lived along its banks for millennia, leaving artifactual evidence of their existence, followed by Spanish explorers and missionaries who began crossing that section of northern Mexico along El Camino Real de los Tejas in the late seventeenth century. As noted in a National Park Service study of the trail corridor: "When Spanish explorers began to travel into Texas and western Louisiana in the 1680s, they followed already existing networks of American Indian trails. Representatives of the Spanish Crown used these paths to reach areas where they subsequently established missions and presidios. Eventually, armies and immigrants followed these routes, which led to Euro-American settlements across the two states." The route was not static over time, however, moving in various directions in a braided pattern to accommodate myriad factors, including environmental considerations as well as changes in transportation modes, settlement patterns, and Indian relations. As the route pushed farther north and east of San Antonio in service to the East Texas missions and later the frontier settlement of Los Adaes (in present Louisiana), the extension known as the Upper Road became a preferred route from the early 1690s to the 1800s. Passing through present New Braunfels and San Marcos, the trail crossed Onion Creek only a few hundred yards upstream from what is now the golf course before turning east toward the Spanish settlement at Nacogdoches.[5]

Skirting the Hill Country to the west and traversing reliable supplies of water, the historic north–south corridor continued as an important route of commerce and settlement as Texas changed throughout the colonial and republic eras to the time of statehood. Eventually, a more northerly route developed from Onion Creek with the establishment of the capital at Austin as well as other towns and cities beyond. With the shift in settlement to the west came a significant new purpose as a primary means of moving cattle to markets and rail lines outside Texas. Early efforts to exploit the vast feral herds of longhorn cattle along the South Texas range began in earnest during the republic era as drovers rounded up stock and headed north, where market demand for beef was exceedingly high. Defined more clearly beyond Austin, where the trail followed earlier existing routes, what came to be known as the Shawnee Trail was the primary means of bovine conveyance from the south by the 1850s. As trail historian Wayne Gard chronicled, it "led from the ranges of southern and southwestern Texas past Austin, Waco, and Dallas. On the north, it kept to the high prairies, skirting the post oak timbers." Traversing the Red River at the Red Bluff crossing near Preston, the route continued through the Indian Territory (present Oklahoma) and followed parts of the Osage Trail across southeastern Kansas and Missouri on its way toward Saint Louis or later market points farther west, including Independence, Westport, and Kansas City.[6]

The introduction of wild cattle proved detrimental to local livestock, however, due to a tick-borne illness referred to as splenic fever, hemaglobinuria, or protozoan cattle fever but known commonly as simply tick fever or Texas fever. While longhorns were immune to the disease, the parasites they hosted carried the infection that would decimate northern herds and lead to the closing of holding pens, shipping facilities, and even trails to Texas cattle. It also resulted in legislative measures to curtail the further introduction of such livestock. The threat ended, along with the cattle drives, during the Civil War. After that conflict, though, a burgeoning market for beef in the North reemerged with a concomitant opening of new rangeland. With antebellum routes no longer viable for transportation, the preferred route out of Texas became a more northerly trail established by Illinois cattleman Joseph G. McCoy in 1867, utilizing the Union Pacific railhead at Abilene, Kansas. As Gard noted: "The trail to Abilene was new only above the crossing of the Brazos River near Waco. Below, it followed the beaten paths of the Shawnee Trail. Some of the herds came from ranges along, or even beyond, the Rio Grande." Upon procurement of manageable herds, he added, drovers "trailed them northward through the brush country, either following the old Beef Trail past Beeville, Gonzales, and Lockhart to Austin or bending westward to San Antonio." From there "feeder trails came in from each side," and near Austin "the drovers took their herds across the Colorado River, most of them using the Montopolis ford, a little below the town." While the trail necessarily narrowed at such major stream crossings, it spread out much wider on the approaches, often covering miles to take advantage of available grasslands and the available water of small streams in the vicinity.[7]

Closer rail lines, including those that eventually reached into Texas, coupled with the opening of new trails to the west and the fencing of previously open lands eventually marked the end of the Chisholm Trail. Although there were sporadic drives north for a few years due to economic factors, the trail essentially ceased to function as a cattle-market route in the 1880s. As Gard observed, though, it left behind a remarkable historical legacy that changed the cultural landscape forever.

> [The Chisholm Trail] had spurred the settlement and stock-
> ing of the northern ranges. It had brought down the price of
> beef for the housewife and helped beef to displace pork as
> the chief meat item on the dinner table. It had hastened the
> building of Western railroads, had increased exports of beef,
> and had given impetus to the industries of meat packing and
> refrigeration.
>
> Too, the trail had brought together people from different
> sections of the country and thus helped to lessen the animos-
> ity left by the Civil War. It had shown Texas cowmen the need
> for improved breeds and had given them the means to bring in
> blooded stock, as well as to improve their ranches. And, like the
> Crusades of the Europeans in earlier centuries, the trail drivers
> had given thousands of young men an opportunity for adven-
> ture and had provided subjects for epic literature and art.[8]

Although millions of cattle made their way to northern markets over the Shawnee Trail–Chisholm Trail system, there are few remaining vestiges of the relatively short-lived enterprise. There have been efforts to mark many of the natural landmarks along the way, but much of the old trail remains too broadly aligned for proper interpretation. Much of the route now lies beneath modern highways, including Interstate 35, which crosses the Onion along the western edge of Onion Creek Country Club. Few travelers on the thoroughfare—or nearby golfers for that matter—have any idea of the important route they share with the past. For those duffers who are aware of the story, however, they can look south from the number-two tee box to gain some appreciation for the countless numbers of explorers, traders, missionaries, settlers, and cattlemen who headed in their direction over the centuries. As they tee off and watch the flight of their golf balls toward the green only a short distance away, they might also reflect on a time when giant sea lizards plied coastal waters extending far above the arc of their shots.

JIMMY AND JOHNNY

In a sport known for proper decorum and gentility, especially in the late 1940s and early 1950s, Jimmy Demaret stood out as a colorful and gregarious character. Although a natural athlete who garnered widespread attention for his impressive tournament wins in an era before the big professional purses, he was more than the "first-class second-rater" some perceived him to be. Still, he relied more on innate ability than on steady regimens of diet and exercise, choosing instead to parlay his celebrity and style into more-lucrative endeavors than golf and golf course design. He became a sought-after entertainer, both as a raconteur and a nightclub singer, and a television sports commentator. The following story about an appearance on *The Tonight Show* with Johnny Carson demonstrates his comedic timing, which endeared him to his many fans and followers. Asked by the late-night host to analyze his swing, Demaret had Carson take a practice swing. As Nick Seitz wrote originally in *Golf Digest*,

> Carson swished a club through the air and looked at him expectantly. Demaret thoughtfully stroked his chin and moved around on Carson's other side.
>
> "Swing again," said Demaret.
>
> Carson did. Demaret moved to still another angle of observation.
>
> "Swing one more time, John," said Demaret, arching his eyebrows.
>
> Carson did.
>
> "What do you think," he asked Demaret.
>
> "Tell you what, John," Demaret drawled, sucking on his teeth. "If I were you I'd lay off for a couple weeks." He paused. Then he added: "And then I'd quit." The audience fell all over itself.

Source: Nick Seitz, "Houston's Odd Couple," in *Under the Lone Star Flagstick: A Collection of Writings on Texas Golf and Golfers*, ed. Melanie Hauser (New York: Simon & Schuster, 1997), 269.

THE COURSE *IN* HISTORY

In the early 1960s, when the idea of a golf course development along Onion Creek first surfaced, the property was part of a ranch owned by Austin contractor Rex Kitchens and his wife, Effie. Rex, an avid golfer who pitched the idea to player and designer Jimmy Demaret, died in 1965, however, and it was not until 1969 that Demaret acquired the land through his partnership with champion Austin golfer Jimmie Connolly and with major financial assistance from Arthur Temple of Diboll (see chapter 13), represented through his Lumberman's Investment Corporation. The course design was largely the work of Demaret, who claimed that "nature was the architect of Onion Creek. I simply followed the natural features of the land." Drawn by the hardscrabble chalk-rock outcroppings; the native oaks, cypress, and pecans; and the clear waters of the creek, Demaret worked with the natural contours of the land to preserve vistas and develop a course that favored accurate tee shots. Construction began in 1971 under the direction of Lee Bilberry of Oklahoma and was completed by the fall of 1973. The formal opening occurred the following April and, given Demaret's celebrity status as both a golfer and an entertainer, featured such luminaries as Frank Sinatra, Bob Hope, Phil Harris, Willie Nelson, Mickey Mantle, and Tennessee Ernie Ford as well as astronauts Gene Cernan and Charles Duke, former Texas governor Allan Shivers, and football coaches Darrell Royal and Paul "Bear" Bryant. There were also, as would be expected, golfing stars such as Demaret and Jack Burke, who together had designed the prestigious Champions Golf Course outside of Houston. The event drew a sizeable paying crowd, with proceeds going to the Texas Ranger Museum, a decision that also brought out fifty or so protestors angered by what they perceived as the racist history of the law-enforcement organization. A newspaper article covering the opening spoke as well to the related housing development that at the time included only three occupied condominiums and fifteen single-family homes under construction.[9]

Given the oil embargo of the 1970s and the development's distance from Austin and away from nearby commercial estab-

A complete information kit of memorabilia associated with the initial Legends of Golf Tournament at Onion Creek Country Club, April 1978. Photograph by Dan K. Utley.

Rice on Demaret

Grantland Rice, the celebrated sportswriter known for his heroic prose and compelling portrayals of sport celebrities, penned the following poem in 1947 in celebration of Jimmy Demaret's flamboyant on-course wardrobe:

> The rainbow ducks behind a cloud and hides its face in shame.
> The redbird, bluebird and thrush look sordid, dull and tame.
> The pelican with startled look, deserts the fish at sea,
> When J. Demaret takes his stand upon the starting tee.
>
> Green, blue and crimson, pink and gold, with purples on the side,
> He makes surrounding flower growth look drab and even snide,
> In one quick look at blazing flame, the rosebuds fade and fall,
> But better still above the rest—the guy can hit that ball.

Source: Grantland Rice, "Jimmy's Raiment, Voice, and Swing Lead Grantland Rice to Pen Poetry," in *Under the Lone Star Flagstick: A Collection of Writings on Texas Golf and Golfers*, ed. Melanie Hauser (New York: Simon & Schuster, 1997), 133.

lishments, the Onion Creek enterprise was not immediately the moneymaker its investors had envisioned. That began to change by the latter part of the decade, around the time Demaret made the club the centerpiece of a new venture in golf. Sources differ on who helped foster the idea with him—some giving partial credit to entertainer Bing Crosby, film and television sports producer Fred Raphael, and others—but the concept for an invitational tournament at Onion Creek for former golf champions soon became a reality after securing proper financial backing and a broadcast commitment from NBC. Known as the Legends of Golf, the tournament made its debut on April 26–30, 1978, featuring a field that collectively represented ten US Open championships, eleven Masters wins, nine British Open wins, and forty-eight appearances on Ryder Cup teams. Noteworthy participants in the first tournament included Julius Boros, Gardner Dickinson, Cary Middlecoff, Sam Snead, and Gene Sarazen as well as Demaret and Burke. In the end, the team of Snead and Dickinson prevailed, with Snead sinking a birdie putt on the last hole to secure the victory and the winning purse of $100,000 for the pair. The Legends of Golf Tournament led to the formation of the Senior PGA Tour (now the PGA Tour Champions) in 1980 and continued to be played at Onion Creek through 1989 before being moved to other venues. The club has also hosted three LPGA tournaments, as well as state tournaments for the University Interscholastic League, and remains a popular private club well known for its challenging holes, scenic beauty, and impressive amenities set against the backdrop of historic Onion Creek.[10]

2

WE'RE STILL HERE

SAN FELIPE SPRINGS
GOLF COURSE, DEL RIO

SCORECARD FROM THE PAST

Currently: San Felipe Springs Golf Course

Historic Name: San Felipe Springs

DETAILS: Nine-hole municipal golf course opened in 1922; distance is 2,988 yards from the longest tees

Location: 1524 E. Highway 90, Del Rio

Historical Context: Prehistoric occupation; early twentieth century military occupation

Historical Type: Natural springs

Period of Significance: Prehistory and sixteenth through nineteenth centuries, 1914–23

Signature Hole of History: Number six is a straight, 341-yard, par-four hole that plays north to south between the historic West Spring and East Spring.

THE COURSE OF HISTORY

Historian Gary L. Pinkerton opened his recent book about Trammel's Trace in East Texas by noting, "For all the places people now travel, someone was the first to be there, the first to observe the natural beauty, the first to gaze across a grand vista." And, he added, "as others followed, their footsteps wore paths to springs or honey trees, to shelter and safety, or to sacred places where the Great Spirit was present." At a prehistoric-site tour along the Colorado River in Central Texas, an archeologist, replying to the standard question about where "the people" went, conveyed a

HOT SPRING   DEL RIO, TEX.

A group of people gathered at San Felipe Springs, Del Rio, for an unknown event, 1887. Photograph by Frederick W. Snow of Chelsea, Massachusetts. Courtesy Texas State Library and Archives Commission, 1/26-1.

somewhat similar metaphysical response by simply saying, "We're still here." This then, at one level, is a story not only of those who were among the first to visit a site but also of those who, appreciating its significance within the natural environment, returned many times over. At another level, though, this is the story of how disparate cultures over the millennia can sometimes link their histories through nature, even when those connections are vague or not clearly understood. In this case, the connecting point is a natural water system known as San Felipe Springs in Del Rio, Val Verde County.[1]

Geologist Gunnar Brune, in his seminal 1981 work *Springs of Texas*, described the San Felipe system as the fourth largest in the state, noting that it included "a group of ten or more springs which extend for about three kilometers along San Felipe Creek northeast of Del Rio." Brune wrote too of possible cultural connections, from a Native American village and sixteenth-century Spanish explorers to nineteenth-century transportation routes and later military and agricultural development. In his survey of the springs, he also recorded, "The largest and best known are No. 1 through 3 on the San Felipe golf course." Of those, the West Spring (No. 2) and the

East Spring (No. 3) had a combined discharge rate of 2,950 liters per second, far greater than the rest of the springs in the system combined.[2]

Broader patterns of similar cultural connections between golf and prehistory intrigued Texas archeologist Douglas K. Boyd, who began to pair his extensive field experience with writings on golf-course design concepts, particularly those of Albert Warren "Tilly" Tillinghast (see chapter 9), considered the dean of golf architects. Tillinghast understood and appreciated these connections, seeing them as enhancements to his "course beautiful" concept. As Boyd observed, the common threads through the years were the landscape and history. "More precisely," he wrote, "old golf courses and archeology are closely linked because of how people used the landscape. Prehistoric Native Americans and historic EuroAmericans settled in these beautiful natural places because they provided shelter and abundant wood, water, and wildlife. When early golf architects chose a course site, it was simply the continuation of an age-old pattern of seeking a highly desirable location." Boyd's particular field of study focused on fifteen early golf courses related to the Edwards Aquifer along the Balcones Escarpment. These stretched from Bell County (Sammons Park, Temple), southwest to Comal County (Landa Park, New Braunfels), and then west by way of several San Antonio courses to San Felipe Springs. Boyd credited the Del Rio course as an early inspiration for his critical analysis of cultural connections, which is fitting since a detailed archeological survey he helped conduct there in the 1990s resulted in much of what is known about the site's prehistory.[3]

Fresh out of Texas A&M University with a master's degree in anthropology in 1987, Boyd joined the Austin firm of Prewitt and Associates, a cultural-resource consulting firm later tasked with investigating the springs area in advance of a proposed water-treatment plant for the City of Del Rio. As he wrote: "We were hired because the Antiquities Code of Texas and the National Historic Preservation Act (1966) required that a search for cultural resources be made and that the effects of the construction project be considered if any important resources were found." Working under the legal purview of the Texas Historical Commission and utilizing the general criteria of the National Register of Historic Places for assessment, Prewitt and Associates conducted extensive archeological and historical surveys of the property, excavating areas as needed for further data recovery of buried features to determine mitigative measures that might be required. Val Verde County is one of the richest in the state with regard to prehistoric cultural resources, so the project archeologists had good reason to anticipate significant deposits. Their suspicions were borne out within the footprint of the golf course when they "uncovered four feet of stratified archeological deposits that revealed continuous occupation during the last 3,000 years."[4]

Such cultural-resource-management (CRM) surveys result in technical reports, termed "gray literature," that are essential planning documents for countless ongoing projects involving a wide variety of federal, state, and municipal entities each year. Designed to mitigate the effects of development projects on significant cultural resources, they generate extensive findings that help in the systematic recording, preservation, and interpretation of historic elements, including intangible aspects like folklore, ethnohistory, and sense of place. Due to the vulnerability of such resources from relic hunters and others who might exploit artifacts for personal

TEXAS ANTIQUITIES

Section 191.093 of the Antiquities Code of Texas states that landmarks and artifacts on public land "are the sole property of the State of Texas and may not be removed, altered, damaged, destroyed, salvaged, or excavated without a contract with or permit from the committee [Texas Historical Commission]." In other words, to avoid legal complications, golfers at San Felipe Springs Golf Course should leave any suspected historical artifacts in situ. Appreciate the heritage of the site, but play on through.

Source: Mark Denton, Texas Historical Commission, Apr. 13, 2017

gain, the CRM reports are generally limited in distribution to those professionals—archeologists, historians, reviewers, planners, and government officials—directly involved in the investigative process. The general, non-site-specific information they contain, however, often makes its way into educational programs, publications (such as this book), museum exhibits, and other accessible venues by means of what is known broadly as public history. As a result, the description herein of the archeological findings at San Felipe Springs speaks to the broad overview of significance.

Analysis of the San Felipe Springs site in the 1990s involved intensive investigations related to geomorphological, archeological (prehistoric and historic), and historical methodologies. For the prehistoric phases over four distinct cultural zones, recovered artifacts and unearthed features included burned rock middens, rock-lined pits, scrapers, manos and hammerstones, gravers, ceramics, and lithic scatters as well as bifaces and caches associated with flint knapping. There were also food-associated elements, such as snail and mussel shells and animal bone fragments. Arrow points identified in the research included those of the Scallorn, Perdiz, Cliffton, Shumla, and Pandale styles, among others. Geomorphology testing indicated that prior to the earliest occupational phases along the springs, the runoff formed a braided, shallow-sided tributary system that evolved to an incised creek with higher banks formed from alluvial deposits and erosion over time. The resulting extensive natural and fertile terraces afforded some protection from regular rainfall runoff, although the "paleo-flood record suggests that one or more floods between ca. 2700 and 1700 B.P. (before present) were of high magnitude." Such massive flooding may have removed earlier evidence of habitation in the area, but it buried and protected such evidence in other areas. Regardless, extant cultural deposits, including charcoal remnants suitable for radiocarbon dating, represented "continual deposition over the last 3,000-4,000 years . . . , denoting Late Prehistoric/ Protohistoric, Late Archaic, and Middle Archaic occupations." The materials were, the studies indicated, largely the "residue left by Toyah peoples." The geographic extent of the identifiable cultural phase was from present North Central Texas to South Texas and westward to the San Felipe Springs area. Its distinction is reflected in an expanded use of improved stone tool technology, a greater reliance on earthenware pottery, and some evidence of limited bison utilization. The Toyah phase in this part of West Texas, however, did not represent a bison-hunting culture per se.[5]

The cultural-contact period in the Del Rio area that marked the interaction between Native Americans and Europeans—technically the beginning of the historic era—dates to the mid-sixteenth century. In the more than four hundred years of this period, the springs have been integral to various episodes of exploration, pioneer settlement, agricultural development, and community growth as well as the support of transportation routes and the establishment of military installations. The last chapter of the latter phase occurred shortly before World War I, with the development of Camp Del Rio, renamed Camp Michie in 1920 for US Army brigadier general Robert Edward Lee Michie, who died in France in 1918. The temporary installation—primarily a tent encampment—

Photograph of the 1997 archeological excavations on the sixth green at the San Felipe Springs Golf Course. Photograph by Douglas K. Boyd; used with permission of Prewitt and Associates, Inc.

served as a small cavalry outpost for Fort Clark, thirty miles to the east in Kinney County, and was initially part of an extensive line of border defenses during the Mexican Revolution of 1910–20. A primary objective of troops stationed at Camp Michie was the security of the rail line crossing the Pecos High Bridge, a strategic point along the vital southern transcontinental route. As Del Rio historian Doug Braudaway recorded in his narrative for a state historical marker commemorating the site, the short-lived camp "overlooked San Felipe Springs and the upper part of the creek on both sides of the creek." It sat on four hundred acres donated through the G. Bedell Moore estate and "was contiguous with today's San Felipe Golf Course." There were ancillary facilities farther south near Moore Park as well.[6]

Camp Michie remained technically operational through 1923, with formal conveyance back to the Moore family, although operations at the site ceased even before then. The imminent transition from military to civilian use was indicated in a January 1921 site inspection and commendation report by Maj. Gen. J. T. Dickman. Addressing his findings to Col. Sedgwick Rice, commander of the 12th Cavalry at the camp, he wrote:

> The new officers' club which has been under construction was formerly opened with a reception and ball on the night of March 18[, 1920]. The officers and leadership of Fort Clark and Eagle Pass and many people from Del Rio and vicinity were invited.... At a meeting of the officers of the regiment it was decided to turn the club into a country club, and accordingly invitations have been sent to many people of Del Rio and vicinity to join as associate members. We are prepared to give full country-club service. An outdoor dancing pavilion has been completed and the work of laying out a golf course around the famous San Felipe Springs is now under way. It is hoped that it will be completed so that the links will be ready for play in the fall.

The effective end of Camp Michie came in October 1921, when Colonel Rice, a decorated veteran of the Indian Wars who had also served in the Philippines and Cuba, led his regiment overland more than four hundred miles to its new post at Fort Brown near Brownsville. He died there four years later and was buried at Arlington National Cemetery.[7]

THE COURSE *IN* HISTORY

Although not mentioned by name in the military reports, the architect at work on this new golf course was John Bredemus, now considered the dean of Texas golf course designers for his work at Colonial Country Club in Fort Worth and other major locations, but the one at Camp Michie marked his first project. The man largely responsible for taking a chance on the young and relatively inexperienced designer was William Moore Abbey, a former insurance executive in Houston who moved to Del Rio and became a successful merchant. An avid golfer, Abbey worked diligently not only to develop a local course for his own interests but also to promote the quality of life in his adopted hometown. After purchasing a hundred acres from the Moore estate in 1921, he joined with local business leaders C. C. Belcher and B. G. Stafford to form the San Felipe Country Club as a membership organization. The new building mentioned in Major Dickman's site report earlier that year served as the original golf clubhouse.[8]

The enigmatic Bredemus has been described by those who knew him best as a loner and a genius, and he seems to have been a true character as well as a superb natural athlete. Born in Flint, Michigan, to Luxembourgian American parents, Bredemus received his education at the prestigious Phillips Exeter Academy in New Hampshire and then for a brief time at Dartmouth College, a hundred miles to the northwest. A great deal of misinformation has clouded the history of his early years, much of which surrounds his athletic accomplishments. What is known for certain, though, is that Bredemus placed second in the Amateur Athletic Union (AAU) all-around competition in 1906 and won the overall championship two years later. His participation in the 1912 competition, however, has resulted in some lingering confusion. That year, representing Princeton University, he came in second in the all-around championship to Jim Thorpe of the US Indian Industrial School in Carlisle, Pennsylvania (Carlisle Indian Industrial School). Bredemus amassed 6,303 points to Thorpe's record-setting 7,476, besting the legendary Native American athlete in the pole vault, hammer throw, and 880-yard walk events. That same year Thorpe won two gold medals at the Olympics in Sweden but was soon stripped of all of his amateur honors when he admitted to playing semipro baseball a few years earlier. As part of the controversial decision against Thorpe and his amateur status, Bredemus received the AAU medals for 1912 as well as the title. He did not, however, receive Thorpe's Olympic medals, as some sources have reported.[9]

Bredemus completed his degree in civil engineering from Princeton, also in 1912, and moved to New York, where he learned to play golf at the Van Cortlandt Park Golf Course (Vanny) in the Bronx, the oldest public course in the country. While he picked up

THE GHOST OF BREDEMUS

In *Billy Boy*, his novel centered on the life lessons of golf, the celebrated writer Bud Shrake introduced course-designer John Bredemus as an angel who befriends the protagonist and provides a historical link to the setting of Colonial Country Club in Fort Worth. The following passage speaks to what Shrake viewed as the lingering spirits of fame and place.

"Let me explain my need for secrecy," Bredemus said. He had finished his dinner, though his plates and bowls were not scraped and licked clean, as Billy's were. "I am constantly and anonymously touring the golf courses I have built to see what changes are being made. What happens, Billy Boy, is I build a wonderful golf course. Then others come in and build a grand, expensive clubhouse, and charge a lot of money to join. Golfers play on my course until they get quite good, and that gives them the privilege to demand changes be made, greens flattened, and so on. These golf clubs organize committees to listen to critiques and come up with notions of their own. Soon the course is being systematically ruined."

"Is Colonial ruined?"

"Oh, my, no, I trust not," said Bredemus. "Colonial was so grand in the beginning, it will be difficult to ruin. But I haven't really walked the course in years. I only took a quick peek today."

"Why have you built all these golf courses if you know people are going to come along and ruin them?" Billy asked.

"Well, they're not all ruined. Intelligent changes are made from time to time. Now and then I am able to influence a player or a greens committee chairman by subtle methods. But even so, yes, I have spent more than half my life building golf courses in Texas. Other than my love of the game and the outdoors, there are two reasons. Golf courses inspire community. And open spaces are the lungs that allow the communities to breathe."

Source: Bud Shrake, *Billy Boy* (New York: Simon & Schuster, 2001), 77.

the game quickly and showed some early promise in regional tournaments, his talents as an athlete did not translate to his success as a professional golfer. Instead, he eventually utilized his engineering skills to design courses, which was the beginning of his legendary talent in the game. After teaching school in the Northeast and working with a design team for the Lido Club on Long Island, Bredemus moved to San Antonio, Texas, in 1919 to accept a job as a school principal. His ulterior motive, though, was to find a place where he could play golf year-round. He worked at the Brackenridge Park Golf Course (see chapter 9) and, with the commission to build the new nine-hole facility in Del Rio, embarked on his career in course design. As the sport was then still in its infancy in the Lone Star State, Bredemus set the early standards as the first golf course architect in Texas. Harvey Penick, the guru of the sport in the state for many years, believed that Bredemus's success came in a broad innate approach to basic design. "John taught me it takes the eyes of an artist to design a course," Penick wrote, "but the skills of an engineer. John was both." He also credited Bredemus with being the state's earliest golf instructor; helping organize the Texas Open, which debuted at the Brackenridge course in 1922; and spearheading efforts to establish the Texas PGA. In writing about his friend, Penick immortalized the quirky character of the elusive Bredemus: "John traveled with just a few clothes, a bag of books, a canvas golf bag of seven clubs, a checkerboard and a sockful [sic] of checkers. . . . Taking off across the state by himself, telling no one where he was going or what he was working on, John built golf courses without leaving records. He didn't want fame. Nobody knew what he did with the money he was making. He wasn't spending it on himself."[10]

In addition to his work at San Felipe Springs, the Texas courses Bredemus designed include Memorial Park, BraeBurn, and Westwood in Houston; Colonial and Ridglea in Fort Worth; Scott Schreiner Municipal in Kerrville; the Conroe Country Club; and the San Angelo Country Club. While working on a design project at Big Spring in Howard County, Bredemus suffered a heart attack and died on May 8, 1946; he is buried there in Mount Olive Cemetery beneath a simple gray granite headstone bearing a Texas PGA logo. Legend has it that Bredemus died estranged from his family and almost penniless, but a friend, Brackenridge Park golf pro Murray Brooks, raised the funds necessary for his burial and monument, which unfortunately bears the wrong date of birth (1893 instead of 1884). As for what he did with the Thorpe medals, Bredemus apparently took that secret to his grave. Penick, who once saw them, believed that the great golf course architect remained true to his pledge to melt them down; they were not found among his final belongings. Forty-five years after his death, Bredemus received posthumous induction to the Texas Golf Hall of Fame as part of the class of 1991, which included Mary Lou Dill, Henry "Lighthorse" Cooper, Hal Underwood, George Hannon, and Bruce Lietzke.[11]

3

A PAGEANT AMONG THE RUINS

MENARD GOLF COURSE, MENARD

SCORECARD FROM THE PAST

Currently: Menard Golf Course

Historic Name: Presidio San Luis de las Amarillas

DETAILS: A nine-hole public golf course dating to the 1930s, with realignments in recent years; distance is 4,730 yards from the longest tees when played as eighteen holes

Location: Off US 190 on Golf Course Road, one mile west of Menard

Historical Context: Fortification established by Spanish soldados in 1757 to support Mission Santa Cruz de San Sabá

Historical Type: Spanish presidio; archeological ruins

Period of Significance: 1757–70 as a presidio; 1937 to present as a protected historic site

Signature Hole of History: Number nine, a par-four, 252-yard hole that parallels the southern boundary of the commemorative area set aside to protect and interpret the remaining presidio ruins.

THE COURSE OF HISTORY

One of the most harrowing incidents of the Spanish missionary period in present Texas played out along the frontier of the San Saba River valley in 1758, almost two decades prior to the American Revolution. Established the previous year as the result of an expedition funded by Mexican mining mogul Pedro Romero de Terreros and headed by his cousin Fray Alonso Geraldo de Terreros, Mission Santa Cruz de San Sabá represented an effort to bring Christianity to the region's Apache Indians. The group was under the military command of Col. Diego Ortiz Parrilla and included many members of the abandoned San Xavier (San Gabriel) missions near present Rockdale in Milam County who had reorganized at San Antonio. Striking out from there to the northwest in April 1757, the expedition arrived at the proposed site of the new mission on the north side of the San Saba River later that month, the priests overseeing construction of a small church while the military corps began work on a presidio a few miles downstream. The distance between the two outposts served to allow the missionaries greater access to the Native Americans, who avoided the presence of soldiers, but it also increased their vulnerability in the remote area. Despite its inherent dangers, this mission-presidio model was utilized successfully in other regions of northern Mexico, especially at San Antonio and along the Rio Grande. What made this particular operation different, though, was the longstanding cultural enmity between the Apaches and the Comanches who vied for dominance in the region.[1]

With no immediate contact from the nearby Apache groups, the mission seemed doomed from the beginning, resulting in the abandonment of plans for a second sanctuary, but work on the formidable stone presidio continued unabated. Within months of their arrival, however, the padres began receiving visitors, which brought a measure of encouragement. But there were underlying and then unknown reasons for this sudden change. As historian Robert S. Weddle wrote, "The story of the Mission Santa Cruz de San Sabá is one of Apache perfidy, Spanish gullibility, and the disastrous consequences of both." To the Apache, the mission served as an eddy in the turbulence of their struggle for survival against their enemies; to the padres, the presence of Indian visitors represented validation of their hard-fought struggle to establish Christianity along the frontier. Despite early encouragement for both sides, however, the evidence soon began to mount that this situation might be decidedly different from appearances. Despite pleas from Parrilla to relocate to the relative security of the fortress, the three remaining missionaries and their assistants remained at their station, albeit with a minimal guard of the soldiers. On the morning of March 16, 1758, with but little warning, a large party of Comanches, joined with allied Bidais, Tonkawas, and others, encircled the stockaded compound and pressed forward. Father Miguel de Molina provided a chilling account of the raid:

> [I was] filled with amazement and fear when I saw nothing but Indians on every hand, armed with guns and arrayed in the most horrible attire. Besides the paint on their faces, red and black, they were adorned with the pelts and tails of wild beasts, wrapped around them or hanging down from their heads, as well as deer horns. Some were disguised as various kinds of animals, and some wore feather headdresses. All were armed with muskets, swords and lances, and I noticed also that they brought with them some youths armed with bows and arrows, doubtless to train and encourage them in their cruel and bloody way of life.[2]

When the warriors managed to breach the stockade walls, those inside met them with gifts in a vain attempt at appeasement. In the tense moments that followed, a Tejas chief and his companions rode out toward the presidio while those who remained began ransacking the mission. Any effort at rapprochement quickly faded in the wholesale hostility that ensued. While Father Molina sought safety in interior buildings, Fathers Terreros and Santiesteban fell mortally wounded along with others, and the raiding party set fire to the stockade and several buildings. Those who remained soon made their way to the church for what appeared to be a final stand, preparing a cannon and continuing to fire on the raiders. Meanwhile, the chief steward, José Gutiérrez, managed to escape under enemy fire and made his way to the presidio to report the attack. As Weddle noted, "Prayers crossed the lips of the besieged, for they knew the hopelessness of a counterattack from the Presidio."[3]

With his command severely depleted due to other assignments, Parrilla nevertheless rallied a number of troops in response, but they met heavy resistance along the way. Some soldiers managed to circumvent these encounters, though, and made their way to the mission, distracting the raiders in the process and allowing those in the church to escape. Back at the presidio, the garrison regrouped and prepared for an early morning attack, but it never came. As reports confirmed that the Indians had withdrawn over the ensuing days, Parrilla took steps to secure the presidio before leading a party of soldiers to assess the damage at the mission site. "Charred remains and ashes marked the spot," Weddle wrote, "where Father Terreros and his companions had risked martyrdom rather than abandon the site of their labors for safety at the Presidio." The soldiers began the gruesome and painstaking task of identifying the bodies and burying the remains. The carnage proved to be complete and overpowering. Despite the dire situation, Parrilla chose to trust that the dispatches he sent to San Antonio for reinforcements would be answered, though the following days filled those who remained with anxiety. Although the couriers successfully made their way to San Antonio, the response from authorities proved less than adequate. Only a small contingent went to aid Parrilla, as the prevailing thought was that any available soldiers should be retained for the defense of San Antonio in light of the sizable raid at the mission. Such an attack never materialized, though, and Spanish military leaders instead prepared for a punitive expedition in 1759, which would reach all the way to the Red River and ultimately result in a sound defeat for the Europeans. The compelling lessons of the attack along the San Saba and the subsequent expedition were two-fold. The first was that the Comanches and their allies, equipped with sufficient weaponry and fast horses, were a formidable force far superior to the Spanish *soldados*. The second was realizing the immediate need to reassess the frontier missionary experiment. There would be future missions, including those serving the Apaches, but none of them would be in the vicinity of the San Saba—and none quite so remote. Nevertheless, Parrilla's isolated presidio remained in operation to maintain the Spanish presence in the region. Reinforced with a stone outer wall and recommissioned Real Presidio de San Sabá in 1761, the fortress nevertheless was obsolete within a few years and finally abandoned by 1770. Its rock ruins remained a landmark in the vicinity, visited by explorers, adventurers pursuing a legendary silver mine in the area, and early pioneers to what became Menard County a century after the destruction of the mission. To the early Anglo-American settlers, the abundant rock supply of the ruins served as something of a public quarry, providing building material for many of the early buildings of the nearby county seat of Menardville (later Menard) as well as local ranches.[4]

With time, the site of the failed mission melded into the natural environment and disappeared from the cultural landscape, as well as the collective memory of those who lived in the area. Its exact location remained one of the state's great archeological mysteries well into the latter part of the twentieth century, although there were numerous attempts to ground truth the site beginning in the early 1900s. Among those who worked diligently to identify the site through the years, either on the ground or through archival records, were such prominent researchers as historians Herbert Eugene Bolton and Carlos E. Castañeda, newspaper publisher and local historian John Warren Hunter, and archeologist Kathleen Gilmore. Each contributed to a greater focus on a general location, but it was not until the 1990s that the investigations proved conclusive thanks to the application of new technologies and the work of a new investigative team representing diverse disciplines. Architect Mark R. Wolf and archeologist V. Kay Hines collaborated on this new study, which included aerial remote sensing with the assistance of pilot Glynn Crain, and later joined with field crews from Texas Tech University to check anomalies their work identified. Everything came together on September 4, 1993, when investigators working in a recently plowed field found sherds of Spanish colonial pottery and pieces of fired daub, which as stated by Dr. Grant Hall of Texas Tech, "convinced us that we had found the Mission Santa Cruz de San Sabá." Additional and ongoing investigations continue to present a more comprehensive understanding of a pivotal event in Texas history.[5]

Bookended chronologically by the various field investigations during the twentieth century, the site of the old presidio piqued the interest of those planning commemorative and interpretive activities in association with the Texas Centennial in the 1930s. As a result, the Commission of Control for Texas Centennial Celebrations allocated eighteen hundred dollars, which Menard

County matched with five hundred dollars, "to acquire the twenty-five acre site and to restore the stone building as it was in 1761." To that end, the commission hired local concrete contractor John Floyd Perry to oversee the "reconstruction" (more accurately a replica) in partnership with another Menard concrete man, Floyd L. Napier. Noted as advisors on the project were Louis V. Kemp of the commission; Lt. Gov. Walter Woodul, also a member of the commission; and historian J. Frank Dobie of the University of Texas; it is unclear to what extent the three provided technical assistance, if any. The contractor crews followed extant architectural remains where evident and worked from plans provided by Menard resident Hewitt Hobson Wheless, a rancher and lumber retailer. As the building took shape above ground, the design became more conjectural, especially with regard to embellishments, but the resulting edifice was a roughly proportional stylized representation of how the frontier fort might have appeared. Given its mass and historical setting within the San Saba Valley, it provided a unique backdrop for commemorating the story of the Spanish mission period and provided museum space for artifacts, related and otherwise.[6]

As the replicated presidio took shape, state and local officials began planning for a special dedication ceremony befitting the site's statewide significance. The centerpiece of the event was an original play by Menard resident Henry Reeve entitled *The Fall of Mission San Sabá*. A New Jersey native, Reeve was a would-be Hollywood actor who had set aside his career ambitions when circumstances in the 1920s took him to Menard, where he fell in love with a young woman named Sophie Luckenbach Mears. The couple made their home in Menard, where they built the Mission Theatre not only for movie presentations but also for plays—mostly mysteries—staged by Henry. His acting abilities made him a logical choice to write and direct the San Sabá pageant, set against the backdrop of one of the state's most historic sites. While Henry Reeve never made it to Hollywood, he had a great nephew who did; actor Christopher Reeve was for many years a true star, perhaps best known for his portrayal of Superman.[7]

On the morning of May 8, 1937, the dedication of Presidio San Luis de las Amarillas got underway at Mission Park, one mile west of Menard. Following an opening march by Cherry's Band of Ballinger, a dedicatory address by the Hon. Walter Woodul, and the christening of the structure by Mrs. Fannie Splittgarber Ellis using San Saba river water, the play began in the presidio courtyard. As the program noted, the drama depicted the "peaceful everyday life of the inhabitants of the fort," then "climaxed" with a scene of the "massacre at the hands of the Indians" as a chapel bell rang out. The program provided further details of the theatrical spectacular:

> Authentic costumes have been obtained from the Centennial in Dallas and the players will be Menard people. Many of the high school students will be Indians in breech clouts and war paint. The members of the American Legion will don the uniforms of the Spanish garrison. The monks will be dressed in robes and even wear pates as was then the custom.
>
> The squaws will wear beautiful leather dresses and the war chiefs will wear feathered bonnets. The color and beauty of a life long since dead will be reproduced for the audience.[8]

Another colorful account of the pageant survives through the writing of Bandera resident J. Marvin Hunter, the longtime editor of *Frontier Times* magazine, who called it "beautiful and impressive." He further noted that the cast consisted of "a band of 75 Indians, 16 Spanish soldiers in costumes used in the Cavalcade at the Texas Centennial Exposition last year, and 250 school children, with thirty or forty people," in the depiction of life along the San Saba frontier almost 180 years earlier. Hunter went on to praise the work of Reeve, and to highlight the technological advances incorporated in the work, he noted, "The entire program was given out by loud speaker, through the courtesy of Gay Copeland, manager of the West Texas Gas Company of San Angelo, co-operating with the Menard Electrolux dealer." Following the pageant, the crowd of about three thousand toured the grounds, viewed the special historical-museum displays, and visited with longtime friends in a homecoming for former residents of Menard.[9]

The pageantry of the day's events was a fitting manifestation of the pride local residents had in the rich history of the valley. In

This amazingly detailed panoramic photo by N. H. Rose captures the crowd that gathered near Menard on May 8, 1937, for the dedication ceremony at the reconstructed ruins of the presidio at San Saba (not the mission as labeled). Taken during the Great Depression at a time marked by unprecedented state efforts to celebrate the rich history of Texas, the picture is an excellent depiction of the community pride and spirit that underpinned this successful project. Courtesy Hunter-Rose Collection, Harry Ransom Center, the University of Texas at Austin.

the middle of the Great Depression, the presidio replica represented the economic promise of the future, one built in part on heritage tourism and historic preservation. Sadly, other factors, including the close of the centennial events, the onset of a second world war, and economic reconsiderations, worked against the historic site. By the late 1950s, the presidio was again in ruins and within the field of play for the Menard Country Club (which included until recently a green within the historic compound). Chronicling the site's post-centennial decline, an Abilene newspaper observed: "There was no caretaker, and vandals broke in and destroyed much of the contents. Treasure hunters added to the destruction by digging up the floor, and today the fort, more familiarly known as San Saba, is a ruin."[10]

Over the years, there were indications that the Franciscan order of the Roman Catholic Church might move to declare the site a shrine, which would lead to annual pilgrimages to San Saba, and there were renewed efforts to open it to tourists. But the most promising development came with two important changes. The

DEDICATION OF MISSION SAN SABA, near Menard, Texas, May 8, 1937. (Copyrighted by N. H. R

first was the realignment of the golf course to protect the site, while the second came later with renewed local interest in the historic site. Continuing archeological investigations and improved visitor facilities, including extensive interpretation, speak to a new era for the ancient presidio, which remains one of the best and most accessible places to get a true sense of the Spanish frontier in Texas.

THE COURSE *IN* HISTORY

A press release in September 1929 told of the successful capitalization of funds for the establishment of a "combination airport, country club and golf course" in Menard. Noting the progressive spirit of the small town, the article observed, "While airplane transportation may as yet be a bit hazardous, it will be so common in the near future that every town that wants visitors will have to have an airport." The news came only weeks before the shock of the stock-market crash presaged a severe economic downturn for the nation and no doubt caused some measure of doubt for those interested in the new project. How and precisely when the

A view through the presidio ruins with a pin flag visible in the distance. Photograph by Dan K. Utley

development got underway is unclear through available local resources, but a newspaper article in 1940 noted that its associated park would be open through the summer thanks in part to the work of the Menard Golf Association. The golf course development probably occurred in the 1940s, the prevailing thought in 1972 when the Texas Parks and Wildlife Department, at the request of the state legislature, conducted a feasibility study of the property regarding its possible development as a state historic site. In the report Dessamae Lorrain wrote, "In 1946, Menard County built a golf course and road through the presidio, destroying historic fabric and establishing a use of the historic site which continues today." Lorrain further noted, "In 1971 the golf course in and around the presidio was 'beautified' by leveling with a bulldozer the entire south wall, the west wall south of the reconstruction, and a large section of the north wall." As a result, "the integrity of the site has been compromised to the extent that its validity as an historic structure is questionable." A few months later the agency concluded that the county should continue to own and maintain

THE NATIVE AMERICAN HERITAGE OF PROFESSIONAL GOLFERS

Not much has been written about the class struggle of Native American golfers, but in many ways their stories coincided with those of African American and Hispanic golfers. Those who sought to be included in the sport in the early days of professional golf faced similar barriers of club and tournament restrictions that discriminated on the basis of race. They faced similar obstacles with regard to professional organizations. Two of the earliest individuals to test the limitations of sanctioned play were Oscar Bunn, of the Shinnecock tribe, and John Shippen, of mixed African American and Native American ancestry. After some initial controversy, both played in the 1896 US Open at Shinnecock Hills, Long Island, New York, thanks to pressure from USGA president Theodore Havemeyer. Shippen finished fifth that year and continued to play in subsequent Opens. Despite such intervention, the leading professional organizations of the time continued to mirror society in general through the ensuing decades. During that time, many Native American golfers associated themselves with the United Golfers Association (UGA), founded in 1926 primarily to support African American players. The organization, however, had an open-membership policy that allowed golfers like Bill Spiller, of mixed African American and Cherokee heritage, not only to compete but also to excel. Thanks in large part to legal actions by Spiller, beginning in 1948, as well as mounting public pressure, the PGA finally abolished its so-called "Caucasian clause" in 1961. By then, however, Spiller had passed his prime as a competitive golfer. The change, though, allowed others greater access to the sport, and in 1969 Orville Moody, a Choctaw, entered and won the US Open at Champions Golf Club in Houston. The next tour win for a Native American came a few years later when Rod Curl, a Winta, prevailed at the 1974 Colonial National Invitational. In 1999 Notah Begay, of Navajo, San Felipe, and

Isleta heritage, also won on the PGA Tour and later became the first full-blooded Native American to compete in the Masters at Augusta, Georgia. Among his competitors on the tour were others, like Tiger Woods and Ricky Fowler, with ancestral ties to Native American culture.

Source: Gregory Bond, "Golf," in *Native Americans in Sports*, ed. C. Richard King, vol. 1 (New York: Routledge, 2004), 130–31.

the site "until its priority for acquisition by the Parks and Wildlife Department is reached."[11]

While there is no definitive documentation for the statement about the 1946 development of the golf course, the consensus among those in Menard County supports that conclusion. The date is also consistent with the organization of the Menard Country Club in the fall of that year. An article on the club in a 1982 county history noted, "The golf course was part of the club at one time, but has since become a separate organization." Such postwar civic improvements were common in Texas, even in rural areas, where construction on city-owned or county-owned land (as in the case of the Menard course) often resulted from local planning utilizing government equipment and crews. But the 1946 date may represent an update of facilities or even a realignment to take in the presidio site, given earlier references to golf at Menard, including some from the late 1930s.[12]

The golf course and the ruins remained intertwined until planning for extensive archeological investigations got underway in the early twenty-first century. Working in close partnership with Menard County officials and interested preservation groups, Texas Tech University archeologists, led by Dr. Hall, began conducting a series of extensive field-school investigations of the presidio site in 2000. Working under authority from the Texas Historical Commission, university faculty and students first joined with amateur archeologists, local residents, and even military personnel from nearby Goodfellow Air Force Base to clear the area of nonhistoric materials in order to open archeological test units designed to differentiate between original Spanish occupation and later reconstructions. The results were immediate and extensive, with a vast array of artifacts from the colonial era. Over the ensuing years, Texas Tech investigations at the site continued to open other areas of the ruins, leading to important new information on the site and also enabling a more accurate reconstruction of the above-ground structures. Concurrent with the archeology, the county proceeded with a redesign of the course. In the overlapping time frame, though, archeologists sometimes had to deal with errant golf balls while players did their best to continue their games amid the excavations. "The ruins are a unique accent to the course," Manager Kevin Eger observed in a 2004 interview, "but it's tough to play around an archeological exploration."[13]

4

RESURRECTION

STEPHEN F. AUSTIN GOLF COURSE, SEALY

SCORECARD FROM THE PAST

Currently: Stephen F. Austin Golf Course

Historic Name: San Felipe de Austin

DETAILS: Reopened with seventeen holes after redesigns in 2016 and 2017 due to storm-induced erosion of the meandering Brazos River; exact yardage figures unavailable

Location: 1130 Park Road 38 in Stephen F. Austin State Park, Sealy

Historical Context: Early Anglo-American colonization of Texas

Historical Type: Mexican colonial town

Period of Significance: 1824–36

Signature Hole of History: Number two, a 155-yard, par-three configuration in which Sweet Creek comes into play, reflects the historically undulating terrain along the Brazos River.

THE COURSE *OF* HISTORY

In existence as a Mexican colonial town only from 1824 to 1836, San Felipe de Austin made a lasting mark on Texas history as a center of early immigration by Anglo-American settlers. Following its burning in advance of the Mexican Army as the Texas Revolution unfolded on the coastal prairies, the settlement failed to regain its prior status as an important political and commercial center and instead developed as a small, dispersed, rural settlement with an agricultural base. Today it is best known for its colonial

The riverine setting of the Stephen F. Austin course, with its ancient trees draped with Spanish moss, provides an important visual background for appreciating the area's colonial history. Courtesy Ken Lund, https://www.flickr. com/photos/kenlund/16260032451.

history, despite limited public access to associated sites and artifacts through the years. This is changing, however, thanks to the efforts of historians, archeologists, and museum specialists tasked with preserving elements of the past for the public. In the field of public history, the umbrella term for such work is "interpretation," which in the historical sense denotes the processes of collecting accurate information and presenting (or interpreting) it for the general public, including heritage tourists, schoolchildren, history enthusiasts, researchers, and others. This account, then, not only reflects the known historical facts and contexts of an important site but also celebrates the work of the public history interpreters—those who strive to preserve the past and keep it dynamic so it remains relevant and viable to future generations. History is not static; instead, it moves and changes continually to reflect evolving social values and frames of reference as well as new investigative programs and technologies. In that regard, San Felipe de Austin is being resurrected—quite literally, thanks to public archeology and history and renewed focus on records—to be discussed in new ways that challenge long-held perceptions of what took place on a small patch of ground almost two centuries ago.

The story of San Felipe de Austin has historical roots in events that took place in San Antonio de Bexár (present San Antonio) in late December 1820. There fifty-nine-year-old Connecticut native Moses Austin, an ambitious entrepreneur and a pioneer of the American lead industry, sought authorization from Gov. Antonio María Martínez to establish a colony of Anglo-American settlers in the province of Texas. Initially rebuffed by the governor and ordered to leave Bexár immediately, Austin reportedly then had a chance encounter with an earlier acquaintance, the Baron de Bastrop, as the two crossed the plaza. Upon confiding in Bastrop about his failed proposal—something the baron clearly understood from his own earlier colonization efforts in Spanish Louisiana—the two planned and eventually secured for Austin formal approval for the colony. Although Austin's son, Stephen Fuller Austin, later wrote his secondhand accounts of the encounter, about which historians have long speculated, it remains at the center of a change in attitude by the Spanish government regarding Texas colonization. It also serves to perpetuate the pivotal role Bastrop likely played in that transformation.[1]

Born in 1759 in Dutch Guiana, Philip Henrick Nering Bögel grew up in Holland as part of the Dutch aristocracy and became a tax collector in a time of political turmoil in Europe. Fleeing his homeland due to possible embezzlement, Bögel, restyled as the Baron de Bastrop, made his way to Spanish Louisiana and West Florida by the end of the eighteenth century. Soon after entering Texas in 1804, Bastrop traveled to San Antonio de Bexár, where he made his home, and in late 1820 began his support of the Austin colonization plan. His support continued even after Stephen Austin took control of the colony following the death of his father in 1821. The following year, despite a revolution that resulted in an independent Mexico, their planning continued. In an effort to facilitate the endeavor on behalf of the new government, Bastrop received an appointment as colonial land commissioner in 1823. The following year, after close consultation with the baron and others, Austin chose to establish his headquarters along the Brazos in a settlement the Mexican governor named San Felipe de Austin for the young empresario and the governor's patron saint (Saint Philip).[2]

Austin first visited the site of the future colonial center in 1821, observing: 'The bluff is about 60 feet high—The country back of this place and below for about 15 miles (as far as we went) is as good in every respect as man could wish for. Land all first rate, plenty of timber, fine water—beautifully rolling." In 1827, just three years after Seth Ingram first surveyed the townsite, pioneer Noah Smithwick settled there and in the 1890s provided one of the most vivid accounts of the frontier settlement. "The buildings all being of unhewn logs with clapboard roofs," he wrote, "presented few distinguishing features. Stephen F. Austin had established his headquarters something like half a mile back from the river on the west bank of a little creek—Palmito—that ran into the Brazos just above the main village." Despite the symmetry of Ingram's orderly survey, the reality on the ground was of a linear configuration along the main road. Comparing it to a funeral procession, Smithwick noted that it was "pretty good as to length, but rather thin." In a somewhat prescient manner, he wrote too of the lingering history of a time and place that now guides those working to interpret the past. "San Felipe de Austin! The shibboleth that flings the door of memory wide; the spell that bids the tide of years roll back, and from the ashes, where it has lain these sixty years and more, conjures up the old town. . . . San Felipe de Austin! Itself but a phantom, what a host of phantoms the name summons back to repeople it."[3]

Among those early pre-revolution residents of San Felipe were many—in addition to Austin, Bastrop, and Smithwick—whose names still resonate in the state's history. They include William Barret Travis, an attorney who figured prominently in the early disturbances that led to revolution and then later led in the defense of the Alamo. There were also Gail Borden, publisher of the important revolution-era newspaper the *Telegraph and Texas Register*; Samuel May Williams, entrepreneur, financier, and Austin's close

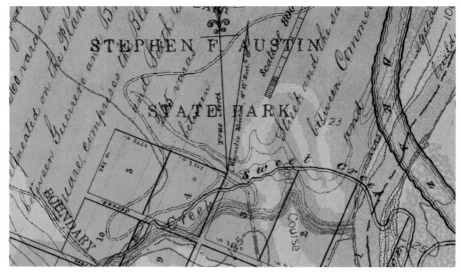

This image represents the early English-translation town plat of San Felipe de Austin, from the General Land Office, overlaid on a recent topographical map to show the relation of Baron de Bastrop's lots 1 and 2 to the current golf course along Sweet Creek. The image design is the work of Michael R. Moore, San Felipe de Austin project historian. Courtesy Michael Rugeley Moore.

confidant who served as postmaster of the colony; and Horatio Chriesman, the colony surveyor and a militia leader. While the enigmatic Bastrop played an important role in the disbursement of grants during the colony's early years, he died at Saltillo in 1827. Although he received several tracts of land for his invaluable service, he likely lived in a house on lot 536 instead of his garden lots, or out lots (numbers one and two), developed in the mid-twentieth century as the Stephen F. Austin Golf Course.[4]

As tensions developed between colonists and the Mexican authorities across Texas during the 1820s and 1830s, San Felipe de Austin became a center of resistance as well as revolutionary protest and preparedness. Delegates to the politically charged conventions of 1832 and 1833 met there to express their grievances against the government. In November 1835, with revolution an irrevocable solution, those assembled at San Felipe drew up a provisional government. A few months later, news of fierce military reprisals by the Mexican government under Gen. Antonio Lopez de Santa

Anna and the eastward flight of Gen. Sam Houston's Texan forces presaged the abandonment of San Felipe and the strategic Brazos crossing, precipitating what came to be known as the Runaway Scrape. On March 20, 1836, two weeks after the fall of the Alamo, Moseley Baker directed his local garrison—reportedly upon orders from Houston—to direct the evacuation of San Felipe and then torch all structures to preclude materials from being used to move troops across the river. Within hours, the colonial town of San Felipe was no more.[5]

When news of the Texan victory on the plains of San Jacinto in late April began to filter back through the region, some planned to return to San Felipe, and for a time the location of the former settlement held promise as a center of government for Austin County. Soon, however, even that promise faded, and Austin's former colonial headquarters gave way over the ensuing decades to other rapidly developing areas, such as the new railroad town of Sealy two miles to the southwest. While municipal development waned at San Felipe, it remained an important historical landmark, albeit one with only buried features from its period of significance. Regardless, state efforts to preserve the site failed to materialize significantly, and it fell to local residents to set aside property to provide a modest means of commemoration, including a small tract near the center of the former town. There residents preserved a well, built a replica of Austin's log cabin, brought in the 1840s-era Josey Store to house exhibits of community history, and with a focus on contributions by schoolchildren, raised funds for a memorial obelisk. In the 1930s the Texas Centennial Commission placed a commemorative granite marker on the property and commissioned a heroic statue of a seated Austin by the noted English sculptor John Angel. With those primary features in place by 1940, the commemorative site conveyed to the State Parks Board (later the Texas Parks and Wildlife Department) along with a nearby recreational area.[6]

In 2007–8 the Texas legislature transferred administration of the commemorative area, now the San Felipe de Austin Historic Site, to the Texas Historical Commission (THC). Utilizing both public and private funds, the THC broke ground across FM 1458 for an expansive museum complex to provide a broader interpretation of the San Felipe story. Central to the museum will be artifact collections amassed through the years by means of professional archeological investigations conducted under the auspices of the Texas Parks and Wildlife Department and the THC. Underground investigations and artifact analysis should continue as an integral part of the new museum program.

In March 2017, 181 years after the fall of the Alamo triggered events that led eventually to the abandonment and destruction of San Felipe de Austin, THC's site manager and public historian Bryan McAuley sat on the front porch of the Josey Store for an oral-history interview. With the steel framework of the future museum looming off to his right several hundred yards beyond the current commemorative site, he talked about plans for an important new phase for the interpretation of the former colonial town. "I've long advocated that we should be a place that defines the visitor experience as it relates to public archeology, and I do think we are going to push the envelop there." Reflecting on the still-unknown aspects of the site, he added this: "Archeologically, we don't know exactly what we're going to find. I hope if we can do enough archeology in front of the people, that that will resonate with them, and that as we learn things, they will see it." Such investigative access at an important historic site will be unique, but the challenge for public historians is even greater. Austin's iconic plat map of the town, for example, is, as McAuley noted, "a projection of a dream, and the reality is much smaller and a much different experience, so we have to be careful to interpret that." Speaking one year before the formal opening of the facility, he shared his vision for the lessons it will help convey. "People who love the story of the Texas Revolution, I'm optimistic, are going to respond favorably to the fact they know very little of it beyond the battles," especially the "nuanced" but pivotal history that took place on a small patch of ground. The story of Stephen Austin may be the draw for many visitors, McAuley concluded, but his hope is that they will be inspired by many other stories, including "William Barret Travis's life before the Alamo, and . . . Celia Allen, who was a slave woman who was given her freedom here and operated a bake oven." Since

San Felipe de Austin artifact. Originally thought to be a military button possibly from a Mexican uniform, upon closer inspection it proved to be from a golf blazer of much later vintage. Button owned by San Felipe resident Steve Packard. Photograph courtesy Texas Historical Commission, San Felipe de Austin State Historic Site.

"HISTORIC BUTTON"

In the course of his work as manager of the Stephen F. Austin State Historic Site, it is not unusual for Bryan McAuley to hear about the discovery of artifacts, either those found near the surface or those unearthed in land activities like gardening. He judiciously researches each item, hoping it might provide additional information about the community's history. In one instance a landowner contacted him about a metal button he believed might be from a Mexican soldier's uniform. What the finder first thought might be crossed swords or pikes turned out to be golf clubs, with the crown above them referencing the historically iconic Royal Blackheath Golf Course of Scotland. Such golfer buttons are still available commercially, and while an artifact of sorts, it relates more to the clubhouse than to pioneer life along the Brazos.

Source: Bryan McAuley, oral history interview by Dan K. Utley, San Felipe de Austin State Historic Site, Mar. 8, 2017.

Bryan McAuley, site manager for the San Felipe de Austin State Historic Site. This picture, taken in March 2017, shows the construction phase of the new Texas Historical Commission museum one year before its formal opening in 2018. Photograph by Dan K. Utley.

the museum is scheduled to open before the publication of this book, this part of the overall story may well serve as both past and prologue.[7]

THE COURSE *IN* HISTORY

Just as local residents proved instrumental in establishing Stephen F. Austin State Park in 1940, they also proved vital to the creation of early amenities on the property. To that end, civic leaders from Sealy, Brookshire, Katy, and Bellville formed the Stephen F. Austin Golf Association in the early 1950s, with George H. Stevenson of Sealy as president. The organization worked with the Texas State

Parks Board for the development of a golf course through a special partnership, with the state providing materials and overall planning and the association handling maintenance and regular supervision. Before the Parks Board gave final authorization, however, it had to deal with a broader issue of equal access to park facilities. The National Association for the Advancement of Colored People and others challenged the practice of exclusion by custom that prevailed in recreation facilities across the Old South. In Texas a bill sponsored by Sen. Warren McDonald sought to codify a formal segregation plan that would set aside existing parks, or parts thereof, as special areas for African American recreation. One of those included in the bill was Stephen F. Austin State Park, whereby "Negroes would take over old picnic facilities or use new grounds leaving the old for whites." Although the bill passed and Gov. Allan Shivers signed it into law, subsequent court orders, including a decision in *Beal v. Holcombe* that centered on golf courses, led to the integration of parks by 1952. The following year the board approved the construction of the first nine holes of a planned eighteen-hole course at the new state park.[8]

Arland Jay Mangum, an officer of the golf association, drew the plans for the original course. An electrical engineer by training, Mangum began working for the Humble Oil Refining Company in the 1930s and rose steadily in management, eventually moving to offices in Katy, twenty miles east of San Felipe. There he was an active civic leader and school board member in addition to his leadership role in the regional golf association. Without formal training in course design, Mangum used his appreciation for and knowledge of the local terrain to lay out a challenging course that included tight fairways and made use of heavy rough, woodlands, and water features, including Bullinger Creek (Sweet Creek) and small lakes and ponds. As he later described it: "The growth was so thick we couldn't use regular surveying instruments.... We had to use compasses. You couldn't see the surveying poles 100 feet ahead of you, the brush was so high." At one point the workers even temporarily misplaced the bulldozer used to clear the fairways. Herbert Schroeder, formerly with the Dallas and Levelland country clubs, served as the first pro of the new course, which for-

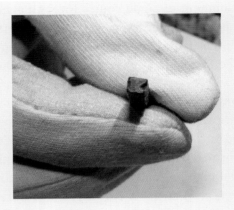

Detail photograph of the historic sort, or movable-type piece, discovered during recent archeological investigations at the San Felipe de Austin State Historic Site. Courtesy Texas Historical Commission, San Felipe de Austin State Historic Site.

"K" TYPE

Recent archeological investigations at San Felipe de Austin under the direction of the THC produced a wide range of artifacts from the village's nineteenth-century period of significance. One of these was a small piece of lead that, upon close inspection, appeared to be the letter K from the kind of set type used by early printers. The artifact is significant because it possibly relates to early printing endeavors at San Felipe. The first of those was the *Cotton Plant* newspaper—the first in the Anglo-American colonies—published by Godwin P. Cotton. A later and better-known publication was the *Telegraph and Texas Register*, put out by Gail Borden Jr., Thomas H. Borden, and Joseph Baker beginning late in 1835. As residents prepared to evacuate San Felipe early in 1836, however, the owners moved their publishing operation to Harrisburg. Unfortunately, the town was in the direct line of the advancing Mexican Army, whose soldiers seized the press and disposed of it in Buffalo Bayou. During the Republic of Texas, Gail Borden reestablished the newspaper, albeit on a different press. Through later difficulties and subsequent owners, it remained in operation until 1877.

Source: Bryan McAuley; "*Telegraph and Texas Register*," Handbook of Texas Online, accessed Mar. 17, 2017, http://www.tshaonline.org/handbook/online/articles/eeto2.

mally opened on Sunday, July 18, 1954. The following September, the wives of club members formed a Women's Golf Association, which featured special play days "with members playing nine holes of golf at 25 [cents]" and "winners receiving a golf ball as their prize."[9]

Work on the back nine did not get underway until the summer of 1971, with "dozer work" by Robert Lange of Brenham. The fully functional, eighteen-hole course opened the following year. The well-maintained facility proved popular for local golfers, including those from the nearby metropolitan area and visitors taking advantage of the park's camping facilities. Whether or not duffers avail themselves of exhibits at the separate San Felipe de Austin State Historic Site, now operated by the THC, they nevertheless play amid a series of interpretive kiosks prepared by the Friends of the San Felipe de Austin State Historic Site and funded through local sponsors. One of the kiosks provides historical background on Baron de Bastrop, the land commissioner who first issued titles to settlers in the Austin colony. Denoting the land's links to the past, it reads in part, "A portion of the golf course... [is] located on two of the lots (Garden Lots #2 and 3) that Bastrop owned in San Felipe." While the course does not bear his name in tribute, Bastrop is nevertheless remembered as the namesake of the county and town in the Colorado River valley northwest of San Felipe.[10]

IN THE SPIRIT OF THE WEST

BUTTERFIELD TRAIL GOLF CLUB, EL PASO

SCORECARD FROM THE PAST

Recent Past: Butterfield Trail Golf Club

Historic Name: Butterfield Trail

DETAILS: Eighteen-hole public golf course; distance is 7,307 yards from the longest tees

Location: 1858 Cottonwoods, El Paso

Historical Context: Nineteenth-century transportation and postal shipment

Historical Type: Overland-mail route

Period of Significance: 1857–62

Signature Hole of History: Number eight is a relatively straight par-four hole situated along an east–west alignment that closely parallels what is believed to be the original route of the Butterfield Trail between the Hueco Tanks and Franklin City (El Paso) stage stops. Golfers tee off in the direction of the east-bound stages coming from California and headed to Missouri or Tennessee.

THE COURSE *OF* HISTORY

On the afternoon of September 30, 1958, a horse-drawn stagecoach slowly made its way through El Paso from the Sears store to the central post office, where a thunderous explosion—the result of an old-fashioned, gunpowder-charged, anvil salute—marked its approach to the city center. Thousands of onlookers gathered to watch the spectacle and to join in the historical celebration that day. Mayor Raymond Telles officially welcomed the stage, its occupants, and its accompanying entourage as the vehicle came to a stop near a makeshift corral constructed of aspen poles and wagon wheels in the El Paso National Bank parking lot. He marked the occasion by presenting the riders with "Conquistador scrolls" commemorating the special centennial event. Among the dignitaries riding in the stagecoach was Ann Butterfield Newman, a descendant of John Butterfield, founder of the Overland Mail Company, the contracting postal service for El Paso—and indeed the American Southwest—for a few years before the Civil War. In another stagecoach, which approached the site by a different route, rode retired teacher Emily Giddings, whose father, George H. Giddings, oversaw the Jackass Mail operations between San Antonio and San Diego, California. Both routes were integral to the development of El Paso. The focus of the festivities that day was on the antebellum role the region played, when for a relatively short time, stagecoaches daily plied the iconic Butterfield Trail, which stretched roughly 2,800 miles from Tipton, Missouri (not far from Saint Louis) to San Francisco, California. Duly proud El Pasoans reveled in the recognition and continued the celebration throughout the day, with a parade, an evening barbecue, period music by the Texas Western College Pep Band, and a mock holdup at Five Points by the Rancheros, a reenactment group judiciously apprehended by the El Paso Sheriff's Posse. Ben F. Dixon, chair of the Butterfield Centennial Commission, in keeping with the theme of the day, spoke of the events leading up to the far west Texas leg of the journey. "We've had a fine trip and have stayed on schedule," he noted. "Haven't run into any Apaches, but we were 'held up' three times by Texas bad men along the way. In Oklahoma we had to sign a peace treaty with the Choctaws before we could proceed. All in the spirit of the West, of course."[1]

El Paso represented the last Texas stop for this unique national commemoration. Other towns in the state celebrating earlier were Sherman, Jacksboro, Albany, Anson, San Angelo, McCamey, Fort Stockton, and Dell City. What they had in common, and what they shared with towns in six other states, was a historical kinship tied to the route of the Butterfield Trail. In the late summer and early fall of 1958, these trail towns—some of which had developed only after the demise of the route—hosted exhibits of related books and artifacts. There were also special screenings of a travelogue entitled *Westward the Overland Mail*, which told of "a desert trail that has begotten a great civilization of farms, ranches, agricultural, commercial and industrial empires and metropolitan communities." Perhaps fittingly, net proceeds from the film showings were dedicated to another trail effort then underway—the "Darien Sub-Committee . . . , daring the fevers and wilds of Panama to construct the final connecting link uniting the Americas by a great through highway from Tierra del Fuego to the far shores of the 49th state." (Pres. Dwight Eisenhower signed the Alaska Statehood Act in July 1958, clearing the path for formal recognition of the new state in January 1959.) Although as a business venture the Butterfield Trail was in operation only from 1858 to 1861, much longer than the equally iconic Pony Express, it nevertheless produced an enduring legacy evocative of Manifest Destiny and American ingenuity. In the continuum represented by the opening of the West, the Butterfield Trail came on the heels of scientific and military expeditions through the Desert Southwest and presaged the transcontinental rail and telegraph lines that soon followed. Despite the brevity of its existence, it represented a pivotal point in US history.[2]

Soon after the US-Mexico War, which formally ended in February 1848 with the Treaty of Guadalupe Hidalgo, which established the southern boundary of Texas and resulted in the expansion of the United States westward to California, communication across the vast territory became an immediate concern. This increased dramatically as news spread about the discovery of gold at Sutter's Mill in California only a few days earlier. What followed was the epic gold rush of 1849, one of the most monumental migrations in US history, as thousands of would-be prospectors, business speculators, and others quickly made their way to the nation's new western coast to seek their fortunes. As there were no transcontinental rail or stage lines at the time, the only viable route immediately available for travelers, as well as for mail and parcel post, was by transoceanic routes to Central America, overland travel across the Isthmus of Panama, and steamship conveyance to California. Given the extensive costs and travel time involved, establishing more-direct overland routes from America's heartland—the western extent of rail lines and government mail service at the time—became the primary objective. It was within this context that a plan for regular stagecoach and mail service across the southwest, as part of a larger transcontinental route, began to emerge in the 1850s.[3]

Born in 1801 at Berne, New York, upstate west of Albany, John Warren Butterfield grew up on a family farm in a transitional era of transportation innovations. He knew firsthand of the nearby Erie Canal, a vital economic mainstay in the region, and through his interest in horses developed an early appreciation for stage lines and livery services that served the area. From his start as a delivery driver in Utica, Butterfield developed a company and eventually acquired his own routes and expanded operations to diversify his transportation services. He was, as trail historians Roscoe P. and Margaret B. Conkling noted, someone who "realized from experience that if certain articles of merchandise or other matter could be transported and delivered with greater dispatch by eliminating loss of time in storage and transit ..., public business would gladly bear the higher tariff rate that such a service would naturally impose." He organized the Butterfield and Wasson Express Company in 1849 and the following year spearheaded a merger with two other firms, headed by Henry Wells and William Fargo, to form the American Express Company. In short order, however, Wells and Fargo formed their own venture, ironically to cash in on the California trade, although the initial contract in that endeavor went to Butterfield, who formed the Overland Mail Company for that purpose.[4]

The lucrative mail-delivery contract Butterfield bid on and secured from the federal government called for him to provide semiweekly service via coaches from Saint Louis and Memphis to San Francisco. The duration of each trip was to be twenty-five days or less along a route determined by the US Post Office, but the location of way stations and stage stops would be up to the company. With just a year to prepare the infrastructure, Butterfield committed a considerable upfront investment, but the payoff would be $600,000 per year over the six-year extent of the contract— more than enough to recoup expenses and make a sizable profit.

Still, the risks of such an undertaking, given the complexities and uncertainties of the natural and cultural environments through the frontier lands, were considerable.[5]

The route would prove critical to the success of the operation, and that decision fell to Postmaster General Aaron V. Brown, a Virginia native and former Tennessee congressman and governor. In the late 1850s, with sectional tensions between the North and the South already at a heightened state, any government action perceived to favor one region over the other drew intense scrutiny and political criticism. By being a southerner favoring a southern route that would, in all likelihood, lead eventually to a similar route for the first transcontinental rail line, Brown precipitated intense debate over his choice. While he argued that his selection offered the best seasonal conditions, northern critics roundly blasted it as corrupt regional favoritism, but ultimately Brown prevailed. In choosing a northern contractor, he may have mollified the opposition to some extent, but in the end his selection of Butterfield was based primarily on experience, although it may also have helped that the New York businessman and Pres. James Buchanan were considered good friends.[6]

For his rolling stock, Butterfield turned to the Abbot-Downing Company of Concord, New Hampshire, longtime manufacturers of a wide range of coaches, including the round-bottomed and brightly decorated stagecoaches so strongly identified with westward transportation. Indeed, the Concord coach served its purpose on various sections of the trail, primarily those stretching out from San Francisco and Memphis through Arkansas. In Texas, however, the rocky terrain and deep sand deposits out west, as well as boggy areas to the east, called for a lighter passenger coach to ensure speed and durability. Known as Celerity wagons, or mud wagons, the light coaches were often canvas-sided and usually pulled by teams of four mules—the preference in Texas—or horses. Designed to accommodate four passengers comfortably, the wagons often carried several more people in addition to luggage, mail, packages, water, and supplies. Named for their speed, these coaches usually traveled at three to five miles per hour.[7]

In the summer months of 1858, company workers built the requisite stations across the route, often referred to as the Oxbow Route because of its severe southerly deviation from its starting points along the Mississippi River. As historian Glen Sample Ely noted in his extensive study of the trail, Texas alone hosted more than fifty stations, each representing minimalist construction of vernacular design, with some millwork coming from regional providers, including some in San Antonio. "Workers constructed the stage stops out of wood, adobe, rock, or a combination thereof. Building a station took about fifteen days with a three-man crew. . . . Each stage stop usually had three rooms . . . with an attached corral." Employees fashioned furniture onsite, while regional merchants vied for provision service. In addition to staples, company stations maintained livestock for butchering. Water sources were generally nearby but with sufficient distance to allow unrestricted access by local Native Americans.[8]

With the primary infrastructure in place and the favorable trail route reconnoitered, the Overland Mail Company began service in September 1858. The first westbound stage entered Texas by way of the Red River at Colbert's Ferry, north of Sherman. From there the route continued on to Forts Belknap, Phantom Hill, and Chadbourne, serving all the settlements in between. It continued across the Colorado and Concho valleys toward the Horsehead

CELERITY ON THE UPPER ROAD

Much of what is known about the Butterfield Trail, especially with regard to site-specific surveys of extant remains, is attributable to the work of a remarkable couple—Roscoe Pratt "Rod" Conkling (1877–1971) and Margaret Badenoch Vear Conkling (1890–1973). A native of upstate New York, where John Butterfield was a local legend, Rod Conkling developed an early interest in the American West and particularly the overland-mail route. Through his work as a mining engineer, he worked in Mexico and South America before moving to El Paso to work with the American Smelting and Refining Company. While there, he met the Chicago-born Margaret Vear, a local music teacher. The couple married in 1930 in a local cave (named appropriately Conkling Cave) and spent much of their free time in the intensive pursuit of in-situ investigations all along the trail from Missouri to California, reportedly wearing out three cars in the process. Their extensive and detailed field notes, as well as photographs of sites and artifacts, provide a remarkable foundation for any study of the trail. They eventually compiled their findings and analysis in a three-volume work, *The Butterfield Overland Mail, 1857–1869* (1947). By that time, the couple had relocated to California, where they died in the early 1970s. The following represents their historical assessment of the Celerity wagons used almost exclusively through the midsection of the trail, including Texas.

The "celerity" wagon was an innovation on the part of Butterfield to provide a lighter and faster type of vehicle for use on the rougher sections of the route, and also to furnish something like an overland mail coach sleeper. The carriage of this vehicle was built on the same lines as that of the regular [Concord] coach, but had smaller wheels. The lower part of the body was fashioned much the same as the regular coach body also, but the top was a frame structure covered with heavy duck, the doors and sides provided with curtains of the same material. This vehicle had a capacity for nine inside passengers only. The three inside seats were so constructed that they could be adjusted and made into a bed. With its low center of gravity this wagon was less liable to an overset than the regular coach. The first consignment of one hundred of these were built by [James] Goold [and Company of Albany, New York].

Source: Roscoe P. Conkling and Margaret B. Conkling, *The Butterfield Overland Mail, 1857–1869*, vol. 1 (Glendale, CA: Arthur H. Clark, 1947), 133.

Celerity wagons, or mud wagons, such as the one depicted in this 1858 illustration, were the preferred mode of transportation by the Overland Mail Company along the western stretches of the Butterfield Trail in Texas. The Overland Mail—Changing Stage-Coach for Celerity Wagon, in Frank Leslie's Illustrated Newspaper, October 3, 1858. Courtesy Special Collections, University of North Texas Libraries.

Crossing of the Pecos River. There it followed along the east bank of the Pecos to a place known as Pope's Well (Pope's Camp), where in 1855 US Army captain John Pope led an expedition of engineers and military personnel in a futile attempt to drill for water on the Llano Estacado. Outside Pope's Well, the trail began a gradual turn to the west, with the next sizable community being the town of Franklin (outside of El Paso). From the Horsehead Crossing to the Franklin stop, the trail passed such landmarks as Delaware Springs, Pine Spring, Guadalupe Pass, the salt flats, the Cornudas Mountains, and Hueco Tanks, the last stage stop before El Paso.[9]

The last Texas leg of the trail followed a route commonly known as the Upper Road, though that section proved problematic because of the scarcity of dependable water sources and the general absence of military protection. As a result, the company abandoned the Upper Road in May 1859 in favor of the Lower Road from San Antonio and Fort Stockton, which branched off not far from the present Butterfield Trail Golf Club and provided some measure of federal military protection via Forts Quitman and Bliss. Even

ORMSBY AT HUECO TANKS

Waterman Lily Ormsby Jr., a twenty-three-year-old reporter for the *New York Herald*, carefully chronicled the inaugural westbound run of the Overland Mail along the Butterfield Trail as the lone through passenger. On the evening of September 26, 1858, he boarded the coach leaving Tipton, Missouri, headed for San Francisco, where he arrived in twenty-three days and twenty-three hours after a journey of more than 2,700 miles. The following account of the stage's arrival at Hueco Tanks (which Ormsby recorded as Waco Tanks) appeared in the *Herald* on November 11, 1858:

> On reaching the Waco [Hueco] Tanks, we found an excellent corral and cabin built; but to our consternation the station keeper pointed to two eight gallon kegs, saying, "that is all the water we have left for a dozen men and as many head of cattle." The Waco Tanks have been reported to be inexhaustible, but the usual droughts had drained them, and the most rigorous search through the mountain[s] did not bring to light any more. The tank had been recently enlarged so as to hold water enough to last a year when the rain next fell, but until that time the station would have to be abandoned unless by chance water could be found in the viciity. We changed horses here and took supper, and a few hours' ride brought us to Franklin city [sic] on the Rio Grande River [sic], opposite the ancient town of El Paso.

It was during the leg from Hueco Tanks to El Paso that the stage passed along the southern boundary of what, more than a century and a half later, is now the Butterfield Trail Golf Club.

Source: Waterman L. Ormsby, *The Butterfield Overland Mail*, ed. Lyle H. Wright and Josephine M. Bynum (San Marino, CA: Huntington Library, 1942), 77.

with this change, the route through El Paso was short lived. In the latter part of the Buchanan administration, sectional disturbances propelled the nation—inevitably it seemed—toward civil war. In addition, the company faced a financial crisis due in large part to stalled congressional action on the post office appropriations that ultimately resulted in the ouster of Butterfield and the transfer of company control to Wells Fargo, which had provided substantial operational loans. Even with that adjustment, as Glen Sample Ely chronicled, sectional pressures proved insurmountable.

> Texas's secession vote in February 1861 prompted Congress a few weeks later to move the overland mail service form the southern route to a central route through the country's mid-section, far away from the Southern states. The Overland Mail Company agreed to switch operations to the central route, and on March 12, 1861, Postmaster General Montgomery Blair officially ordered the change. It took a few weeks for the news to filter down to all the stations along the line, but by early April, Butterfield was pulling out of Texas.

The company sold its Texas sites and equipment to George Giddings, who continued local mail service until 1862, when the Union Army took control of the trans-Pecos region. With that, the Butterfield Trail passed into history, although its legacy has endured through the years. Vestiges of its brief but significant existence is still evident in museum artifacts, archival records, preserved stagecoaches, and in the ruts that have remained as historical scars on the land, such as those found within the Butterfield Trail Golf Club.[10]

THE COURSE *IN* HISTORY

Although the Butterfield Trail Golf Club is one of the newest courses featured in this book, it is noted for its colorful heritage through marketing and course layout, "The history of the old west merges with plans for the future of El Paso at the beautiful Butterfield Trail

Golf Club," declares the club's website, which also includes a brief history of its namesake trail. Even its address number, 1858, is a reference to the year stages and wagons first started moving through the area on the transcontinental route.

The course is the work of legendary golf course designer Tom Fazio. Growing up in Norristown, Pennsylvania, outside Philadelphia, he learned the golf business by helping his uncle, a designer and former golf professional of some renown, George Fazio. His apprenticeship paid off, and in time he started his own design business, which has now become one of the most successful firms in the world. Honored several times by *Golf Digest* as the "Best Modern Day Golf Course Architect," Fazio holds the distinction of having more of his layouts formally designated as among the best in the nation than any other designer. His courses in the *Golf Digest* list of "America's 100 Greatest Golf Courses" in 2015–16, for example, include the Wade Hampton Golf Club in North Carolina, Butler National Golf Club in Illinois, Shadow Creek Golf Course in Nevada, and the Estancia Club in Arizona. Among his Texas courses, in addition to Butterfield Trail, are the Canyons and Foothills courses at Barton Creek Resort and Spa in Austin, the Jack Rabbit course of Champions Golf Course in Houston, Stonebrier Country Club in Frisco, and Dallas National Golf Course. As noted in company literature, the architectural philosophy of FAZIO Design is to develop links that play off their natural environments by "creating harmonious transitions from existing topographical conditions, developing courses that offer golfers of varying skill find a challenging yet enjoyable experience." As Fazio told one interviewer: "I'm still the traditionalist who doesn't believe in gimmicks like railroad ties, moving a lot of earth if avoidable, any trick or deception that's just too penal in nature. I believe in a redemptive view of mankind, a tolerance which punishes golfers, but is forgiving enough that when they make mistakes they're not sent into Dante's inferno of oblivion." His respect for the environment, both natural and cultural, results in what one client described as "instant patina." Such a description is fitting for his design of Butterfield Trail, which celebrates the desert environment and visually provides historical references to the past.[11]

COHO'S HORIZON

CROSS TIMBERS GOLF COURSE, AZLE

SCORECARD FROM THE PAST

Recent Past: Cross Timbers Golf Course

Historic Name: John Jeremiah "Coho" and Nancy Jane Smith Farmstead

DETAILS: Eighteen-hole public golf course; distance is 6,734 yards from the longest tees

Location: 1181 S. Stewart Street, Azle

Historical Context: Dispersed agricultural settlements in North Texas during the late nineteenth and early twentieth centuries

Historical Type: Farmstead

Period of Significance: 1860s–1940s

Signature Hole of History: The eighteenth green is in close proximity to archeological vestiges of the Smith farmstead. Interpretive markers, signage, and kiosks in the area provide basic historical information on the family and buried features.

THE COURSE OF HISTORY

In the process of overlaying one cultural landscape—like a golf course—on another—perhaps a historic farmstead or a prehistoric campsite—evidence of the earlier landscape or horizon most often gives way surficially to new features on the land. Where the changes on the earlier landscape are marginal, with only minimal disturbance of historic features, the site is said to have archeological integrity—that is, buried beneath the new horizon, in situ, can be unmistakable, albeit fragmented, records of past lifeways that professional cultural-resource

A fairway view along the eighteenth hole, the signature hole of history for the Cross Timbers course. Photograph by Stanley O. Graves.

specialists can detect, analyze, and interpret with great accuracy. Such is the case with the Cross Timbers Golf Course, which contains extant remains—below and above the ground—of a farmstead that existed from the time of the Civil War and remained occupied until around World War II. Archeological investigations have yielded information on how this farm family lived during that approximately eighty-year period, and historical records, including oral histories and folklore, give life to the basic footprint on the land. These two elements thus become one, each complementing the understanding of a relatively small piece of history within broader concepts that are relevant to larger stories of cultural history.

Much of what is known about the evolution of agricultural history in Texas is the result of a legal and scientific process known as cultural resource management (CRM). Formally, it came about as the result of the National Historic Preservation Act of 1966, signed into law by Pres. Lyndon B. Johnson. The genesis of the legislation goes back much further, however, and reflects a growing public alarm, particularly in the boom era following World War II, that significant elements of our collective past had been lost in a relatively short time to new highways, airports, rail lines, pipelines, and related infrastructure funded or regulated by public money. Specifically, Section 106 of the act called for careful investigations and review of the consequences any federal "undertaking"—either through review or funding—had on cultural resources. Since 1966, states and other public entities have enacted similar processes for protecting the past through mitigative measures that can include historical research, oral histories, detailed photography, measured drawings, archeological reports, and simple avoidance of features. The Texas Historical Commission is the agency designated to review projects conducted on state lands or on properties owned by entities of the state, such as counties and municipalities. While the legal implications are much broader in scope, this was the mechanism in place when the city of Azle began planning for a municipal golf course in the 1990s. As a result, under a Texas Antiquities Permit, the city contracted for a site review by AR Consultants of Dallas, which completed its report, "Cultural Resources Evaluation of the Azle Municipal Golf Course," in 1993. Archeologists Brenda B. Whorton and S. Alan Skinner were the primary investigators as well as the authors. Their findings for what is formally known as the Coho Smith Site (designated by archeological trinomial 41PR27) served later as documentation for a commission marker that provides historical interpretation for both golfers and heritage tourists.[1]

According to Whorton and Skinner, the site "serves as a good example of a small, post–Civil War North-Central rural Texas farmstead which has several unique features." Its significance comes not only from the archeological features, described in detail later, but also through historical association with a unique character in Texas history—Coho Smith. John Jeremiah Smith lived a complex life, marked by what seems to be an overwhelming wanderlust mixed with a compelling sense of adventure. Born in 1826 in Pennsylvania, he moved with his family, led by immigrant patriarch James Smith from Rotterdam, Holland, to Carroll County,

COHO AND CYNTHIA ANN

Captured at the age of nine during an 1836 Comanche raid in present Limestone County, Texas, Illinois-born Cynthia Ann Parker grew to maturity with her captors and adopted their culture as her own. The wife of Chief Peta Nocona and the mother of Chief Quanah Parker, she was rescued, along with her daughter Topasannah (Prairie Flower), by Texas Rangers along the Pease River in 1860. Although Cynthia Ann returned to live with members of the Parker family near Birdville in Tarrant County, she had great difficulty readjusting to the lifestyle of her childhood and continually sought opportunities to return to her tribal family. Given her inability to remember English, her cousin, William Parker, sought the services of a translator, which led them to Coho Smith, who had learned the Comanche language during his own captivity. Smith's poignant description of meeting Parker is a compelling reminder of the sadness she long endured:

> We had went about 100 yards when I saw a little smoke. It was at a place where a large tree had been cut down to make clap-boards [sic] and the hearts of the board timber were lying there. She was sitting on a bunch of the hearts with her elbows on her knees and her hands to her face. An old sunbonnet hid her face. A little child was sitting on the ground making a little coral [sic] with small sticks and talking to its self [sic] in Comanche . . . . A little fire was burning near.

At first wary of Smith's presence and intentions, as with others who sought to help, Parker was overcome with joy upon hearing him talk in her adopted language. Excitedly responding in a mixture of Comanche and Spanish, she spoke with him until the "we [sic] small hours," as Smith recorded, incessantly seeking his assistance in escaping and offering him all manner of reward from her Comanche family upon her return: "The last thing I remember hearing was her saying, 'Si le doy o mi gene si le doy, todos las muchachas que si quire, pero bonito y buen mosos.' (I will give you, or my people will give you, all the girls you want, but pretty and well made)." Despite the hope Smith must have represented to her, he rejected her pleas, leaving Parker once again despondent and feeling trapped. Tragically, despite countless efforts by family members and other supporters, and even the promise of assistance from the state legislature, she never fully accepted her plight, but she also never returned to her Comanche family. Cynthia Ann Parker died in Anderson County around 1870 and was initially buried there. Subsequently, her remains were reinterred in Oklahoma, first at Cache, then finally at Fort Sill, where her son, Quanah, is also buried.

Sources: S. C. Gwynne, *Empire of the Summer Moon: Quanah Parker and the Rise and Fall of the Comanches, the Most Powerful Indian Tribe in American History* (New York: Scribner, 2010), 187–89; A. C. Greene, "Texas Sketches: Cynthia Ann Parker Saga," *Dallas Morning News*, May 11, 1984, 21A; Iva Roe Logan, ed., *Cohographs by Coho* (Fort Worth: Branch-Smith, 1976).

Missouri, in the 1830s. There, after James drowned in the Missouri River, his son apprenticed as a cabinetmaker to learn a trade as well as English, since he spoke only Dutch. Lacking a formal education, Smith quickly picked up the language, as well as several others then prevalent on the US frontier. In the early 1840s he first made a trip into Texas, returning later to connect with North Texas pioneer John Neely Bryan and assisting him in laying out the original plat for what became Dallas.[2]

In a letter to the *Dallas Morning News* in 1903, Smith provided details of his work with Bryan, who had obtained rights to 640 acres of land through the Peters Colony. Working with him and others, Smith helped build the first houses in the new community. When it came to the task of laying out the townsite, he noted that the only compass was "a pocket one with a two-inch needle." He added: "We made our surveyor's chain of an old bed cord, and went at it, laying off the town of Dallas. Neither of us had any experience in laying off a town, so we laid off the public square first (and entirely too small, by the way)." From the square, the team proceeded to lay out streets and blocks to the north and then to the south. In the process the men came across "an old woman" cooking in the shade of a large hickory tree who asked, "Gentlemen, do you know what day this is?" When she informed them that it was the Sabbath, they checked their notes, concurred, and duly quit work for the day. Smith concluded his letter thus: "Most of the old pioneers are dead. I am still in the land of the living, by God's grace." He was seventy-six at the time.[3]

In 1845 Smith moved south to the Mexican state of Coahuila, where he was reportedly "adopted" by a wealthy family. Imprisoned briefly for running contraband tobacco, he was later captured by a Comanche raid in the Santa Rosa area. During his captivity, he received a lance wound to his left knee, an injury that left him permanently crippled. As a result, Smith acquired the moniker "Cojo"—Spanish for lame—which he Anglicized to "Coho," a name he readily used in correspondence. He eventually escaped and returned to Missouri, where he married Nancy Haney and worked as a painter and farmer. What followed was a series of adventures that connected him to gold mining on the West Coast and to the filibuster expeditions of William Walker in Cuba and Central America. He also became a Texas Ranger, serving until his honorable discharge in 1860. Parting ways with his wife and their five children, Smith was in Parker County, Texas, by 1861, when he wed Nancy Jane Hoggard. Together they established their homestead in the dispersed farming settlement near Ash Creek, southwest of what developed later as the town of Azle, where they raised their own eight children. Eschewing the sedentary life, Coho continued his adventures far afield, working for a time in the mercantile and freighting businesses in Mexico but ultimately returning to Parker County, where he worked as a teacher, farmer, gunsmith, and cabinetmaker. He also worked to develop his homestead, which grew to include an expanded cabin, stone-lined well, root cellar, springhouse, and what is believed to have been a family fort. An inveterate keeper of journals, he carefully chronicled his rich life; these writings and drawings became the basis of a book entitled *Cohographs by Coho*, now among the rare works of Texana. Coho

Smith died in 1914, and Jane Smith died two years later. Daughter Rosa Smith Harris subsequently took possession of the home, and her family resided there until the 1940s, when the property conveyed to Floyd I. Scrimshire, who owned a nearby dairy. For a half century, Scrimshire grazed his cattle on the land and leased tracts to others for agricultural and caliche-quarrying activities. He made improvements to the land, including stock tanks, and used the old Smith home for hay storage.[4]

With time, the unoccupied farm deteriorated, and native vegetation gradually overtook the site. By the 1990s, the structural remains were difficult for archeologists to detect in an initial survey, even though they knew some details of the site through the mapping work of the Tarrant County Archeological Society. Whorton and Skinner provided details of the intensive surveying required at the overgrown and forgotten site:

> A hands-and-knees foray into the [covering] plum thicket revealed that there was a pile of rock located in the area and also noted the presence of several rocks that might be foundation rocks. In addition, further survey located the mouth of what appeared to be a root cellar, and along the creek we noted a dry-laid limestone rock wall that had been built across a short gully. Almost by accident we discovered another pile of cut limestone rock in a heavily overgrown cluster of old trees located just west of the well. The discovery of these apparent features along with oral history about this location indicated that we had located a house site and/or school site that might date to the period just after the Civil War.... In all, the area north of the dirt road contained evidence of a two-room residence with a chimney in the east end, an unusually constructed root cellar, a hand-dug well, a spring house, a series of one-stone-high rock "walls" that define work/living spaces around the residence, and a dry-laid rock wall constructed in a gully just south of the creek.[5]

The root cellar, a feature commonly found on farms of similar eras in Texas, proved to be of particular interest to the investigators because of its unusual configuration. Excavated by hand into the rock and clay found on the site, the cellar was approximately nine feet across at its widest point, with small cavities that flanked the entryway. "In plan view," Whorton and Skinner reported, "the cellar is irregular in shape but might be visualized as a three-lobed clover leaf." Also of interest was evidence of a springhouse, which utilized flowing water to cool stored food and dairy products. The investigations located stone remnants of what may have been, according to family and local history tradition, a family fort. What proved inconclusive, though, was evidence to support stories that the Picket School, so called because of its vertical picket construction, was located on the site or had been an earlier use for the house. In order for that to be proven, Whorton and Skinner concluded, additional testing beyond the survey investigations would be necessary. As with most CRM archeological investigations, limited site testing is preferred since full excavations destroy the resource, so answers to such questions remain buried, perhaps for some future investigations utilizing different, noninvasive technologies. Regardless, the survey produced evidence sufficient to afford a measure of protection for the Smith farmstead and to facilitate the placement of a state historical marker for the Coho and Nancy Jane Smith Farmstead Site in March 1996. The inscription speaks to both the story of pioneer settlers of the Azle area and to the value of historical archeology in providing tangible links to the past.[6]

The Course *in* History

Final planning for the Azle Municipal Golf Course got underway following the completion of the cultural resource report and other investigations. To design the course, the city hired Jeffrey Brauer, a noted golf course architect with a national reputation. Brauer grew up in suburban Chicago, where like many youthful would-be golfers, he frequently accessed local courses on Mondays, when they were closed. Setting his sights on a career in golf course design, he focused his studies and, after attaining a degree in landscape

Kiosk and historical markers interpreting the site of Coho and Nancy Jane Smith's homestead. The eighteenth green is in the background. Photograph by Stanley O. Graves.

architecture from the University of Illinois, went to work for well-respected Chicago-area course designers Ken Killian and Dick Nugent. When he began feeling the need to find his own projects to test his innovative ideas, Brauer decided to move to the South at the age of twenty-nine. "I went to the local library to look at phone books," he remembered, "and Dallas was the only major city without a yellow page listing for Golf Course Architects, so Dallas it was." Rising quickly in the business, he developed a unique design philosophy that drew from historic courses he had played and studied. "I lean to playability, visibility, and receptivity," he noted. "In computer terms, I am mostly 'What you see is what you get.' In general, on any given course, I believe holes are too much alike, rather than too different, so I do borrow from classic ideas of every era, and you might call my style 'eclectic.'"[7]

Brauer remained active in the American Society of Golf Course Architects, for which he served as president, and a promoter of continuing education and a leader on such issues as environmen-

THE MOO CREW

Norm Peterson, sports editor for the *Hood County News* in
Granbury, once compared Robert Landers's golf swing to
something from a "failed sobriety test," while *Sports Illustrated*
writer Austin Murphy thought the "brusque three-quarter
swing" looked more like "a man trying to kill a cornered rat."
Murphy added that the Azle man perfected his unorthodox
style by relentlessly hitting golf balls in his pastures, "an aro-
matic practice range that gives fresh meaning to the expres-
sion crappy lie." Landers was a Parker County farmer who
reportedly took up the game of golf in his twenties and quickly
became something of a phenomenon by consistently winning
local tournaments. In 1994 he signed up for the Senior PGA
Tour Qualifying Tournament (also known as Q-School) and
gained national attention by finishing sixth in the standings,
thereby earning his professional card for the following year.
As Peterson chronicled, Landers "played 33 events that year,
finishing 77th on the money list." The following year he played
fewer tournaments but won more money, his best finish being
fourteenth place in Ohio. All the time he continued to keep his
farm in operating order. Playing with clubs he reconditioned
himself, Landers "took the world of polyester slacks and pas-
tel pullovers by storm," despite his usual attire of Wrangler
jeans, tennis shoes, and Cross Timbers Golf Course shirts.
Garnering a sizeable band of followers called the Moo Crew,
he brought a great deal of attention to his home course in
Azle during his brief stint on the senior circuit.

Sources: Norm Peterson, "Landers Saw the Cities; He'll Take the Farm," *Hood
County News* (Granbury, TX), Apr. 4, 1998, 13; Austin Murphy, "Moo Debut:
Farmer Robert Landers Was a Hit in His First Senior Event," *Sports Illustrated*,
Feb. 13, 1995, online source.

tal sustainability. He has garnered a wide range of recognition for his courses, including the Giants Ridge Golf Club in Minnesota, the Links at Sierra Blanca in New Mexico, and the Canterberry Golf Course in Colorado. In addition to the Cross Timbers course, which opened in 1995, among his other Texas courses are Cowboys Golf Club in Grapevine, Bluebonnet Hills Golf Course in Manor, the Squaw Valley Golf Club in Glen Rose, and the Wilderness Golf Club in Lake Jackson.[8]

CONCEIVED IN CHAOS

THE CAMPUS COURSE AT TEXAS A&M, COLLEGE STATION

SCORECARD FROM THE PAST

Currently: The Campus Course at Texas A&M

Historic Name: Agricultural and Mechanical College of Texas

DETAILS: Eighteen-hole public golf course located at the southeast corner of Texas A&M University; distance is 7,008 yards from the longest tees

Location: 1 Bizzell Street, College Station

Historical Context: Early higher education in Texas

Historical Type: Land-grant college

Period of Significance: 1876 to the present

Signature Hole of History: Number four is a 353-yard, par-four hole with a slight dogleg to the right, bounded by water and bunkers, with fairway bunkers guarding the green. It has seen relatively little change since originally designed by Ralph Plummer. Relative to the history of the university, though, the fifteenth green is in an area that yielded artifacts during excavations associated with the course redesign. These included broken dishware from Duncan Dining Hall, built in 1939, when part of the golf course site served as a garbage dump.

THE COURSE *OF* HISTORY

Early in his two-volume centennial history of Texas A&M University, historian Henry C. Dethloff wrote: "Conceived during the chaos of Civil War and delivered during the pain of Reconstruction, the A&M College somehow survived the wolves, the political machinations and spoilsmanship of the Radicals, and

Number two green on the Campus Course at Texas A&M. Courtesy Texas A&M University Press.

Teeing ground of hole number 3 on the Campus Course at Texas A&M. A par 4, 427 yards from the maroon tees. Courtesy Texas A&M University Press.

the purges of the Democratic Redeemers to become Texas' first public institution of higher learning." Setting the context in another time, though, he noted that the roots of the story reached much further back. The goal of higher education as a defining element of progressive people emerged early in the days of the republic, first carried out by such pioneers as the Methodists at Rutersville and the Baptists at Independence. Although there were calls for republic and later state support of the initiative, and indeed some measure of progress on that front, other pressing issues crowded out the objective until shortly before the Civil War. In 1858 the legislature passed a bill, which Gov. Hardin Runnels signed, providing a general means of funding for the long-sought University of Texas. Before its effective implementation, however, intense sectional strife split the nation, and Texas seceded to join the Confederate States of America. As a result, the state was not initially included in the federal land-grant-college legislation known as the Morrill Act of 1862.[1]

The namesake of the land-grant legislation was Vermonter Justin S. Morrill, a US representative and later senator whose idea for a system of federal support for colleges teaching agriculture and industrial arts partly drew on the ideas of Illinois College professor Jonathan B. Turner and others. Morrill brought to these the political acumen to make it a reality in Congress, despite considerable dissent from his colleagues and even an earlier veto by Pres. James Buchanan. When subsequent legislation passed and Pres. Abraham Lincoln signed it into law, the Morrill Act set into place the policies for establishing and funding land-grant schools under state compliance measures and provided general parameters for program offerings as well. Iowa was the first state to meet the requirements for consideration, which led to what became Iowa State University, but the first school deemed fully operational under the legislation was Kansas State Agricultural College (later Kansas State University) in Manhattan. Following the Civil War, the benefits of the Morrill Act conveyed to the readmitted southern states as well, albeit slowly due to the complications of Reconstruction. When Texas finally received approval of its application, signifying that it met the programmatic requirements, it then entered the five-year timeframe to have the school open and fully functional. Despite some initial interpretive differences on the exact date for opening the school, the state persevered. Acting under the understanding that the resulting college would fall under the operational umbrella of the University of Texas, Gov. E. J. Davis named three commissioners—George B. Slaughter (who replaced initial appointee McDonald Lorance), John G. Bell, and F. E. Grothaus—to select and secure a campus site within three months, utilizing funds from the sale of federal land scrip. Hoping to locate the school within what was then the projected center of population growth, the commissioners heard offers involving sites in such locales as Grimes County, Austin County, and Brazos County. Despite some political wrangling that could have resulted in Beeville as the school's home, the remote Brazos County site near Bryan prevailed. This location afforded the commissioners relatively open prairie land near the Brazos River and proximity to the Houston and Texas Central rail line, recently extended from its temporary terminus at nearby Millican.[2]

In 1871 Bryan was relatively new, having only recently succeeded Boonville as the seat of government. Although Brazos County was one of the poorest in the state at the time, progressive-minded political leaders pushed for due consideration and made every effort to secure the college, which they believed would set a positive course for the area's economy then dependent largely on livestock and farming. Three specially elected men represented the town in the ensuing negotiations, with Harvey Mitchell taking the lead as discussions later intensified. Deeds filed on June 23, 1871, formally sealed the deal. These included three tracts totaling 980 acres from Mitchell, one tract of 1,226 acres from J. Frederick Cox, and one tract of 210 acres from "Mrs. Rebecca Rector and her husband, Nelson W. Rector." Of the conveyances, only the Rector property then had land under cultivation. Bryan thus provided 2,416 acres, allowing the college to move from paper and planning to reality. Securing the property proved relatively easy in comparison to the broader tasks that followed. Preparing the grounds and developing the curriculum proved somewhat daunting for those charged with transforming the prairie land to a viable college campus worthy of the public investment.[3]

Part of this prairie acreage had served as a staging area for cattle shipments via rail to northern markets. Principally post-oak savannah, the property appeared to be "adapted to the purpose almost as if designed by nature, or prescribed by a most skillful connoiseur [sic]," as the commission architect and treasurer reported to his colleagues upon a personal tour of the grounds. The natural environment of the site, though, posed its own challenges, particularly given the diverse wildlife that included deer, rabbits, scorpions, snakes, and other critters. "Packs of wolves challenged the intrusion and trappings of civilized man into their domain," Dethloff noted, and even after the college began functioning, close encounters one might otherwise anticipate along the prairie margin still occurred, including wolf attacks on unsuspecting students within the campus proper. Nature no doubt also played a part in construction setbacks due to the underlying and undulating clay soils so susceptible to deluges and dry spells, but there was also the human factor. Construction work began as soon as possible but soon proved inadequate. With more than half of the budgeted $75,000 expended on bringing the main building foundation to grade, an inspection revealed that the work failed to meet safety standards, resulting in its removal and reconstruction on new specifications. In an 1873 letter to the governor, construction inspector A. S. Broadus reported, "The foundation walls have already given way, even without the building being on them, in one place opposite one of the cisterns, the wall has sunk at least six inches below the level and cracked in several places."[4]

No less challenging than the environment and the work site, though, was the task of creating an educational program that was the first of its kind in the state in addition to adequate educational models for scientific farming and industrial management, which were still emerging fields of study nationally. Demand drove development, outpacing the available educational materials and qualified instructors, which were especially limited in the South following Reconstruction. To address those concerns while also seeking to establish the physical campus with limited funds, the college board sought a president who would have proven leadership qualities and serve as a draw for prospective students. The members first offered the job to former Confederate president Jefferson Davis, who still engendered widespread pride and respect in post-war Texas. "When I was asked to accept the presidency of the Agricultural and Mechanical College of Texas," Davis recalled, "I consented. I could not picture a more pleasant and satisfactory occupation than to be enabled to aid in instructing the youths of Texas, many of whose fathers I knew personally. . . . Some of the wisest counselors from my side were soldiers from Texas." His initial acceptance proved short lived, however, due to the concerns of family and friends who feared the task would drain his energies and keep him away from his beloved Mississippi. "I finally yielded," Davis admitted, "and declined the presidency with regret." While turning down the offer, he suggested his friend T. S. Gathright, then the superintendent of public instruction in Mississippi, who accepted the position once offered.[5]

Against seemingly insurmountable odds, the board, president, staff, and workers persevered and planned to welcome the first students on September 17, 1876. When that day arrived, however, only six young men "reported for matriculation," causing school officials to delay the formal opening until October 4, now recognized as the official commencement of the college. Enrollment for the first session eventually topped one hundred, and the school became a viable reality after five years of preparation. The early promise of success did not preclude other serious setbacks in the early years, including farmer protests over an initial lack of agricultural classes, but overall the concept of the land-grant system worked well in Texas, as it did in other states. The Agricultural and Mechanical College of Texas (renamed Texas A&M University in 1963) thus became the state's first public institution of higher education, seven years before the formation of the University of Texas, which existed only on paper during A&M's formative years. Eventually the two schools became separate institutional systems, although they shared in the state's impressive and sustaining Permanent University Fund.[6]

Through the ensuing years, A&M built on a strong foundation of academic excellence and garnered national recognition as a premier military school. Growth in the first half of the twentieth cen-

A lone golfer playing on the Campus Course in the late afternoon hits a shot back toward the 1932 Administration Building in the late 1950s. Courtesy Texas A&M University Rec Sports.

tury was steady and impressive but proved even more dramatic as the result of progressive long-range planning soon after World War II, when such factors as the GI Bill and a burgeoning national economy resulted in increased enrollment and innovative new programs. In the decade between 1948 and 1958, the campus at College Station expanded rapidly to meet the new demands of a world-class institution. Beloved campus landmarks added during those years include the Memorial Student Center (1950), the original G. Rollie White Coliseum (1954), an upper deck for Kyle Field (1954), the A&M Press building (1955), and various other structures and facilities for the instruction of the sciences, agriculture, engineering, business, and education. It is within this context of unprecedented growth and development that a tract of open land on the southeast corner of campus took on new life as a golf course, whose vast cultural landscape has also capably served as part of the university's impressive and welcoming "front door."[7]

THE COURSE IN HISTORY

Golf was a popular sport among cadets at Texas A&M long before construction of the Campus Course. There were some early short-hole courses in the area, and after 1916, students had access to the Bryan Country Club (now Bryan Municipal Golf Course) on West Villa Maria, which for many years served as the golf team's home course. Plans for a closer, on-campus site began in the late 1930s but lingered through the World War II years. The idea became a reality in 1948, however, when the Student Life Committee donated $4,000 and the Association of Former Students $25,000 toward the total project costs of $75,000 for development. The university kicked in the remainder and the following year contracted with noted golf architect Ralph Plummer to begin the design work.[8]

Plummer proved to be an ideal architect for the project for several reasons. Known for a quick turnaround, competitive (low) design fees, and minimal landscape disruptions, he had also attended Texas A&M. A native of the Fort Worth area, Olaf Joseph Plummer (he later changed his name to Ralph) nurtured an early appreciation for golf while a caddy at the Glen Garden Country Club and later as a somewhat successful professional. But in course design he met his calling, working early on as a close and trusted creative assistant and construction overseer to legendary designer John Bredemus. Nicknamed Rabbit for his speedy work ethic, Plummer relied more on intensive onsite observation than on detailed drawings, designing courses that were accessible to the average golfer and that reflected as much as possible the natural terrain. He favored long fairways, utilizing existing trees and contours and introducing bunkers only sparingly while highlight-

Ralph Plummer, original designer of the Campus Course, Texas A&M University. The photo is signed and dated December 6, 1950, when the course formally opened. Courtesy Texas A&M University Rec Sports.

ing open greens and lengthy running approaches; longer approach shots, he believed, called for larger greens. His designs also incorporated such elements as prevailing crosswinds and the arc of the sun to maximize favorable play for golfers. Given his training with Bredemus, Plummer was not only the designer but often also the builder, or at least an involved overseer. In addition to the Campus Course, he designed such noteworthy courses as Preston Trail and Prestonwood (Creek Course) in Dallas, Lakeside Country Club in Houston, Elkins Lake near Huntsville, and the Tryall Golf and Beach Club in Montego Bay, Jamaica.[9]

Working in general consultation with a college advisory committee composed of experts in agronomy, landscape design, recreation, and construction, Plummer and his team began working on the Texas A&M project in January 1950. Completed in July of that year, the new grounds had time to grow in and stabilize before formal dedication at year's end. Despite it being a cold and windy day, a crowd of students, faculty, local residents, and former students were on hand at 1:30 P.M. on December 6 for the official opening. The ceremonious first tee off was by members of the Aggie's Southwest Conference championship team from

1926: A. O. Nicholson, H. W. Brehmer, J. C. Landon, and Ellis Wilson. Nicholson, then a Dallas banker, was something of a golf legend at the time, as his exhibition round at the new College Station course marked the 807th he had played in all parts of the world; he would increase that number substantially in the ensuing years. Also part of the opening festivities were golfers Alice and Marlene Bauer, billed as the "Beauteous Bauers." Born in South Dakota, the sisters had gained national fame not only for their barnstorming golf presentations but also for competing professionally. Along with noted Texas golfer Babe Zaharias, they were among the thirteen women who established the Ladies Professional Golf Association (LPGA) in 1950.[10]

This aerial photo of the Texas A&M University campus, looking west around 1957, shows the relatively new golf course in the lower left quadrant. The detail reveals the openness and flat terrain of Plummer's design, with few trees and traps to impede golfers. Courtesy Texas A&M University Rec Sports.

Have Clubs, Will Travel

Alfred Oscar "Fred" Nicholson (1906–83) was an avid golfer
with few serious contenders. His unique contribution to the
game was not his level of play—available records indicate that
he was in the ten or lower handicap range as an adult—but his
unwavering lifelong goal to play more courses than any other
amateur golfer. In that regard he fell short. Massachusetts
native and traveling salesman Ralph A. Kennedy, the so-called
Iron Horse of Golf, documented 3,165 unique courses, finishing his run at the Hamilton Inn Golf Course in Lake Pleasant,
New York, in 1953. Close contenders to Kennedy include Alex
H. Findlay, who played 2,388 courses, and Jack B. Redmond,
whose exact total is unknown but probably was considerably
north of 2,800. Although Nicholson logged slightly less than
2,000 courses, he sustained the quest from his first round in
1919 until shortly before his death in 1983, remaining one of
the most prolific players of the game.

A native of Shamrock, in the eastern Texas Panhandle
and where he first played golf, Nicholson set an early goal of
surpassing the total number of courses amassed by his father,
O. T. Nicholson, who played around 500. By the time of his
discharge from the US Army as a colonel following World War
II, the younger Nicholson had 503 courses to his credit, including ones in Egypt, Morocco, Tunisia, Mexico, and twenty-nine
states, and set a new goal of 1,000. Later a banker by profes-
sion in both Shamrock and Dallas, he reached 1,365 courses
in 1964 and, given the death of Ralph Kennedy in 1961, could
honestly claim to be the most prolific course amateur alive.
Nicholson's total at the time included courses in all fifty states
and several additional countries, including Scotland, Switzer-
land, Canada, and the British West Indies. While he put family
and business before his hobby, when he played golf, Nicholson maintained a strenuous pace, as noted in a 1958 article in
USGA Journal and Turf Management: "He has added as many
as ten new courses in three days while on vacation in Okla-

homa; one day he added three courses in Maine, Rhode Island and New Hampshire. On several occasions he has played four courses in a day. In his most intensive period he added 38 courses in 15 days." After playing the Gatesville Country Club in 1973—his 1,665th course—the former Aggie champion replied "Lord, no" to a reporter's question about whether or not he would eventually run out of courses to play. "They're building them faster than I can play 'em."

Sources: "Gatesville Course 1,665th Played by Shamrock Golfer," *Gatesville (TX) Messenger and Star-Forum*, Sept. 20, 1973, 22; James M. Shevis, "Have Clubs, Will Travel Proclaims Avid Golf Fan," *Brownsville (TX) Herald*, Aug. 28, 1964, 11; Nancy Jupp, "Man of a Thousand Golf Courses," *USGA Journal and Turf Management*, Aug. 1958, 14–15; Ted Morello, "Texas Army Colonel Rides Golf Bag 'round World—500 Courses," *Daily Capital Journal* (Salem, OR), July 25, 1946, 2017; John Sabino, Golf's Iron Horse: *The Astonishing, Record-Breaking Life of Ralph Kennedy* (New York: Skyhorse Publishing, 2017), Kindle ed.

Texas A&M boasted a student population of approximately 6,675 by the fall of 1950, and the course and other campus improvements served as key components of plans for future growth and development. To keep the new facility accessible to students, the original greens fees were fifty cents for single play, with a $7.50 semester membership available. Faculty, staff, and former students paid slightly more: seventy-five cents for single play and $27.00 for a nine-month membership; their guests paid a $1.00 fee. In general, USGA rules governed all play, though there were additional course rules, including:

3. Shirts must be worn at all times. . . .
5. Each player must be in possession of a set of clubs.
6. Wearing of shoes with high heels will not be permitted on the course. . . .
8. Holes must be played in consecutive order.

"Babe Sees Trouble for Bauer Sisters"

The following excerpt is from a United Press story that ran in various papers in April 1950, several months before the Bauer sisters' appearance in College Station, following news that they would join the professional-golf circuit.

SAN FRANCISCO—The glamorous Bauer sisters—Marlene and Alice—will infuse new life into the ranks of the nation's women professional golfers, cocky Babe Didrikson Zaharias said today.

But in the same breath, she predicted that the young club swingers would find the going very tough on the professional circuit.

The Bauer sisters, along with the rest of the country's top-ranking feminine golfers, will tee off in the first leg of the $17,000 Weathervane cross-country tournament at Pebble Beach tomorrow and Sunday.

"Sure, Alice and Marlene are glamorous kids," said the forthright Babe, "and they are going to help make women's professional golf more important.

"But I honestly don't think they'll cut much of a swath in the professional ranks. In the first place, they don't hit a long enough ball." The colorful Babe also predicted that the girls would find it a bit different playing for cash.

"I wish the Bauer sisters all the luck in the world—but they might as well know the facts."

Source: *Pittsburgh Press*, Apr. 28, 1950, 35.

The southeast corner of the Old Horse Barn, located several yards offsite across a road, served as the first golf shop and offered facilities for club repair and club storage as well as retail space for equipment and supplies and for the sale of "light refreshments." Joe G. Fagan served as the original pro-manager, and Clyde Harrison was the greenkeeper.[11]

Plummer's original design for the Campus Course prevailed for more than a decade, but by the late 1960s, it needed updating and some minor redesign due to erosion, overplay in certain areas, and deferred maintenance. Construction began on a new onsite clubhouse in 1969, and in the early 1970s golf designer and pro player Jackie Burke received a contract for changes that included rehabilitated greens and tees, installation of an extensive irrigation system, and the addition of three ponds and fifty-four bunkers. The resulting redesign considerably shortened the course to 6,244 yards.[12]

Burke's redesign of Plummer's plan served the university well, both as a golf course and as something of a field lab for the school's renowned turf-management program, into the twenty-first century. Underlying conditions remained, principally heavy clay soils, which worked against even the program's best efforts, and these eventually led to a call for a major new redesign. Jeffrey D. Blume, a 1989 graduate in landscape architecture, and Dave Elmendorf, a star Aggie football and baseball player in the 1970s, worked with course operator Sterling Golf on a comprehensive new design that once again lengthened the course and brought in new elements to enhance the terrain, promote improved landscape management, and offer new challenges for golfers. "One of the things I wanted to do was bring in a style of architecture to the state of Texas that hasn't really seen that much of," Blume noted. "It's sort of an early American style golf course. The characteristics are elevated greens, lots of bunkers and very understated movement in the fairways. There are not a lot of those in Texas." Blume began his work by moving a lot of dirt to provide new elevations and swales and to top the course with a substantial layer of sand to promote more-sustainable grass cultivation. The most prominent visual changes in addition to the length (now 7,008 yards) were a new lake and considerably more bunkers (now 154) that challenged golfers while also serving to direct the visual flow of the course.[13]

What is perhaps the most abiding historical element of the Campus Course is the Aggie family it represents. From its inception in the decade following World War II to the present, it has been shaped and nurtured almost exclusively by those who learned their professions from professors and staff members who lent their expertise for the cause. From Plummer to Blume, even as other schools closed their onsite courses or never took on the challenge, there has been a trans-generational sense of place about the Campus Course despite its changes. Such continuity speaks to a heritage that, although conceived in chaos, has survived against the odds and even prospered. In that regard, it is part of a much larger story.

BATTLE IN THE CANYON

CANYON COURSE AT MEADOWBROOK GOLF COURSE, LUBBOCK

SCORECARD FROM THE PAST

Currently: The Canyon Course at Meadowbrook Golf Course

Historic Name: Yellow House Canyon

DETAILS: An eighteen-hole public course (thirty-six holes, including the adjacent Creek layout, originally Squirrel Hollow) northeast of downtown Lubbock; distance is 6,522 yards from the longest tees

Location: 601 Municipal Drive, Lubbock

Historical Context: Buffalo hunting, late-nineteenth-century Anglo-American–Native American warfare on the southern plains

Historical Type: Battlefield

Period of Significance: 1877

Signature Hole of History: Given the nature of the historic site, all holes share in the overall story of the Yellow House Canyon Fight, but number one, a par-five, 593-yard hole, gives golfers a strong test from the start. For historical perspective, playing roughly south in the general direction of the 1877 battle site, number eight is a par-five, 477-yard hole.

THE COURSE OF HISTORY

Yellow House Canyon, or Yellow House Draw, is a significant natural cut in the Caprock Escarpment north and east of Lubbock that stretches into Crosby County and farther southeast. The name comes from a natural feature in Hockley County known as Casas Amarillas. The canyon is an erosional feature caused in part by the

Yellow House River and other streams that drain into a complex to form the headwaters of the Brazos River. It is an area of relatively flat plains flanked by pocket canyons, steep walls, minor draws, eroded ledges, and boulders. In historic times it was a landmark well known by Anglo-American hunters and Native Americans, who followed the native buffalo (American bison) across the plains, albeit for different reasons. The animals were a vital source of food and clothing for Native Americans, providing materials for ceremonial and utilitarian purposes as well. For Anglo-American buffalo hunters, the shaggy hides were the prize and, as historian William C. Griggs noted, were like "gold dust waiting to be panned." In their quest for the money part of the animals, as they viewed it, the hunters saw little use in the meat and bones, often salvaging only the tongue for immediate consumption and leaving the rest to decompose. To the Indians, such wanton destruction was not only unimaginable and unforgiveable but also precipitated an end to their freedom and way of life. The commercial harvest of buffalo, especially during what has been termed the Great Slaughter of the 1870s, became a flashpoint between the two cultures.[1]

One of the legendary encounters on the Texas plains during that decade took place at Yellow House Canyon. The events that spawned the skirmish, however, began much farther afield in different locales. One was the 1876 establishment of Camp Reynolds, also known as Rath City, in what is now the southern portion of Stonewall County. This supply settlement for the buffalo trade grew up around a store opened earlier by Charles Rath, who had abandoned a similar operation at the ill-fated Adobe Walls farther west. Small bands of hunters and skinners ventured out from this and other buffalo camps into more remote areas to set up frontline hide camps, bases from which they hunted their prey and collected hides. One such man was a hunter named Marshall Sewell (Sewall), originally of Pennsylvania. Fellow hunter John R. Cook described him as an educated man who, although not a "professed Christian," treated others fairly and courteously and refrained from drinking, smoking, and cursing. Cook also noted that he was "a man of hopeful, optimistic tendencies," which may have accounted in part for his actions on February 1, 1877. Alone and without reason to fear for his personal safety, Sewell set up his hunting stand along a sizeable buffalo herd in the area of present Dawson or Borden Counties. From his vantage point, he reportedly killed buffalo at will with his long-range .45-caliber Creedmoor Sharps rifle, ceasing only when he ran out of ammunition. As it turned out, though, Sewell was not alone; observing his harvest that day were a number of Native Americans gravely disturbed by the slaughter they had witnessed.[2]

While a series of concerted state and federal actions, including punitive military actions by Col. Ranald S. Mackenzie, resulted in a general subjugation of Native Americans along the southern plains by the mid-1870s, unique and extenuating circumstances led to the presence of a small tribal band in the area of Sewell's camp in February 1877. A Comanche and Apache band from Fort Sill, Indian Territory, was in Texas, with or without official dispensation, to hunt buffalo in order to augment their meager government pro-

This 1878 photograph, which shows Charles Rath atop a stack of buffalo hides somewhere in Kansas, documents a typical hide-yard operation of the type that utilized buffalo pelts harvested from the Texas plains and other locales. Visible in the left rear is the press used to prepare the hides for rail shipment. Courtesy Legends of America Photo Prints.

visions. The leader of the group was a Quahadi chief, Black Horse, who directed the attack on Sewell as he endeavored to connect with his approaching companions for resupply. Among the Indians that day was captive Herman Lehmann, who provided an account of the aftermath of Sewell's death: "We then went back to the body of the hunter we had killed and took two scalp-locks from his head, cut a gash in each temple, and thrust a sharp stick through his stomach." Buffalo hunter Cook was among those alerted about the attack and tasked with investigating the action. Arriving near the site around midnight, he and his companions buried Sewell in a shallow grave the following morning and covered it with mesquite branches. Within two hundred yards of the corpse, Cook observed, lay "21 bloated unskinned buffalo carcasses."[3]

Back in Rath City, a punitive expedition, including Cook, soon formed and on March 4 headed out against the tribal band. After a number of thwarted efforts and only a single encounter with an Indian scout, the group eventually identified the Indian encampment at Yellow House Canyon on March 18 and prepared for battle. Griggs noted that "the hunters tightened their horses's [sic] girths and tied their hats to the rear of their saddles" before dividing into three groups to maximize surprise. Upon the order to charge by Hank Campbell, the hunters sprang their trap. At first the attack went as planned, with the Indians caught off guard and forced to scatter. As they realized that they far outnumbered the rapidly advancing hunters, however, the Indians valiantly rallied, temporarily driving them back to seek the safety of canyon outcroppings, from which they laid down a withering fire that then forced their foes to fall back as well. Soon an extensive prairie fire, set by the Indians to provide themselves cover, broke the ensuing lull in the fighting. Amid the smoke appeared first one rider, who the hunters quickly shot dead, and then another, who was believed shot from his horse but managed to escape. The second rider was Herman Lehmann, who later wrote of that moment: "My horse was killed. I dropped down behind him and fought there for a while, but it got too hot for me and I ran back to the bluff but in the run I was shot in the leg. I was using a long-range buffalo gun at the time and I think I hit the mark with it several times." Lehmann added that he and his Indian companions made several assaults, but the hunters successfully repelled each one. Aware of the overwhelming odds against them, the hunters sent several men out in an effort to secure reinforcements, but at least one, described as a "big fat black man," faced quick capture by the Indians. Cinched tightly by them in tribal regalia, including a war bonnet, and forced to run back to his line, the man fell dead from shots by his companions, who mistook him for one of their foes.[4]

What had been a ten-hour battle came to an indecisive end with nightfall. Under the cover of darkness, both groups fell back to safer positions, with the hunters setting fires along the way as a means of diversion and in hopes of obscuring their trail. There were no further encounters, however, and the men returned to Rath City on March 27, concluding a twenty-three-day expedition. News of their fight spread quickly, and in early May a detail of the Tenth Cavalry, out of Fort Griffin and under the command of Capt. P. L. Lee, encountered the tribal group at Silver Lake (Quemado) in present Cochran County, forcing its surrender and subsequent return to Fort Sill. The fighting at Yellow House Canyon, while producing no conclusive victory for either side, nevertheless remains a significant event in Anglo-American–Native American relations on the Texas plains, making the end of an uncertain era punctuated by myriad cross-cultural hostilities. What followed in due course was the settlement of the last frontier in the state, an area defined in large part by a rich history strongly associated with its indigenous people.[5]

Historians have long conjectured about the exact location of the battle, which likely centered on grounds south and southwest of the modern Canyon Course. While the supposed battlefield represented the nexus of the 1877 encounter, the fighting extended well into present Mackenzie Park, and the various movements of hunters and warriors, especially in the early phases of the encounter, no doubt crossed what is today the golf course. These early maneuvers—in effect a series of thrust-and-parry actions from both sides during the course of the engagement—depended on the cover of canyon walls and outcroppings that today form a natural backdrop for the area's cultural landscape.

Nearly fifteen years after the fighting in Yellow House Canyon, the relatively new town of Lubbock was designated the seat of government for Lubbock County in 1891. The city grew steadily in its early years but began to experience rapid growth in the 1920s, in part because of the new Texas Technological College (Texas Tech) and its development as a railroad and hospital center for the southern plains. In 1920 the population was 4,051 people, but in just ten years that number increased almost five fold. A reflection of that growth was the announcement in the *Lubbock Morning Avalanche* in September 1928 of a new municipal golf course. Slated for development in Yellow House Canyon "on the new Plainview–Amarillo highway," it reflected the sponsoring work of local real-estate dealer John W. Jarrott. Building contractor W. G. McMillan supervised the work, and "Boney" Bonebrake of the Hill Crest Country Club in Amarillo designed the layout. Arthur Allen "Boney" Bonebrake, only twenty-eight years old when he took on the Lubbock project, was something of a golf phenomenon in the plains. Born in Topeka, Kansas, in 1900, he held a number of course records in his home state before becoming a golf instructor and taking up the job of designing courses on his own. Little is known of Bonebrake otherwise, for he tragically died of heart failure at Borger, Texas, in 1930, only two years after his work at Meadowbrook and just nine days after his thirtieth birthday.[6]

The course in Yellow House Canyon—now the Canyon Course of Meadowbrook Golf Course at Mackenzie Park—opened on April 12, 1929, as a nine-hole course, but work began immediately on a second nine that opened for play that September. A newspaper advertisement at that time boasted of "perfect greens and Bermuda fairways" a "mere four minutes drive from the main business district of Lubbock." It also included an inset entitled "Attention Ladies" that noted: "This course is ideal for your game. Additional tee boxes have been installed near the hazards so that you might cross easily and without the necessity of long shots. You'll like this course after you play it."[7]

Meadowbrook became a major component of a larger recreational area in 1935, when the federal government announced plans for a Civilian Conservation Corps (CCC) unit to develop surrounding acreage as a state park named for Colonel Mackenzie, whose cavalry forces traversed the general area in the 1870s in expeditions against various Native American groups. Following CCC project protocols, the City of Lubbock secured rights to the proposed site—547 acres—that included the course and a small city park. Additionally, the county offered Shannon Park and its existing amenities as well as the use of its heavy machinery for road building and other infrastructure work. Federal approval for a state park (designated SP-52) came in the spring of 1935, and the first enrollees camped at the site in July of that year. The young men were members of Company 3820(V), a unit composed of World War I veterans (thus the "V" in the designation). The initial company failed to develop as planned, though, and in 1936 the CCC

No Pushover for Duffers

About this time next year, a lot of golfers are going to be having a lot of fun playing on the new Meadowbrook golf course.

Because that's the kind of a course they're building at Meadowbrook these days—a golf course for pleasure. It is being designed to give Mr. and Mrs. Average Golfer a chance to shoot some ego-tickling scores.

By that we do not mean that the new Meadowbrook course when it is opened for grass greens play next spring, will be a pushover for all the duffers in town, an easy mark for the better than average players, a careless frolic for the par-busters. To play the course correctly one must be armed with virtually every shot known to golf, because there will be times and occasions calling for every club in the sack and every angle of backswing.

Source: From Collier Parris, "A Golf Course for 'Fun,'" *Sportometer, Lubbock Evening Journal*, June 2, 1939, 4.

reorganized it as a "white junior" unit of younger men. The personnel at the park changed continually, but the company remained in place until 1941, when the nation's attention focused on possible involvement in another world war. During their time at Mackenzie Park, the "CCC boys" built stone entrance portals, roads and trails, bridges, a refectory, and large swimming pool. According to historian James Wright Steely, chronicler of the Texas state park system, the state retained ownership of the land following the completion of the work of the CCC, and the City of Lubbock oversaw the daily operations of Mackenzie Park. That arrangement changed in 1993, "when the state traded its land for property at Lubbock Lake Landmark State Historical Park." Since then full ownership and responsibility of the park has resided with the city.[8]

During the years of the CCC operations at Mackenzie Park, the city expanded and improved Meadowbrook to make it more appealing and challenging. Work began in 1939 to lengthen the course overall and to add new grasses and an irrigation system. As local sportswriter Collier Parris reported:

> The new greens, fellow duffers, are going to be very neat. In situating them, [course manager W. G. "Bill"] McMillan and Professional Joe Byrne have utilized natural topography, contours and hazards. Some of them are in very tricky spots indeed and if one shoots over and past them, one is going to exercise one's vocal organs in no uncertain terms; some of them lie flat enough, some curve upward from the back, based on the natural curves, rises and falls of the grounds; some are wider in front than in the rear, and vice versa. But all of them are big, strong healthy fellows that should make putting a pleasure.[9]

Through the ensuing years, the city has contracted for redesigns of the course, most notably by designers Warren Cantrell (1950s) and Bob Lohmann (around 1990). Lubbockite Cantrell, a native of Hill County, interned as an engineer with the noted Abilene architect David S. Castle. In 1928 he designed the Stamford Country Club, staying on as a pro and then later serving as the pro at the Abilene

GONE TO THE DOGS

Pro-Manager John J. (Jay) McClure of Lubbock (Tex.) Meadow-brook GC has a prairie dog sanctuary right next to his municipal course. The dogs are protected and are one of Lubbock's main tourist attractions. However, McClure estimates that even though the prairie dogs are well fenced in, with wiring going down 10 feet under a high masonry wall, they escape and set up new diggings on the course and driving range. He estimates that over 10,000 golf balls have been lost down the dog holes on the driving range alone.

Source: From Herb Graffis, "Swinging around Golf: News of the Golf World in Brief," *Golfdom*, Aug. 1965, 78.

Country Club. He continued as a golf designer and worked on such courses as Ranchland Hills in Midland, Tascosa in Amarillo, and Rolling Acres in Corpus Christi. In Lubbock he designed the Hillcrest Country Club, redesigned and worked as the pro at Meadowbrook, and was the golf coach at Texas Tech in the 1950s. A prominent leader in professional associations, he twice served as president of the Texas PGA. When interviewed in 1957 about his distinguished golf career, he recalled in particular his friendship with some of the game's greats, including fellow Texans Byron Nelson, Ben Hogan, and Gene Sarazen. "You know," he said, "most of the great golfers have been Texans anyway." Cantrell died in 1967 at the age of sixty-one and was posthumously inducted into the Texas Golf Hall of Fame in 2010.[10]

A SCULPTOR IN THE PUMP HOUSE

BRACKENRIDGE PARK GOLF COURSE, SAN ANTONIO

The noted San Antonio architect Ralph Haywood Cameron designed the clubhouse for the Brackenridge Park Golf Course in the early 1920s. Among Cameron's other local landmarks from the same era are the Medical Arts Building (1926), Grace Lutheran Church (1928), and the Academic Building at Randolph Army Air Field (1929). Photograph by Dan K. Utley.

Located in a picturesque setting adjacent to the historic Borglum studio, the Texas Golf Walk of Fame commemorates many of the sport's legends associated with the lone star state, including course designer John Bredemus, class of 1991. Photograph by Dan K. Utley.

The upper reaches of the San Antonio River, from its headwaters south to the area around Mission San Antonio de Valero (the Alamo) and beyond, has a strong association with the early history of the region dating back to the eighteenth century and the time of Spanish colonialism. Then, an elaborate series of *acequias*, or races, carried community-sustaining water from the spring-fed river for residential and agricultural purposes. As San Antonio steadily grew into a major commercial center through the time of Mexican rule, the republic era, and into statehood, the river continued to be its primary source of water, with improvements to its waterworks providing better access and delivery systems to meet increasing demands. In 1877, following a period of sustained growth during the post-Reconstruction years, French émigré Jean Baptiste LaCoste formally started the San Antonio River Works, with a twenty-five-year supply contract to the city. Necessitating a sizable capital outlay up front, LaCoste's venture reflected much promise but delivered relatively little financial return on the investment, which placed him in considerable debt. Among those who stepped up to ensure the effort's viability was George Washington Brackenridge, who owned the headwaters of the river and thus had a vested interest in the waterworks. A successful San Antonio investor and banker, Brackenridge accepted company stock in return for his venture capital and in time acquired controlling interest in the company. By 1883, he was its president, and under his direct supervision, the enterprise not only survived but thrived.[1]

A native of Indiana, Brackenridge completed his academic training at Indiana University and Harvard College before following his family to Jackson County, along the Texas coastal plain, in the years before the Civil War to work as a surveyor. During the war, however, he sided with the Union and made money as a cotton broker and a treasury agent, returning to Texas at the close of the conflict and settling in San Antonio. There he established the San Antonio National Bank in 1866 and began purchasing property along the upper reaches of the San Antonio. At the river's

Timeout at Twelve

From the late 1920s until the late 1960s, when the routing of a new highway curtailed business as usual, Austrian native Elizabeth Schriever operated a sandwich stand known as The Oaks, which served food to Old Brack golfers adjacent to the twelfth green. The stand, housed in a separate building behind the Schriever home on Terry Street, featured a menu of homemade sandwiches, lemonade, and local beers. As the latter were not permitted on the course due to deed restrictions, the backyard venue became a popular resting place for duffers. Course chronicler Reid E. Meyers noted that "golfers developed a protocol to finish playing #12, sit at the tables for ten minutes" to enjoy a food-and-beverage break, "then move on to #13 tee. The next foursome would do the same. Play stopped at the Oaks as a part of every round of golf."

Source: Reid E. Meyers, *The Ghosts of Old Brack: A Pictorial History of the Brackenridge Park Golf Course* (St. Louis: Mira Digital Publishing, 2010), 53–58.

Sculptor Gutzon Borglum in his studio around 1910, prior to his San Antonio commission. Library of Congress Prints and Photographs Division, Washington, DC, http://hdl.loc.gov/loc.pnp/cph.3a37262.

source, he built a home for his mother and named it Head of the River, later conveying the homesite to the Sisters of Charity of the Incarnate Word for development of a college, now the University of Incarnate Word. Brackenridge used his incredible wealth to further a wide range of philanthropic causes, including programs to enhance educational opportunities for women and African Americans. His primary beneficiary, however, was the University of Texas, to which he donated both money and his extensive personal library. He funded construction of Brackenridge Hall (B Hall, since razed) on the present campus, donated considerable acreage along the Colorado River (which later included Lion's Municipal Golf Course), and served on the school's board of regents from 1886 to 1919. His activism in education also led him to serve as president of the San Antonio Public School Board.[2]

In large part, Brackenridge's philanthropic nature eventually resulted in his gift of land to the City of San Antonio for the public park that now bears his name, although there were other mitigating circumstances. He had successfully directed the waterworks and made it a viable operation, overseeing construction of a series of raceways and pump houses that moved water from the river to a reservoir (at what is now the San Antonio Botanical Gardens), from which a gravity-flow system aided in wide dispersal for public use. Over time, though, the system proved inadequate to meet the heavy demands of the growing city, and the widespread use of wells along with sustained periods of drought combined to lower the water table. As he pragmatically revealed to a friend, "I have seen this bold, bubbling, laughing river dwindle and fade away.... This river is my child and it is dying and I cannot stay here to see its last gasps.... I must go." In 1899 Brackenridge donated much of his river acreage to the city, stipulating that it be used in perpetuity for public recreation and maintaining a reversion clause that would give the land to the University of Texas if his wishes were not fulfilled. An avowed prohibitionist publicly, though he imbibed on a limited basis and maintained an extensive wine collection, he further stipulated in the deed that there should be no alcohol sales on the park property, a factor that frustrated city officials for years. Another complicating factor was that Brackenridge retained the water rights and continued to maintain the waterworks until selling out in 1906. Nine years later the city took over the operation, but by then the lower pump house, built in 1885, was obsolete and vacated. It remained so even as workers developed the surrounding land for the Brackenridge Park Golf Course, which opened in 1916.[3]

In 1924 the pump house gained new life through adaptive reuse as an artist's studio. The artist was Gutzon Borglum, who moved to San Antonio from Atlanta to work on a commissioned statue for the Texas Trail Drivers Association. Widely known as an accomplished sculptor and painter, he is now best remembered for his most monumental pieces—Mount Rushmore in South Dakota and the Confederate Memorial at Stone Mountain, Georgia— which were still years away and would be completed by other artists. Born in Idaho in 1867 and classically trained in art in San Francisco and Europe, John Gutzon de la Mothe Borglum was an enigmatic national figure known for his fiery temperament and freewheeling lifestyle among the rich and famous. As historian Gilbert Fite described, Borglum was "iconoclastic, rebellious and strong-willed," an outspoken troublemaker with an uncompromising proclivity for realism in his works. He was a harsh critic of American art at the turn of the twentieth century, eschewing classical forms for what he felt should be a separate nationalistic identity. "We won't look at anything unless it wears a helmet or Greek sandals," he observed, "and a young man with an original idea must starve to death or commit suicide, while the greatest stories of the world, the stories of America, go unrecorded in our public parks and galleries." Borglum's unyielding attitudes often put him at odds with his patrons, a situation evident on the controversial project that consumed his time immediately prior to his move to Texas (and probably hastened his decision). While work was underway at Stone Mountain—the initial *bas relief* carving of Gen. Robert E. Lee's head having been completed in 1924—Borglum clashed repeatedly with the overseeing executive committee, which fired him in February 1925. Responding in anger, the artist destroyed his working models and fled the state under threat of arrest. Although clearer heads eventually prevailed, the con-

The 1885 Pump House No. 2 for the San Antonio Water Works later served as a studio for the noted sculptor Gutzon Borglum. The rusticated stone structure, listed in the National Register of Historic Places, is located adjacent to the seventeenth green. Photograph by Stanley O. Graves.

troversy followed Borglum to Texas in the summer of 1925, when there were large-scale and well-organized efforts, primarily from anonymous sources, to have him removed from the San Antonio commission. As the local newspaper reported, Mrs. R. R. Russell, who headed the women's auxiliary charged with raising funds for the trail-driver monument, eventually put the matter to rest when she received a letter from the head of the Atlanta chapter of the United Daughters of the Confederacy "absolving Borglum from all blame in the controversy."[4]

With the Stone Mountain matter behind him, Borglum received permission to use his own money to rehabilitate the old pump house for his working studio. Originally built in a time when even public-utility buildings often reflected a measure of design integrity, the structure, with his modifications and the park setting, served as an ideal backdrop for artistic endeavors. Listed in the National Register of Historic Places in 1981 for both its architectural and historical significance, the building reflects a strong sense of place and time. The original portion of the structure is composed of ashlar-cut (quarry-face) limestone articulated by dressed-stone detailing. Embellishments include stone lintels and sills as well as voussoirs, or tapered-stone archways, that provide architectural interest and character. The Borglum changes are evident in a gabled addition on the north side, sheathed in stucco and wood battens, and topped with four skylights to bring more light into the interior studio space, as did a tripartite window system. A prominent interior feature was the addition of a U-shaped loft.[5]

During Borglum's time in San Antonio, the old pump house served primarily as his winter studio. There the sculptor worked on a model for the new local monument, although it was never built in full scale as designed and the model not cast until 1940; today the monument is on display at Pioneer Hall in Brackenridge Park. While in San Antonio, Borglum also worked on other Texas projects, including a collaboration with the Texas Highway

TILLY IN TEXAS

Albert Warren "Tilly" Tillinghast, designer of the famed Brackenridge Park Golf Course, is revered in golf history as one of the game's greatest course architects. Born in 1874 to a Philadelphia rubber baron, he had a rambunctious and spoiled childhood, including participation in the city's notorious Kelly Street Gang. At the age of twenty-one, when he was but a novice golfer, Tilly made his first trip to the iconic sports shrine Saint Andrews in Scotland. There he fell under the spell of legendary "Old Tom" Morris and developed a lifelong passion for the game, not only as a player but also as a devotee of its rich history and course aesthetics. Although Tilly dabbled in design as early as 1898 after returning from his second trip to Saint Andrews, his career as a golf course architect really began with a family friend's request to help with a layout at Shawnee in Delaware, Pennsylvania, in 1910. The course opened in 1911 to rave reviews, and Tillinghast was soon in great demand to design and construct courses for America's burgeoning new pastime. From its New York City office, the A. W. Tillinghast Golf Construction Company soon produced an astounding portfolio of iconic courses, including Baltusrol in Springfield, New Jersey (1922); Quaker Ridge (1918) and Fenway (1924) in Scarsdale, New York (1924); Winged Foot in Mamaroneck, New York (1923), and culminating with Bethpage in Farmingdale, New York (1936–37). It was early in this run that the mayor of San Antonio, Clinton Brown, requested that Tilly design a municipal course for Brackenridge Park. His work there began in 1915, and the rugged, wild land along the San Antonio River left quite an impression on the easterner. "It was covered with thick growth of mesquite and ouisache [sic] wood," Tilly remembered. "There were huge pecan trees, which were spared whenever possible—and there were other things as well, such as wood ticks, coyotes, wolves, rattle-snakes, and 'bad hombres.'" The latter refers to an encounter the designer had with a convict laborer the city delivered to help with clearing the site. It appears that Tilly had concerns about the slow pace of construction and asked if at least fifty more men could be enlisted. The mayor and police chief accommodated with the overnight arrest of that exact number of men involved in local cockfights and crap games. One of the detainees quickly attempted to escape, in the process breaking Tillinghast's nose with a wooden handle he had slipped off his grubbing hoe.

Despite his run-ins with Texas lawbreakers and the native flora and fauna, Tilly went on to design other impressive layouts in the Lone Star State. They included Brook Hollow in Dallas (1920), the first course in the state to have complete fairway irrigation, and those at Fort Sam Houston (1916) and the Alamo Country Club (1922) (now Oak Hills) in San Antonio. He also designed the Cedar Crest Golf Club in Dallas (1921), the Corsicana Country Club (1926), and additions to the Rivercrest Country Club in Fort Worth (1921) and Bob-O-Links in Dallas (1936).

In the mid-1930s, at the height of the Great Depression, the PGA hired Tillinghast to inspect courses across the country that employed association-member professionals. From August 1935 through the fall of 1937, he completed two criss-crossing loops of the country, making proposals for improvements at hundreds of courses. Many of his inspections on both trips occurred in Texas, where he visited courses in Lufkin, Houston, Galveston, Tyler, San Antonio, Austin, Waco, Corsicana, Fort Worth, and Big Spring. His suggestions often focused on eliminating bunkers, which he termed "Duffer Headaches," believing that the unnecessary proliferation of such hazards slowed play, were costly to maintain, and generally frustrated the average golfer. As a result of his inspection reports, Tillinghast claims to have eliminated nearly eight thousand of the dreaded "headaches."

Herewith are samples of Tilly's recommendations for several Texas courses:

- At the Big Spring Municipal Course in West Texas, he spent three hours going over the fairways, suggesting several changes, but noted that it was one of the best he had seen in the state.
- In Austin he visited the Austin Country Club and advised pro Harvey Penick on a new green for the 112-yard eleventh hole, then later in the day advised Harvey's brother, Tom, at the Lions Municipal Course.
- At the Z. Boaz Municipal Course in Fort Worth, he recommended the gradual planting of trees in clumps "to relieve the monotonous flatness of the course."
- Returning to the Brackenridge Park course he had designed twenty years earlier, Tilly seemed disappointed in its overall condition. "So popular is the Brackenridge course and so heavy is its play," he wrote, "that the city appears to [have adopted] the policy of 'standing pat.' I believe it could be much improved by up-to-date contouring in many places."

Tilly Tillinghast's influence on golf courses across the United

States was immense, and his work in Texas was certainly no exception. From the many courses he designed or expanded to the others for which he provided consultation and recommendations, his genius remains evident across the broad landscape of Texas golf more than a century after his earliest work in the state.

Sources: Albert Warren Tillinghast, *The Course Beautiful* (Short Hills, NJ: TreeWolf Productions, 1996); Albert Warren Tillinghast, *Gleanings from the Wayside*, 3rd ed. (Short Hills, NJ: TreeWolf Productions, 2001); Albert Warren Tillinghast, *Reminiscences of the Links* (Short Hills, NJ: TreeWolf Productions, 1998); Ron Fimrite, "A Mad Master, A. W. Tillinghast, the Architect of Winged Foot, Was Known for His Outstanding Courses and Outlandish Lifestyle," Aug. 25, 1997, *Sports Illustrated*, accessed online Nov. 25, 2016, http://www.si.com/vault/1997/08/25; A. W. Tillinghast Association website, www.tillinghast.net; World Golf Hall of Fame website, http://www.worldgolfhalloffame.org. While the nickname for Tillinghast is shown in various publications as either "Tillie" or "Tilly," the authors used the latter in accordance with the Tillinghast Association. The goals of the nonprofit society are "to share the accumulated research and knowledge on A. W. Tillinghast—his fascinating life, his remarkable golf courses, his charismatic and humorous writings, and his foundation principles to Modern Golf Course design and construction." The authors recognize the kind research assistance of the association, especially John Yerger, with regard to this chapter and sidebar and chapter 10, on the Riverside Golf Course, also in San Antonio.

Department on roadway beautification in the Rio Grande Valley and work with Corpus Christi officials on an elaborate seawall installation, which was never built as proposed. It was at the pump house too that he began the initial design work and model building for what would be his magnum opus—Mount Rushmore. By 1934, the South Dakota project occupied most of his creative time, and so following a minor dispute with city officials over the maintenance of his studio, he left Texas to pursue that and other projects. Although his time in the Alamo City had been productive, his departure came with some personal misgivings about his treatment overall—not unusual for Borglum, who often felt misunderstood or his genius underappreciated. As he later confided to a friend: "I don't think I have ever been in a town where the crooks and 'respectable people' are so like scrambled eggs, and we have made a fearful blunder to think that the 'honorable' people—the people of wealth and position—were with us. They weren't." Such outsider feelings followed him to Mount Rushmore, where, Fite noted, he "fought regularly with the National Park Service" and "saw those individuals as ignoramuses in an ox-like civilization which had no appreciation of true culture." Frustrated to the end of his career, Borglum died of a heart attack in Chicago in 1941. It then fell to his son, Lincoln, and others to finish his colossal works years later.[6]

When Borglum left San Antonio, administration of the studio fell to the Witte Museum, with the intention of continuing its use by artists. To that end the San Antonio Art League partnered with the museum to establish a school at the studio under the directorship of the noted artist Henry Lee McFee. Born in Saint Louis, Missouri, McFee gained prominence as one of the founders of the celebrated art colony in Woodstock, New York. Influenced by the modernist style of Paul Cézanne and known primarily as a painter of still-life compositions, he once observed that such subjects did "not have to rest and I do not have to gossip as I work." McFee's association with the pump-house studio was short lived, leaving for California in 1940, but his work in San Antonio helped establish the groundwork for high-caliber art instruction in the city. Following his departure, the studio continued to serve local artists until the early 1960s, when the city closed the building. In recent years restoration efforts, with support from the San Antonio Conservation Society and other groups and agencies, have revived its utility as a unique public-event and meeting space.[7]

PECAN TREE HAZARD ON OPENING DAY

J. L. Bowler, playing with J. E. Glover, "bagged" a caddy who was sampling pecans in the top of a tree on the seventeenth hole. He [Bowler] was making a long mid-iron approach for the green and hooked the ball into the trees. The caddy came down with a thump, but suffered no material injuries.

Source: "Humor in Tournament," *San Antonio Light*, Sept. 24, 1916, 4.

Stylistically, the Brackenridge Park Golf Course reflects the original eighteen-hole design of Albert Warren "Tilly" Tillinghast, one of the nation's legendary course architects of the early twentieth century. Administratively, it began as a general concept between Mayor Clinton G. Brown, early parks commissioner Ludwig Mahncke, and his successor, Ray Lambert. These were men of both vision and action in public service, and they utilized all available resources to construct the course as quickly as possible. When Tillinghast first visited the site on October 1, 1915, clearing work was already under-way utilizing multiple city crews as well as specially conscripted prisoners. Rather than spend an inordinate amount of time onsite, Tillinghast made his initial conceptual drawings based on his tour of the partially cleared terrain, then fine-tuned them at his Philadelphia office. Meanwhile, city crews finalized the prepara-tion work under municipal supervision, with input from local golf committees. With the city's dual concerns of expediency and costs no doubt in mind, the local newspaper reported, "When the entire course has been laid out in this manner, it will be possible for the project to be prosecuted without the supervision of the golf course architect."[8]

Work on the course remained on schedule through the spring and summer of 1916, the formal opening occurring in September, almost exactly a year from the time when workers first began grubbing brush on the land. Constructed in an era when golf was still a relatively new phenomenon in Texas and centered on pri-vate clubs, the Brackenridge Park Golf Course provided unprece-dented public access to the sport. The layout, which spanned the river and central waterworks channel while tightly meandering through dense stands of native trees, added to the sport's popu-larity as an enjoyable—albeit frustrating for some—outdoor activ-ity. It also secured Tillinghast's stature as the preferred golf course architect, and he returned to the Alamo City several times to work on local courses and later to inspect them for the PGA.[9]

Building on its early success and dynamic leadership, Brackenridge Park garnered a well-deserved and widespread reputation as a prime venue for golf. Adding to its prestige was the completion of an impressive and expansive clubhouse in 1923. San Antonio historian Maria Watson Pfeiffer noted in the historical sections of the 2008 National Register registration for Brackenridge Park that local architect Ralph Cameron had utilized rubble stone, brick, timbers, and concrete to reference the Tudor style, with features that included arches, gables, a round tower with conical roof, and half-timber finishes. While modern for its time yet suitably rustic for its South Texas setting, the design evoked the European heritage of golf.[10]

Completion of the new clubhouse came on the heels of the inaugural Texas Open the previous year. Initiated in response to the journalistic campaign of local sportswriter Jack O'Brien and aided by Brackenridge golf pro John Bredemus, who later became the state's dean of golf course designers, the open was the first professionally sanctioned tournament in the state. Bob McDonald, known as the "Silver Scot," won the first contest, taking home what was at the time a sizable purse of $1,633.33. Soon after, the fledgling San Antonio Golf Association took over the administration of the tournament, and later winners of the Texas Open at "Old Brack" included Byron Nelson (1940), Ben Hogan (1946), and Sam Snead (1948, 1950). The tournament moved to new facilities in 1960, the year Arnold Palmer began a three-year stint as the winner.[11]

Beginning in the 1950s, Old Brack and the Olmos Basin wetlands were at the center of controversial plans for construction of a proposed highway (281) connecting the city center to the airport on the far northern side. Litigation, local activism, legislation, and negotiations delayed the project until the 1970s, but when work finally commenced, it necessitated a redesign of Tillinghast's original layout on the back nine. Recent restoration work, however, has mitigated that alteration, allowing for a return to the initial configuration where practicable. Now a century old, the Brackenridge Park Golf Course continues to be a popular municipal venue in large part due to its rich history, which extends far beyond its design by one of the nation's leading golf architects.[12]

THE BACK NINE

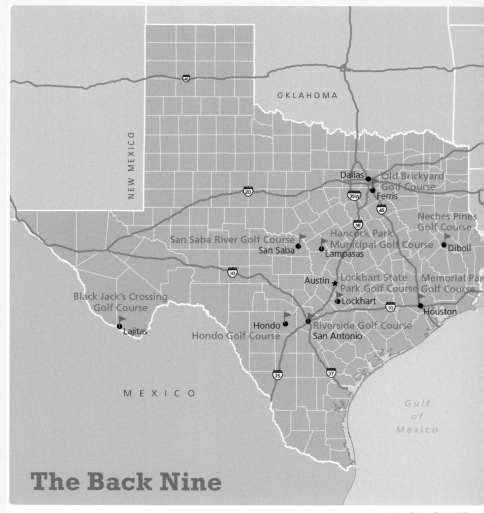

OKLAHOMA

NEW MEXICO

Dallas • Old Brickyard Golf Course

Ferris

Neches Pines Golf Course

San Saba River Golf Course
San Saba •

Hancock Park Municipal Golf Course
Lampasas • Diboll

Austin ★ Lockhart State Park Golf Course

Memorial Park Golf Course

Black Jack's Crossing Golf Course
Lajitas • Lockhart •

Houston •

Hondo • Riverside Golf Course
Hondo Golf Course San Antonio

MEXICO

Gulf of Mexico

The Back Nine

Map by Molly O'Hallorar

10

ROUGH RIDERS AT RIVERSIDE

RIVERSIDE GOLF COURSE, SAN ANTONIO

SCORECARD FROM THE PAST

Recent Past: Riverside Golf Course

Historic Name: Riverside Park

DETAILS: Eighteen-hole course plus nine-hole par-three course along and divided by the San Antonio River; distance of the eighteen-hole course is 6,694 yards from the longest tees.

Location: 203 McDonald, San Antonio

Historical Context: Private park; site of Camp Wood during Spanish-American War preparations

Historical Type: Urban park; military training grounds

Period of Significance: May 1898

Signature Hole of History: Number six is a left-dogleg hole adjacent to the Spanish-American War memorial. Composed of several carved stones, this monument is immediately to the east of the fairway but outside the perimeter fence. Unmarked, it is in a small group of trees on the west side of Roosevelt Avenue in the block between Wharton and Uvalde Streets.

The Spanish-American War Memorial adjacent to the Riverside Course. Pin flag visible in the background. Photograph by Dan K. Utley

THE COURSE OF HISTORY

The tranquil urban setting of Riverside Golf Course, traversed by the San Antonio River and an undulating landscape featuring a relatively tight front nine shaded by large trees and a more open back nine, belies its historic role as a short-lived but nationally significant military training ground. While the general area has an important historical pedigree that reaches back to the Spanish colonial era—specifically Mission San Francisco Xavier de la Nájera, in operation for local tribal groups from only 1722 to 1726—it is the occupation by the First US Volunteer Cavalry for a few weeks in May 1898 that resonates most with heritage tourists today. The story unfolds against the backdrop of declining relations between Spain and the United States that led to war during the first term of Pres. William McKinley at the close of the nineteenth century. The conflict stemmed from a global readjustment of imperialism, as older world powers struggled—militarily, politically, and financially—to maintain far-flung and increasingly complex colonial interests. Exacerbating the somewhat tenuous hold of the old order was the rise of newer world powers, principally the United States.[1]

For years political unrest in its Latin American colonies had troubled Spain, although the island of Cuba retained favored status despite some brief uprisings. With renewed agitation during the 1890s, the Spanish crown took steps to enforce stronger control, including concentration camps and focused military actions against those it deemed insurrectionists and sympathizers. Such actions met with even greater resistance from those fervently pressing for their independence. Reports of Spanish atrocities against Cubans quickly spread to the nearby United States, where the "yellow press" of the era took up the cause and used its sensationalist reporting to enhance political and social sympathies among its readership. Despite a rapidly growing public call for action, the US government during the administrations of McKinley and his predecessor, Grover Cleveland, remained on the sidelines despite an expressed commitment to the Monroe Doctrine, which expressly discouraged foreign (that is, European) involvement in the Western Hemisphere. While ignoring historical ties that reached back to early colonial times, US leaders by the late nineteenth century found it increasingly difficult to cope with a rapidly changing political environment with its own evolving world vision. Pressure intensified early in January 1898, when the United States responded to an intense Havana riot by sending the battleship USS *Maine* to Cuba to assert the country's stakeholder status and provide protection for American tourists and businesses there. The spark that set the course of war came on the evening of February 15, when an explosion ripped through the massive ship, killing 260 crewmembers and sending it to the bottom of the harbor. Deemed the result of a mine, the sinking of the *Maine* further engaged the yellow press in its call for action that, despite some initial failed efforts at diplomacy, eventually persuaded President McKinley to seek a war resolution from Congress, which he received on April 20. In subsequent days the US Navy, at the time the mainstay of American military preparedness, moved quickly to set up blockades of both Cuba and Spanish-held territory in the Philippine Islands. Although the crisis had now escalated into a global confrontation, the island ninety miles off the coast of Florida remained the primary focal point of immediate military action. "Remember the Maine" served as the rallying cry for the requisite surge of enlistment for both the Regular Army and volunteer units in what would be a major test for US power.[2]

Because the United States had downscaled its standing army in recent years, one provision for filling the ranks in quick order was to authorize the development of volunteer forces separate from the Regular Army and state militias. Francis Emroy Warren, a Republican senator from Wyoming and a Medal of Honor recipient for battlefield gallantry during the Civil War with the Forty-Ninth Massachusetts Infantry at Port Hudson, Louisiana, shepherded the legislation through Congress. Of particular interest to Warren was the organization of three volunteer cavalry regiments from the West. As he envisioned, and as the enabling provisions from the secretary of war noted, these western units would be composed "entirely of frontiersmen possessing special qualifications as horsemen and marksmen." The First Regiment, which became the best known of the three, was also the only one to see action in Cuba. Authorization for recruitment fell to the unit commanders, with active enlistment from the western states and the territories of Arizona, New Mexico, and Oklahoma (the former Indian Territory). Chosen as leaders of the First US Volunteer Cavalry were Capt. Leonard Wood, the president's medical advisor, and Assistant Secretary of the Navy Theodore Roosevelt, two friends—both staunch Progressives—who had been among the strongest proponents in Washington for war with Spain. Although Secretary of War Russell Alger first offered the command to Roosevelt, the assistant secretary declined, citing his lack of command experience, but suggested instead Dr. Wood, who had prior infantry experience during the campaign against Geronimo in the Arizona Territory. In reality, both men seemed to lack the military credentials to lead such an effort, but the immediacy of the situation, coupled with their obvious leadership qualities, undeniable resolve, and fortuitous political connections, put them in the right place at the right time. Consequently, the regiment formed in April, with Wood serving as colonel, responsible primarily for unit organization, recruitment, and tactics, and Roosevelt, as lieutenant colonel, in charge of training. Despite the regimental structure, it was the flamboyant and ebullient Roosevelt—a popular politician, western rancher, police commissioner, author, and War Department official—who immediately captured the attention of the public and the media. As a result, the regiment quickly reflected his larger-than-life persona from the beginning, drawing overwhelming numbers of would-be recruits and resulting in the monikers of "Teddy's Texas Tarantulas," "Teddy's Terrors," and others before their final popular recognition as the "Rough Riders," a phrase commonly used in the cowboy culture of the American West.[3]

One of the earliest command decisions was to establish a training camp near San Antonio, Texas. The reasons were many but included the proximity to Gulf ports, the ready availability of horse stock on nearby ranches, the presence of a federal armory to aid in the transfer of ordnance, and a ready community of experienced cavalrymen who could assist in the procurement and training of horses. To the latter purpose, the government set up a horse-purchasing board at San Antonio early in May. Colonel Wood arrived in the Alamo City by train on May 5 and, after visiting with officers at Fort Sam Houston, made his way three miles south of town to Riverside Park, where he would have his training facilities. Located along the course of the San Antonio River, the park began as a private operation under lease to the Alamo Electric Street Railway Company. Immediately to the east were the grounds of the San Antonio International Fair, which included a large exposition hall that would serve as a staging ground, headquarters, and temporary barracks for what became known as Camp Wood. Although the fair remained a viable local event in the fall of each year until 1911, Riverside Park was effectively abandoned by the time Colonel Wood arrived. An effort a few years earlier to convert the site into a cemetery had failed to materialize, and the grounds would not become a municipal park until the late 1920s.[4]

While Wood steadily and efficiently went about the business of setting up the camp at Riverside, Roosevelt finalized his work in Washington before traveling by train to San Antonio, where he arrived on Sunday, May 15, and was greeted by the colonel. The two men then walked to the Menger Hotel by the Alamo to meet with their regimental officers. Later Roosevelt rode by buckboard to the camp, where the recruits, as well as a large crowd of townspeople, had gathered to see him tour the site. Roosevelt biographer Nathan Miller noted the scene:

> The camp was humming with activity. Men had been detailed to squadrons, troops, and squads. Somehow, horses, uniforms, supplies, weapons, had been pried out of a Quartermaster Department that was near collapse from the unexpected strains placed upon it and reluctant to divert scarce matériel to a volunteer regiment. Wood had even obtained new Krag-Jörgenson magazine carbines rather than the single-shot Springfields left over from the Indian wars that were issued to many units. As a result of his efforts, the Rough Riders were among the army's best equipped regiments.[5]

Roosevelt also found an impressive collection of ready recruits not only from the frontier states and territories but the Northeast as well, including several fellow New Yorkers. Among them were such noteworthy individuals as William "Bucky" O'Neill, former sheriff of Prescott, Arizona; Dodge City marshal Ben Daniels; Hamilton Fish Jr. of Columbia, grandson of Pres. U. S. Grant's secretary of state; William Tiffany, of the noted jewelry family and considered a "leader of cotillions"; and Dudley Dean, "said to be Harvard's best quarterback ever."[6] There were, as originally intended, a large assortment of western wranglers, hunters, trappers, Native Americans, and miners. Some boasted colorful names such as Cherokee Bill, Rattlesnake Pete, Tough Ike, and Prayerful James, but there were also a number of eastern social elites that included members of the Somerset Club of Boston and the New York Knickerbocker Club, well versed in such skills as yachting and polo playing. Given the location of the training exercises, it followed that the ranks would include a sizable number of Texans. Roosevelt described it thus: "We drew a great many recruits from Texas; and from nowhere did we get a higher average, for many of them had served in that famous body of frontier fighters, the Texas Rangers. Of course, these rangers needed no teaching. They were already trained to obey and to take responsibility. They were splendid shots, horsemen, and trailers." Recruitment continued at an unprecedented rate until the regiment, initially designed for 780 men, soon reached more than 1,000 in its ranks.[7]

It was a strange assortment well beyond the original vision of politicians or military leaders, but it seemed to work because all were of a single purpose in their resolve to prevail against Spain. Regardless of their background, the men shared the impetuosity of their field commander. "We were young and full of vinegar," one trooper remembered, "and it was tough trying to fill twenty-four hours in camp with a war going on. We were sure it would be over while we were drilling out there at Camp Wood." The colonel observed: "These men are wild. If we don't get them to Cuba quickly to fight the Spanish there is a great danger they'll be fighting themselves."[8]

The intense routine of the camp presaged the need for rapid deployment to Cuba before the end of May. The days began with "Reveille" at 5:30 A.M., followed by care of the horses and preparation for the morning drills. After lunch came more drills, inspections, and reviews. Each day concluded with the evening meal at 7:00, tattoo at 8:30, and "Taps" at 9:00. Interspersed with these activities was the steady pace of supply procurement, sometimes necessitating four or five trips daily to Fort Sam Houston, northeast of the city, to pick up horses, primarily of local stock though with some untamed broncos and others described as "half-thoroughbreds." Drives of small herds through San Antonio thus became standard events as the cavalrymen continued to prepare for war. At the camp, to deter would-be rustlers interested in procuring the best mounts for themselves, the regiment imposed a color-coded system for particular units. Company A, for example, used bays exclusively, while Company B had sorrels, Company C had browns, Company D had grays, and so on. While there was some unavoidable duplication within the twelve companies and some minor exceptions to the general rule, this system of order remained the norm throughout training.[9]

DEATH AT CAMP WOOD

The first Rough Rider casualty occurred at Camp Wood on May 26, 1898, when Irad Cochran Jr. died from injuries sustained when he fell from a horse during drills a few days earlier; military records list his official cause of death as spinal meningitis. Only nineteen years old at the time of the accident, Cochran was a private in Company E from New Mexico Territory. A native of the Pembroke area east of Concord, New Hampshire, he served as a clerk in the town of Las Vegas, New Mexico, at the time of his enlistment. The family had moved to the eastern part of the territory years earlier for his father to serve in the management of the vast Preston Beck Land Grant.

Following a funeral service in the main fair building at Riverside, Cochran's body was returned to Las Vegas for a service in the local Episcopal church on June 1 and burial with full military honors in the city cemetery. According to an Albuquerque newspaper account, the young soldier was "one of the most popular young men ever reared" in Las Vegas. Among those attending his hometown services were members of the New Mexico National Guard and the Grand Army of the Republic, along with representatives of the Knights of Pythias, Elks, Junior Order of United American Mechanics, and the local fire department. Personally paying his respects also that day was the territorial governor, Miguel Antonio Otero, who was among those who had proposed the formation of what became the Rough Riders. In 1899, when members of the unit gathered in Las Vegas for their first annual reunion, they dubbed Lincoln Park as Camp Cochran in honor of their fallen comrade.

Sources: "Burial of Irad Cochran, Who Died at San Antonio," *Albuquerque Citizen*, June 1, 1898, 3; Irad Cochran military records, National Archives, Washington, DC; Miguel Antonio Otero, *My Nine Years as Governor of the Territory of New Mexico, 1897–1906* (1940; repr., Santa Fe: Sunstone, 2007); Tom Hall, *The Fun and Fighting of the Rough Riders* (New York: Frederick A. Stokes, 1899); "Lincoln Park—Landmark in Las Vegas," *Las Vegas (NM) Optic*, July 1, 1975, 6.

The decision to set up the volunteer camp south of town instead of closer to Fort Sam Houston, where the Regular Army trained, proved to be a sound one. In addition to serving the purpose of avoiding any possible conflict between the various regiments, it also placed the Rough Riders farther from the temptations of such camp establishments as saloons and the red-light district. For the most part, the volunteers restrained themselves in those regards, but with time there were increased incidents of "ruffian behavior" and encounters with local law enforcement. The most celebrated of such occurrences occurred during a public concert at Riverside Park on the evening of May 27, four days following the receipt of orders to ship out via rail to Tampa for deployment to Cuba. Presented in honor of Roosevelt and the Rough Riders, the concert featured music by a brass-and-drum band under the direction of "Professor" Carl Beck that included popular military marches and the unofficial theme song of the regiment, "There'll Be a Hot Time in the Old Town Tonight." The event, as reported nationwide by the news media, came dangerously close to uncontrolled chaos.

One thousand people were present, the night was pleasant and everything went merrily till [sic] Prof. Beck had his band play "The Cavalry Charge," which is accompanied by pistol firing. Some members of the band had revolvers loaded with blank cartridges, which they were to fire at a signal given during the rendering of the piece. When they fired the pistols one of the rough riders was heard to shout, "Help him out, boys." With this, several pistols from the outskirts of the crowd blazed forth and then the fusillade began. Then the lights went out and confusion and excitement reigned, terminating the concert and breaking up the crowd.

Given the nature of the recruits, the intensity of the training, and the pending deployment, such episodes seemed imminent. "It is beginning to dawn on the public," the article concluded, "that the rough riders, while comprised in part of society youth and men from all walks of life, who are both gentlemen and material for gallant soldiers, they also include as hard a lot of cowboys and Indian half-breeds as the western territories could furnish."[10]

At 3:00 A.M. on the morning of May 29, the Rough Riders began the process of dismantling Camp Wood and making their way to the rail line three miles distant. Shortages of rail coaches and other unforeseen obstacles delayed the departure, but the following morning the fully loaded troop train got underway to Tampa, where the regiment joined up with the Fifth Army Corps, under the command of Maj. Gen. William R. "Pecos Bill" Shafter. Further delays occurred at the final staging area, but the volunteers finally went ashore at Daiquiri, Cuba, on June 22. Ironically, despite their extensive cavalry training at Riverside, they entered the war zone as a dismounted unit. Two days later the regiment saw its first major action in the Battle of Las Guásimas. Soon after, Wood received promotion to brigadier general, transferring command of the Rough Riders to Roosevelt, now a colonel. Joining up with other US forces moving against the town of Santiago, the men were part of the successful assault on the San Juan Heights that marked the beginning of the end for the brief war. Despite the fact that their pivotal action actually occurred on Kettle Hill during that assault, the Rough Riders remain more commonly associated with the charge on San Juan Hill. Roosevelt exhibited remarkable leadership and bravery during his brief command; for his gallantry, he later received the Medal of Honor.[11]

The Spanish-American War formally ended on August 12, 1898, with the United States firmly entrenched as a world power and the undisputed protector of the Western Hemisphere. In the course of events that followed, it would be up to Pres. Teddy Roosevelt to build on that recently attained and hard-fought status. At war's end, though, Roosevelt happily joined his men as they celebrated victory, then soon after went through the formalities of disbanding the regiment. The end of the Rough Riders came on September 15 at Montauk Island, New York. Riverside, the training ground where they first came together as a unit, reverted to its former use as a park, although without any development by San Antonio until the 1920s, when work began on the golf course. In the interim the newly opened Brackenridge Park (see chapter

9) became the city's favored recreational site. In the years following the war, the national historical significance of the park faded from public memory as San Antonio only enhanced its status as one of the nation's vital military centers during the world wars of the twentieth century. Briefly renamed in honor of the legendary leader of the First US Volunteer Cavalry, the grounds once again became Riverside with the development of a newer Roosevelt Park elsewhere. Appropriately, though, the new road completed to the old campgrounds became Roosevelt Avenue. Today, though, the site of Camp Wood along that thoroughfare is far better known for its golf course than for its unique role in American military history.[12]

Throughout his life, Roosevelt remembered his time at Riverside with fondness when he reflected on the esprit de corps it helped engender. "We had enjoyed San Antonio," he recalled,

> and were glad that our regiment had been organized in the city where the Alamo commemorates the death fight of Crockett, Bowie, and their famous band of frontier heroes. All of us had worked hard, so that we had had no time to

Pres. Theodore Roosevelt, center, with former members of the Rough Riders at a reunion in San Antonio, April 1905. Photograph by Henry C. Clogenson. Library of Congress Prints and Photographs Division, Washington, DC, http://hdl.loc. gov/loc.pnp/cph.3a21300.

be homesick or downcast; but we were glad to leave the hot camp, where every day the strong wind sifted the dust through everything, and to start for the gathering-place of the army which was to invade Cuba.

In 1905, as president, Roosevelt returned to the site to participate in a Rough Rider reunion. Following a speech at Alamo Plaza on April 7, he participated in a grand parade down his namesake road for dinner and reminiscences with his former comrades at the old fairgrounds. It would be the former commander's last trip to San Antonio prior to his death in 1919.[13]

THE COURSE *IN* HISTORY

Riverside Municipal Golf Course opened in 1929, with a nine-hole layout north of the San Antonio River that covered much of the footprint of the Camp Wood training grounds. Although sources differ on the original designer, given the various changes to the course, the initial nine holes were actually the work of George Adolph Hoffman. A native of New Jersey, Hoffman was at various times in his career a playing professional, golf course owner and operator, and designer. For many years he lived in San Antonio, where he designed the golf layout at Olmos Basin. He later moved to El Paso and designed the Ascarate course there.[14]

The era in which the Riverside course debuted led to an interesting association with one of golf's legendary designers, Albert Warren "Tilly" Tillinghast, and resulted in at least one source attributing the layout to him. One of the premier course architects in the first part of the twentieth century, Tillinghast designed such notable facilities as Baltusrol in New Jersey, Bethpage and Winged Foot in New York, and the San Antonio courses of Oak Hills, La Oma (Fort Sam Houston), and Brackenridge. At the height of the Great Depression, though, golf courses and their designers, as well as the PGA, like most businesses were facing hard times. In the mid-1930s, PGA president George Jacobus, of Ridgewood, New Jersey, formulated a plan to help his friend Tillinghast and in the process provide greater assistance to association members, at the same time increasing the organization's visibility and viability. Jacobus hired Tillinghast as a consulting landscape architect to visit golf courses nationwide—wherever there were affiliated members—to offer free advice and planning. Accepting the challenge with remarkable energy and purpose, the designer visited more than four hundred courses from 1935 to 1936, including Riverside, and compiled detailed reports on their conditions. Writing from the Alamo City on January 6, 1936, he mentioned his initial meetings with PGA member Murray Brooks, the salaried professional for the city courses:

> Afterwards I went over the Riverside course with course superintendent, Sam Brown. This course was laid out some five years ago over good and adequate ground. It is a better course in may [sic] respects than Brackenridge. It has amply large turfed teeing grounds which should prove to the city that it is quite possible to maintain such. However I was able to give Brown a number of suggestions for the improvement of six of the nine holes. I found him very appreciative and understanding.
>
> Murray Brooks is a splendid fellow and after wishing him all the luck in the world, I prepared to continue on to Austin.

Tilly offered no further elaboration on his suggestions, but it is worth noting his favorable comparison of Riverside to his own design of Brackenridge, which he felt had been mismanaged since completing his work there. Despite that observation, though, the south-side course never seriously competed with the one on the near north side as one of the city's most popular recreational sites.[15]

In 1961 the city added an additional two holes to Riverside, making it an eleven-hole course. Seven years later city staffers Harold Henk, an agronomist, and Vernon Schmidt, a landscape architect, collaborated on a comprehensive redesign of the links, overseeing the addition of seven holes south of the river to complete the eighteen-hole complex. Their work also included full development of a par-three course at the location. Henk, a native of Seguin and a Vietnam veteran, as an avid golfer particularly appreciated the assignment. Although he was aware of the Rough Rider connection to the site, he never came across any related artifacts during construction.[16]

DIVOTS

Given the massive scope of landscaping and land reuse since the days of Rough Rider training in 1898, Riverside Golf Course lacks what the National Register of Historic Places refers to as "archeological integrity"—that is, any association with the site's historical period of significance long ago gave way to construction, terracing and contouring, and land reclamation. That does not preclude the presence of disbursed buried deposits, though, no matter how remote the possibility that any artifacts might surface during a match. Still, more than one duffer on a course built on a historic site has speculated about the thin line between plowing deep divots and conducting field investigations with "long-handled trowels," otherwise known as irons and wedges. Golfers should remember that harvesting artifacts on public land is illegal—it is also improbable. If there remains historical detritus at Riverside, though, it might conceivably fall into one of the following categories.

AMMUNITION

Corroded brass shells from the time of Camp Wood would likely be from a caliber .30-40 US Army cartridge fired from the Krag-Jørgenson model 1898 carbine that the Rough Riders carried. Designed by Norwegians Ole Herman Johannes Krag and Erik Jørgenson, the "Krag" was adopted by the US military in 1892 as a replacement for the heavier .45-70 Springfield single-shot rifle then in service. Favored for its smooth operation, the Krag provided satisfactory service during the Spanish-American War, although its muzzle velocity failed to match that of the 7-mm Mauser rifle preferred by Spanish troops and was slower to reload and fire. Nevertheless, it continued in limited use by the US military through World War II.

As the regular cavalry utilized the newly adopted Krag carbine at the time of the regiment's formation, Wood and Roosevelt used their considerable political influence to secure the same armament for their volunteer troops, although officers of the regiment received new lever-action M1895 Winchester rifles firing the same .30-40 cartridges. Standard sidearms were Colt .45s. Two Colt-Browning M1895 tripod-mounted 7–57-mm machine guns, donated by recruits, and a newfangled Dudley-Sims dynamite gun provided additional, although often unreliable, firepower.

BLADES

Undoubtedly, some of the men continued to carry their own favorite Bowie knives, but the army also issued Cuban-style machetes, believed to be more practical battlefield tools in jungle warfare. Some officers obviously continued the tradition of using swords, such as the 1872 model cavalry saber Roosevelt complained about dragging between his legs as he raced into battle at Las Guasimas. Because of that experience, he would leave it behind for the more famous San Juan Heights battle a few days later.

CLOTHING ACCOUTREMENTS

Other less-lethal equipment of the Rough Riders consisted of blue flannel shirts, haversacks, Mills cartridge belts, and army-issue canteens, with the letters "US" printed on the front. Their most distinctive uniform fixture was the Stetson felt slouch hat. Made in a style commonly used by the military since the Civil War, these were wide-brimmed hats that often had one side pinned up to allow room for shouldering a rifle. Khaki trousers held up by canvas suspenders and low-heel boots covered with buttoned leggings rounded out their attire.

SADDLES AND TACK

As viewed in the broadest sense of field equipment, the largest component each volunteer had was his horse and the associated saddle, bridal, riding gloves, scabbard, bags, and blankets. Coincidentally, despite the rigorous cavalry training, the last of the required saddles arrived at Camp Wood just as all of the soldiers loaded the horses and pack mules onto train cars for the arduous four-day trip to Tampa. In one of the many ironies of this "splendid little war," all the animals were destined to be left behind for lack of transport to Cuba, and the volunteer cavalry ended up fighting on foot. Roosevelt's personal horse, Texas, did make the trip to the front, where the colonel made use of him in battle. In general, the Rough Riders used a modified McClellan saddle, designed by army officer George B. McClellan before the Civil War. Lighter and leaner in construction than the typical western working saddles, with pronounced pommels and horns more familiar to the frontier recruits of the regiment, the military-style saddle nevertheless prevailed in the training process.

Sources: David Traxel, 1898: *The Birth of the American Century* (New York: Vintage Books, 1998); Henry B. Russell, *An Illustrated History of Our War with Spain: Its Causes, Incidents, and Results Embracing a Complete Record of Military and Naval Operations from the Beginning to the Close of the Conflict with Descriptions of Battles, Sieges, Exploits, and Achievements of Our Army and Navy* (Hartford, CT: A. D. Worthington, 1898); Theodore Roosevelt, *The Rough Riders* (New York: P. F. Collier and Son, 1899); "Rough Riders," Wikipedia, accessed Mar. 2016, https://en.wikipedia.org/wiki/Rough_Riders; Jeremy Anderberg, "Outfitted & Equipped in History: American Rough Rider," Aug. 1, 2013, Art of Manliness, accessed Mar. 2016, http://www.artofmanliness. com/2013/08/01/outfitted-equipped-american-rough-rider/; "Arms of the Rough Riders," The Rough Riders: 1st U.S. Volunteer Cavalry, accessed Mar. 2016, http://www.frfrogspad.com/rough.htm#Arms.

11

ALONG THE HEALING WATERS

HANCOCK PARK MUNICIPAL GOLF COURSE, LAMPASAS

SCORECARD FROM THE PAST

Currently: Hancock Park Municipal Golf Course

Historic Name: Hancock Springs and the Park Hotel

DETAILS: An eighteen-hole public golf course, with the original nine holes (now the back nine) established in the years following World War II; distance is 6,029 yards from the longest tees

Location: 700 Naruna Road, Lampasas

Historical Context: Settlement and recreation

Historical Type: Resort, camp, and municipal park

Period of Significance: 1883–1890s as a mineral-bath resort; early twentieth century as church camp

Signature Hole of History: Number thirteen, a par-four, 297-yard hole with a left dogleg, requires golfers to fly Sulphur Creek in the vicinity of the historic Hancock Springs bathhouse, which can be a hazard for right-handed players with a pronounced hook.

THE COURSE OF HISTORY

Important landmarks to Native Americans and pioneer settlers, and possibly to Spanish explorers as well, the abundant mineral-spring system of Lampasas along Sulphur Creek became the focal point of a community named Burleson beginning in the early 1850s. Within only a few years, the legislature determined that

Sulphur Creek bisecting the Hancock Park Golf Course. Photograph by Stanley O. Graves.

there was sufficient settlement in the area to establish Lampasas County and designate Burleson, renamed Lampasas as well, as the seat of government. Despite the Civil War, the area held much promise for growth and permanence during the years following Reconstruction. The Gulf, Colorado, and Santa Fe Railway reached the town in 1882, and for two years Lampasas served as the terminus before the railroad began extending the route farther west. That short interlude proved a defining moment for the small county seat after a railroad syndicate that included John Sealy and Walter Gresham chose to invest heavily in the area's potential as a spa and resort. Almost from the earliest days of settlement, stories circulated about the curative and therapeutic power of the seven springs feeding into the Sulphur Creek drainage. Influenced by such widespread accounts and by the abundance of the water source, the railroad men hoped to tap into the burgeoning national health phenomenon of "taking the waters." Believing that with proper facilities and skillful promotion to attract a prosperous

LEWIS HANCOCK, GOLFER

The scion of Austin pioneer families, Lewis Hancock (1857–1920) grew to prominence as a business, political, and civic leader in the capital city. A successful banker and the owner of an opera house, he served as both city alderman and mayor. He was also an avid golfer, and it is for that interest that his legacy endures for many in Texas. Although his family owned the land on which Hancock Park Municipal Golf Course in Lampasas is located, he sold the property decades before the development of the links. In Austin, though, he took the initiative to develop one of the state's earliest courses. At a meeting at the Driskill Hotel in November 1899, he formally called on his business friends to help finance and plan the endeavor. As a result, the Austin Golf Club incorporated the following January. Site researchers Margaret Hereford and Gregory Smith noted that the original nine-hole course "was rough, with sand greens—no sod, and no earth moving—but was ready for amateur tournament play on February 22, 1900." In 1913 the course expanded to eighteen holes, utilizing property northeast of the original fairways. The Austin Country Club, as the governing organization came to be known, moved to new facilities in the 1940s, and the earlier site became a municipal operation, Hancock Golf Course. Over time the city sold the second nine holes for commercial development (now the Hancock Shopping Center) but retained the original nine, making significant improvements through the years. Considered "the oldest continually-operating golf course" in the state, Hancock's course was listed in the National Register of Historic Places in 2014 for its significance in the areas of entertainment and recreation.

Sources: "The Funeral of Mr. Lewis Hancock," *Austin American*, Feb. 15, 1920; Margaret Hereford and Gregory Smith, Hancock Golf Course National Register of Historic Places Registration Form, 2014, Texas Historical Commission, Austin.

clientele for a spa, Lampasas could become the Saratoga of the South. To that end they entered into a joint venture to construct an elaborate tourist complex on an expansive rise north of the creek in the vicinity of present South Spring Street. The centerpiece of the operation was a massive frame hotel that reflected the ornate, high-style design of the Victorian era.[1]

The Park Hotel dominated the landscape of surrounding Hancock Park, named for the Hancock family—brothers George and John and George's son, Lewis—previous owners of the 200-acre tract. As Janet Mace Valenza noted in her study of early Texas spas and resorts, the Park Hotel included "more than two hundred electrically lighted and carpeted rooms, a reading and writing room, a music room, a dining room with seating capacity for 150, three parlors, and a billiard room with four tables" as well as an outdoor dancing pavilion. Historic photos show a polychromatic, double-galleried porch that reportedly extended three hundred feet in length, topped by a gabled-roof system and squared towers that added verticality to the hillside massing. Connecting the facility to Hancock Springs, a few hundred yards to the south, was a board-walk that led to a footbridge that took bathers across the creek to a stone bathhouse. The operation was evocative of the Beach Hotel in the coastal resort of Galveston and contemporaneous with the Athenaeum Hotel in Chautauqua, New York, the model for an educational and recreational vacation community the investors envisioned for Central Texas as well. As Valenza noted, the Park Hotel was "the epitome of grace and elegance rarely seen in small frontier towns." It thus became a preferred destination spot for vacationers, those partaking of the therapeutic baths, and cultural and social elites who enjoyed the nearby horseracing, Chautauqua-like literary events, and state and national conferences held on the grounds. The rapid success of the venture spawned related developments in Lampasas, including those associated with other springs, and the Park Hotel expanded as well to accommodate the influx of visitors.[2]

Despite the countless diversions available to those who enjoyed the area during its heyday as a resort, Hancock Springs served as the heart and soul of the visitor experience. In his seminal work

Springs of Texas, Gunnar Brune documented the local geology that produced the various mineral springs, noting that cavernous sub-surface Cretaceous formations allowed for the storage and movement of vast pools of water. Given the pervasiveness and geologic complexities of the limestone substructure and its water currents, Brune concluded: "In general the water is a calcium bicarbonate type, but it may contain large amounts of sodium chloride. It ranges from fresh to moderately saline, is hard to very hard, and alkaline. It may contain much hydrogen sulfide gas, which imparts a 'rotten egg' odor." It was the sulfur content, he added, that gave rise to the tributary's name (although with a different spelling). Now obscured by the bathhouse remains and the later addition of a downstream dam, the Hancock Springs continue to flow abundantly, serving as a primary source for the municipal water supply.[3]

Despite the success of the Park Hotel and the related business activity it influenced, the resort venture proved to be short lived. The decline came gradually at first, following construction of the rail line beyond the city that opened up travel to more exotic places farther west. Within a decade of its opening, the Park Hotel no longer had the unique draw it once enjoyed as the traveling public sought other locales, even other resort options. In 1894 the local Centenary College, founded around the time of the hotel's construction, began leasing the property for its programs. The final blow came on the evening of February 27, 1895. As an ice storm gripped the town, freezing pipes and making roads difficult to maneuver, the old hotel caught fire and, with the local fire department unable to respond in force, burned to the ground. The devastating fire marked the end, not only of the college but also of any pending plans to revitalize some measure of the tourist trade around the once-grand hotel. With its main means of promotion and support gone, Hancock Springs became anachronistic and something of a local curiosity. It lingered for a few years before closing, but its story did not end there; it would be reborn as part of a more localized recreational plan through the years. First, however, it served another role as part of a summer-camp operation.[4]

A view from the twelfth green toward the historic remains of the bathhouse complex. Photograph by Dan K. Utley.

Stabilized remains of the historic bathhouse at Lampasas. The circular feature visible in the water indicates the location of the springs. Photograph by Dan K. Utley.

In July 1905, as the result of an idea proffered by J. H. Dickson, a deacon of the First Baptist Church, the Central Texas Baptist Encampment began operations at the park site. The purpose was to bring together the ideas of summer camps, evangelistic camp meetings, and elements of the Chautauqua concept, which coincidentally had grown out of the Sunday-school movement of the late nineteenth century. Once again Hancock Park became the centerpiece of a successful enterprise, this time one that attracted the attention of Baptist leaders statewide. In 1907, while gathered at Lampasas, the governing body voted to acquire the property for a permanent encampment, assuring the local citizenry and churches "that the park would be run on a broad plan and not with a narrow sectarian scale." The following year the Baptists completed the construction of a large tabernacle known as the Dickson Auditorium, named in honor of the local deacon who first envisioned a religious camp at the site. A new swimming pool, which doubled as a baptismal font, came in 1911. Then in 1913 the land conveyed to the Hancock Park and Assembly Company, which renamed the park for member A. P. Anderson. As such it grew to include sites for tent camping and small cottages, a grocery store, concessionaires, a commodious dining hall, and of course the baths, although there were no provisions for "mixed bathing" by the sexes. Doctrinal religion prevailed in the encampments, as one pastor noted: "Saint and sinner camped side by side and it was a difficult thing for the sinner to go away without a knowledge of the Lord. Sometimes whole families were saved and that was when the Methodists would shout and the Baptists would holler 'AMEN!'"[5]

A growing presence on the grounds through the years was a summer-school offering by San Marcos Academy, a Baptist institution in Hays County south of Austin. Known as Camp Marlamont— an amalgamated name comprised of "Mar" for Marcos, "la" for Lampasas, and "mont" for the Lampasas hill country—it served to provide educational opportunities to academy students for scholastic credit. Advertising statewide under the slogan "The Best Is Not Too Good," the camp essentially offered a unique outdoor classroom setting with the "highest cultural, moral and religious influences." With a program that included morning instruction and afternoon recreation, with time too for the fine arts, the summer academy was advertised thus: "For students not evenly graded. For those who are backward. For those who have been compelled to drop out. For boys and girls who do not want to waste a summer." It proved to be another successful program in the park, but in 1929, without adequate reasoning for their decision, the Baptists abruptly opted to sell the site to a private concern and purchased additional land in Wimberley, closer to their main campus in San Marcos. Now once again known as Hancock Park, it operated under private administration until the city acquired the property in 1936 and embarked on plans to develop the site as a municipal recreational facility. For a brief time during World War II, the city made the park available for the exclusive use of US Army personnel from nearby Camp Hood (now Fort Hood), but at war's end it again became a municipal park operated by Lampasas.[6]

The Course *in* History

As befitted a growing and progressive community in the years following World War II, city planners envisioned a wide range of uses for Hancock Park. Part of that planning included the development of a nine-hole golf course with assistance from the Lampasas Country Club. The chosen tract along the west and north sections of the park placed it immediately adjacent to the old bathhouse structure. Formal dedication of the new park features, including the golf course, baseball fields, picnic and playground areas, and new and rehabilitated structures such as the Hostess House at the swimming pool, occurred over four days in late June 1948. It was a big occasion in the county seat, whose residents saw it as a sign of a new era of promise and prosperity; local businesses closed in the afternoons so their customers and employees could attend the festivities. Speakers included such dignitaries as Congressmen Lyndon B. Johnson and O. C. Fisher and Gov. Beauford H. Jester. As one newspaper reported, though, Johnson upstaged Jester when his arrival by helicopter drowned out the governor's speech, causing him to cut it short.[7]

Designers of the original nine-hole course were local lawyer John Camp Abney, who served as county judge and mayor, and former city manager Dan Nixon; a Mr. Dillingham (first name unknown) oversaw the construction. Their initial work, while commendable, suffered through the years due to devastating floods that heavily damaged the park as well as the city. Most significant early on was the monumental Mother's Day flood of 1957, which damaged much of the downtown area. Other floods since that time have also taken their toll on the course, requiring extensive rehabilitation work, but the city has always reopened and even expanded the facility. Nine new holes, now called the front nine, opened in 1996 utilizing designs by Jepp Willie. Among the ten or so individuals who have served as superintendents of the course since it opened in the 1940s is Alric Cradoc January, whose son, Don January, won ten PGA tour titles and enjoyed a successful career on the Senior PGA (Champions) Tour as well (see chapter 1).[8]

12

NUTS!

SAN SABA RIVER GOLF COURSE, SAN SABA

SCORECARD FROM THE PAST

Currently: San Saba River Golf Course

Historic Name: Risien pecan bottoms

DETAILS: Eighteen-hole course; distance is 6,904 yards from the longest tees.

Location: East of San Saba via US 290 and County Road 102 along the San Saba River

Historical Context: Agriculture

Historical Type: Cultivated pecan groves

Period of Significance: Early to mid-twentieth century

Signature Hole of History: Number eighteen (number nine on the 1970s plat), a 538-yard, par-five hole with a dogleg to the right and a final approach over water that leads golfers back to the clubhouse. Along the way, they play beneath a canopy of old pecan trees that once belonged to propagator and entrepreneur E. Guy Risien.

THE COURSE OF HISTORY

Given that the town of San Saba is the self-proclaimed "Pecan Capital of the World," despite competition from a number of other historical centers of nut production in the state such as Seguin, Goldthwaite, Brownwood, and Bastrop, it would not be out of place to find a pecan tree or two on the local golf course. Golfers, however, are probably unaware of the species encountered along the fairways, being much more focused on immediate concerns like tree placement, trunk density, shade distribution, and leaf clutter

The backdrop of large pecan trees on the San Saba course. Photograph by Stanley O. Graves.

Signage for hole eighteen, the signature hole of history on the San Saba River course. Photograph by Stanley O. Graves.

than on selective breeding or silvicultural management. Yet the relationship of the sport to trees is part of a larger context in which humans and trees coexist for mutual benefit. Environmental historian James M. McWilliams noted: "When humans and plants enter into a relationship, a level of humility is forced upon us as we become integrated into unfamiliar natural processes. A mutually beneficial balance, . . . [while] never perfect, is the only way to ensure that the relationship—much less the plant itself—enjoys some semblance of longevity." Speaking specifically to nut-bearing trees like the pecan and the relational symbiosis they represent, he added: "For most of history, humans have propagated nuts. Nuts, in return, have generously, if more passively, improved the health of humans. They have thrived. We have thrived."[1]

The pecan trees that crisscross the San Saba River Golf Course in a somewhat regular and linear fashion serve as reminders of the formative days of pecan production in Texas. The historical connection is not insignificant, for the Lone Star State is currently the nation's second-ranking producer of pecans and has at times been the undisputed leader. Additionally, what has traditionally been good for the Texas crop has proven to be beneficial for other states as well, particularly those farther west, where pecan production faces enhanced climatic and environmental challenges. Nuts are big business in Texas. To appreciate how San Saba came to be at the epicenter of the industry, both regionally and nationally, it is important to understand the natural range of pecan trees dating back to prehistoric times. As McWilliams observed in his authoritative work on pecans, trees of the species *Carya illinoinesis* proved uniquely adapted to favorable growing conditions found in only a few distinct areas of North America, but where they gained a foothold, they became dominant early on. The lineage, reflective of that dominance as well as the species' adaptability and tenacity, is impressive.

> Pecans belong to the family Juglandacae, the pollen of which first appeared in the late Cretaceous period, about 135 million years ago. About 80 million years later the phylum Hicorae

SAN SABA COUNTY COURTHOUSE

Deeds and documents recording Edmond E. Risien's extensive alluvial, pecan-producing lands along the San Saba and Colorado Rivers, including that fertile bend destined to become the San Saba River Golf Course, are housed in the County Clerk's Office on the second floor of the historic San Saba County Courthouse, less than two miles west of the course. Construction of the courthouse coincided with an era of increased agricultural development in the county, influenced in large part by the pioneering work of Risien. Formally organized in 1856, San Saba County derives its name from early Spanish exploration of the area and the Mission Santa Cruz de San Sabá and presidio upstream on the San Saba River near Menard (see chapter 3). The current 1911 building, the third to occupy the San Saba town square, reflects a general design concept not only as a seat of county government but also as a social and business center. Over the main north and south porticos, the bold inscription "SAN SABA" beneath an encircled Lone Star and the county's motto, "From the people to the people," attests to the structure's broadly encompassing roles.

On the advice of local architect and builder Walter R. Smith, the San Saba County Commissioners Court selected W. Chamberlain and Company of Birmingham, Alabama, and Fort Worth, Texas, to design the current courthouse. Chamberlain's company, as well as the firm of Churchill and White, had earlier submitted preliminary designs for the bidding process, but the final contract called for "Full Plans, Specifications and Detail Drawings." Chamberlain had recently designed the Deaf Smith County Courthouse in the Panhandle town of Hereford, and the commissioners may have been familiar with that classical-revival structure. According to the *San Saba Star,* the company made "a specialty of courthouses, having designed over 60 of them and have [*sic*] done work in ten states." Cham-

A 2016 photograph of the San Saba County Courthouse, San Saba. Completed in 1911, the building features classical detailing in its design. In 2016 a full restoration began under the direction of the firm Architexas of Dallas and Austin, with funding from San Saba County and the Texas Historic Courthouse Preservation Program of the Texas Historical Commission. Photograph by Stanley O. Graves.

berlain worked quickly, and on July 25 the commissioners accepted his plans and authorized solicitation for bids.

The structure is one of a hundred extant Texas courthouses built between 1900 and 1940 and grounded in classical detailing. Domes, grand columns, and pediments evoke a classical era rooted in interpretations of Roman classical styles. The particularly Texas rendition of the style has been dubbed "Texas Renaissance" by Texas Tech architectural historian Willard B. Robinson and "Academic Eclecticism" by Jay C. Henry, an architectural historian with the University of Texas at Arlington. Like other courthouses of the day, the San Saba building reflects the move toward classical elements, with its domed clock tower, ionic capitals, two-story columns, and dentated cornices. The rusticated ground floor and corner quoins, however, recall lingering Richardsonian Romanesque influences not apparent on the earlier Deaf Smith County building. In San Saba the courthouse's elevated entrances with broken pediments over the doors as well as a rectilinear floor plan are other hallmarks of the style. While Chamberlain may have used some elements of a stock plan for the building as a whole, he certainly tailored the finished product to San Saba County. The building finishes were modern and technologically advanced for the time. The pressed-brick exterior cladding followed the courthouse trend, even though wood and locally quarried stone were the materials of choice in the rest of the town. Painted and scored plaster and woodwork defined interior finishes, and plaster and pressed metal served as ceiling materials.

The county's great pride in the plans for the new building was evident in a lengthy 1910 newspaper article about the structure that included a rendering. It would, the article noted, be constructed of "concrete and stone and brick. . . [with an] $800 bell and with a clock of fine movement which will have four skeleton dials which will be 7 feet in diameter each.... [The building will be] fireproof and absolutely up-to-date." Further, it would include a "vacuum cleaning system" and a fire line with fifty feet of hose, modern plumbing, and steam heating. Among the most advanced features was an internal communication system that ensured each office would "be provided with an inter phone, so that an official can talk to any room in the house."

In addition to the governmental functions the building served, it also provided meeting space for the agricultural society and fraternal organizations as well as demonstration rooms. There was a large restroom for women on the first floor, complete with fireplace, providing an unusually comfortable space to congregate. Reports mentioned that farm equipment and products were often on display in a large community room on the ground floor and on the courthouse square grounds. Other groups such as the San Saba Brass Band and the Home Demonstration Club also took advantage of the complimentary community accommodations.

San Saba County became nationally prominent in the nut industry due to the horticultural work of Risien and others, who also established pecan trees on the courthouse square. In accordance with the county's publically inclusive motto, the bounty of these trees are, by recorded decree, left for gathering by the local citizens and cannot be commercially harvested by the county government.

Sources: Mavis P. Kelsey and Donald H. Dyal, *The Courthouses of Texas* (College Station: Texas A&M University Press, 1993); *San Saba Star*, Aug. 12, 1910; San Saba County Commissioners Court Minutes, June 29, 30, July 25, 1910; Willard B. Robinson, *The People's Architecture: Texas Courthouses, Jails, and Municipal Buildings* (Austin: Texas State Historical Association, 1983); Jay C. Henry, *Architecture in Texas, 1845–1945* (Austin: University of Texas Press, 1993); Williams Company, "San Saba Courthouse Master Plan," Feb. 2000, submitted to the Texas Historical Commission, Austin.

sprouted across loosely connected landscapes that would eventually cleave into North America, Asia, and Europe. Sixteen million years later the genus Carya, which encompasses all hickories (including the pecan), came into being. This genus died out in Europe by the Pleistocene period (2 million years ago) but took deep root in limited geographical ranges across Asia and North America.[2]

The pecan tree became a permanent fixture of the natural landscape in parts of North America, though, where it was often a territorial determinant along ridges of rich alluvial soils, such as those deposited over the millennia by relatively low-banked tributaries like the San Saba River. While the natural species distribution reached from Illinois in the north to the coastal regions along the Gulf of Mexico, the prevailing range stretched from Central Texas across the South to Alabama and Georgia. Where it grew naturally, McWilliams observed, the pecan was a "climax tree species," meaning that it favored its own shade to that of others and thus "elbowed out potential competitors for the privilege of darting skyward and basking in direct sunlight." In its natural state, the tree was a fierce competitor, a factor that ensured its sustainability through the years in its native habitat.[3]

Geographer Jane Manaster provided an anthropological overview of human utilization of the nut in Texas, a relationship she speculated reaches back about eight thousand years. Referencing the example of excavations at Baker's Cave along the Devils River in Val Verde County, she noted that archeologists discovered seeds and leaves in situ with cultural artifacts "in strata dating from 6100 B.C. to about 3000 B.C." but added that they were not evident in earlier hearths at the site. Such findings, while inconclusive with regard to commodity range and specific utility, nonetheless provide a relative starting point for the early cultural uses of the nut. Manaster and others have conjectured that the pecan was an integral part of hunter-gatherer societies, both as a draw for animals and as a human food source. Native Americans likely ate them raw or pulverized and dried them for use in breadstuffs or drinks. Nomadic groups in Central Texas no doubt carried them as they traveled, as Manaster noted, perhaps introducing them to other areas and expanding the species range, certainly through trade if not limited agriculture as well. McWilliams wryly observed, "It is with some justice (and not a little irony) that today's most popular cultivars are named after Native American peoples: Pawnee, Cheyenne, Kiowa, Mohawk, Choctaw, and Wichita, to name only a few."[4]

While the archeological record of the pecan is still being uncovered and analyzed through increasingly sophisticated means of scientific detection, the nut's place within the written record has long been established. Throughout the South especially, both Spanish and French explorers recorded details of the native nut and of its use by regional tribes, often comparing the pecan to the walnuts or hickories of Europe. As settlers began moving into the region following the early contact period, additional accounts emerged of seasonal harvesting and food usage, with distribution and trade increasing substantially as a result. There were also marginal but purposeful efforts to manage the supply through passive cultivation. Through that process, which represented some minimal human direction on a natural resource, settlers identified significant stocks of productive trees and isolated them by removing competitive vegetation. This was, in effect, a primitive form of enforced natural selection favoring the stronger and more prolific trees. Stands of weaker specimens, viewed as invaluable for food production, building materials, or fuel, often gave way to tilled fields or fenced pastures. Many such trees also disappeared in the boom era of timber production, which in Texas ranged from roughly the 1880s to the 1920s, as a mindset of "cut out and get out" prevailed in the exploitation of the state's woodlands. Soon, McWilliams observed, native pecan trees were "living in a state somewhere between the wild and the sown," which "conferred higher yields while maintaining genetic diversity and, in turn, healthy trees."[5]

As food usage of pecans increased, so too did the demand for more consistent production, which in turn drove market pressures and commodity prices as well as the need for more human intervention on a large scale. Passive cultivation thus gave way to planting experimentation, hybridization, and scientific farming. Early efforts to enhance selection and viability through the controlled planting of preferred seed stock proved to be erratic and ineffective since pecans do not grow "true to type"; that is, each seed produces a unique tree that does not directly reflect the preferred qualities of the parent. Such experiments proved both costly and time consuming, with results often not fully realized for eight to ten years, the period of first yield after the initial planting. As a result, the preferred techniques of asexual propagation soon coalesced around budding, grafting, and topworking—the process of grafting onto the main branches and directing growth through such techniques as selective pruning.[6]

Early on, pecans proved to be resistant to accepted methods of propagation used successfully in agriculture for centuries. As market demand drove the need for improved varieties and increased productivity over the availability of native stock, however, experimentation took on new significance. In the early 1820s the work of South Carolina potter Abner Landrum, who advocated a change in the seasonal approach to grafting, seemed promising but failed to gain traction in the antebellum years. During that same time, however, a significant development occurred that radically altered the nature of pecan production, paving the way for its development as a true industry. The genesis of change occurred in the 1840s in southeastern Louisiana at Oak Alley Plantation, primarily a sugarcane operation. There owner Jacques Telesphore Roman in effect provided a new experiment station for Dr. A. E. Colomb, who hoped to renew his previous efforts to graft scions, or freshly cut shoots and branches, from a specific tree widely prized in the region for the larger size and thinner shell (paper shell) of its nuts. To assist with the technicalities, Roman relied on his slave gardener Antoine, who proved to be the ideal person for the testing because of his agricultural skills and knowledge of local flora. Deftly, the gardener employed the use of cleft grafts, which allowed him to bond the smaller scions with larger branches of the host stock, for the first time successfully grafting two types of pecans for greater—and generationally sustainable—production and marketability. With time the Oak Alley orchards expanded considerably, thanks to the pioneering work and careful nurturing of Antoine. In 1876 a later owner of the property, Hubert Bonzano, exhibited at the Centennial International Exhibition in Philadelphia, where his pecans—to be known as the Centennial variety—received special recognition. With that and subsequent attention to new varieties in Louisiana and Georgia, a new era of commercial production emerged. Sadly, the true horticultural progenitor of the transition remains largely unknown.[7]

Despite the burgeoning commercialization, such adaptation was slow to develop in Texas, where the abundant and seemingly limitless native inventory prevailed, precluding for a time the need for crop diversity. Consequently, the early spread of cultivars and planned orchards centered on states of the lower South. When such change finally came to Texas, though, it was significant and served as a benchmark for the industry nationwide. The story reflects a wide range of influences, from opportunity and hard work to geography and serendipity. It begins with the curiosity of a young émigré to the United States, Edmond E. Risien.

Born in 1853 in the coastal community of Deal near Dover in Kent County, England, Risien traveled to America in the early 1870s. Trained in his homeland as a cabinetmaker, he arrived in Galveston with the intention of moving on west to California. Following a brief visit with relatives in Limestone County, though, he instead traveled only 150 miles west to the town of San Saba, the relatively young seat of government for San Saba County, organized in 1856. The town held great promise as a developing center of commerce for a widespread agricultural area of Central Texas when Risien arrived in 1874. Perhaps attracted by the possibility for immediate financial opportunities or bolstered in a larger sense by the hopeful business climate that pervaded the state at the end of Reconstruction, he decided to stay. Settling on property east of San Saba along the banks of Mill Creek, he entered into a partnership with Dr. J. C. Rogan, one of the town's founders, to develop the community's first waterworks. Under the terms of their 1878 agreement, Rogan would provide hydraulic equipment for a dam Risien would maintain and operate. The collaboration, which soon involved others, proved successful, and over time Risien expanded the complex with additional milling capabilities and created a bathhouse and swimming hole nearby that became focal points for local recreation and community gatherings. In 1879 Risien wed Elizabeth Lyne, also a native of England residing in San Saba, and the couple made their home on nearby property.[8]

Naturally inquisitive, Risien closely observed the local trade commodities, which included native pecans harvested along the San Saba River bottoms. He analyzed their characteristics and, being an entrepreneur and innovator, decided to do what he could to improve the crop. He began first by offering a monetary reward for the best local specimens, which he hoped to cultivate on his own. The prizewinner turned out to be the owner of land along the confluence of the Colorado and San Saba Rivers, where one tree in particular provided a remarkable bounty of large pecans. Given the exploitive and remarkably wasteful means of harvesting common at the time, however, the landowner had simply felled the tree's larger limbs to provide greater access to the nuts on the ground, thereby severely limiting future viability. When Risien asked why he had done this, the owner replied, "I left one limb so I'd have something to stand on to cut off the others to get the pecans." In this era of natural abundance and before the advent of widespread conservation measures, few except Risien even questioned the practice. Eventually, systematic pecan threshing became the norm, proving to be more productive and less destructive to the trees. In the days before mechanization and the introduction of tractor-powered tree shakers for commercial harvesting, the use of threshing crews paid on shares (sharecropping) was the common and preferred method. Men threw rope lines over the larger limbs and tied foot loops to hoist young boys—generally light, agile, and fearless—high into the upper reaches of the trees; armed with stout sticks, they flailed away within the canopies, dislodging nuts to the ground for harvesting by other field hands. Unfortunately, though, before pecan threshing became popular, large numbers of viable, productive trees simply gave way to needless destruction in the pursuit of harvesting. Such was almost the case with the San Saba mother tree.[9]

In an effort to salvage what he could of the prized tree, the Englishman bought the property for his own use. In the years ahead, he nurtured the mother tree, which survived under his care, and used it to experiment with varying forms of grafting and topworking. Through his meticulous testing and research and his innovative grafting techniques, Risien successfully propagated the mother tree and introduced such improved pecan varieties as San Saba, Western Schley, San Saba Improved, and Squirrel's Delight, among many others. His work put him at the forefront of local and regional production and made him a leader in state and national efforts as well, particularly in the drier climates of the western United States. Risien was "a pioneer in top-working large pecan trees," introducing "the technique of grafting juvenile buds from controlled crosses into large bearing trees to reduce the period of juvenility." In an industry marked by a lengthy time of initial high-risk venture, being able to provide an economically viable alternative years earlier was crucial to widespread investment. It was thus largely through his efforts that the reach of commercialization spread well beyond the natural range of the pecan tree.[10]

This Farm Security Administration photo by Russell Lee depicts a pecan-thrashing scene near San Angelo, Texas, around the 1930s. Library of Congress Prints and Photographs Division, Washington, DC, http://hdl.loc.gov/loc.pnp/fsa.8a27732.

Risien lived a long and productive life, receiving countless accolades for his work, including a proclamation from the Texas legislature. He continued to expand his business, adding a nursery in 1888 and using innovative and attention-grabbing marketing techniques, such as providing samples of his products to such international luminaries as Alfred, Lord Tennyson; Queen Victoria; and John Hay, at the time the US secretary of state. Risien also figured prominently in the establishment of the Texas Pecan Growers Association, which held its first state conference in San Saba in 1921. Upon Risien's death in 1940, the administration of his business passed to his family heirs. His son, Edmund Guy Risien, known locally as "Mr. Guy," took a particular interest in the business and became its more prominent spokesman and promoter. The young man had worked closely with his father in the family orchards and brought an even-greater level of business acumen and marketing to the operations; he continued the family's close involvement in the trade association as well, serving as its president in 1945–46. Like his father, the younger Risien promoted the San Saba business on a global scale—garnering widespread publicity in return—through gifts to Britain's Princess Elizabeth and others.[11]

Risien took up his father's example of community service as well, though he became more widely known in different circles for his penchant for letter writing and his resulting stature as something of a rural philosopher. His writings reflected, sometimes in inflammatory fashion, his positions from the extreme right wing of Texas social thought, expressing plainly his strongly held beliefs on everything from race relations and public education to wars in Europe and Vietnam. In 1947 Risien compiled a number of his essays, interspersed with borrowed poetry and news of the pecan business, into a monograph entitled *How to Run the Universe*, which he distributed widely. Additionally, he was a prolific letter writer,

RUNNING THE UNIVERSE FROM SAN SABA

The following are excerpted quotes from E. Guy Risien's self-published 1947 monograph, *How to Run the Universe*, which included poems, pecan-industry reports, and the author's candid thoughts on a range of topics from liquor, Latin, and foreign missions to suntans, immigration, and world peace.

IMMIGRATION

There are reports of lobbying, subtle propaganda, and political pressure by several other races that have gained entrance into the country in considerable numbers, to get the immigration laws relaxed and more of their countrymen admitted. And they will probably be assisted by a good many wealthy people and large land owners in order to get cheap labor.

ENGLAND

As for "British Imperialism" which many people who are probably trying to get their hands on every dollar and every acre of land they can, thinks this is so terrible and awful. What individual or what nation, that was not "imperialistic" ever amounted to much or became great? If the United States had not been imperialistic there would still be only thirteen colonies.

LATIN

Practically all progress and achievement is the result of some ones [sic] power to imagine and think, so it seems to me that less time should be spent in memorizing, and more in developing the power to imagine and think, and that Latin might be thought of as a sort of ball and chain and hindrance to progress, which students would get along much easier and faster if they were released from: If I say any more someone might get the idea I do not think much of Latin.

As I only reached the eighth grade in school and never had any kind of degree, I am probably exposing a great deal of ignorance on this subject.

LIQUOR

There is a story about three men that came to a locked door. One who had been smoking marijuana which seems to distort the vision, thought perhaps they could crawl through the keyhole, and one who had been using opium, wanted to take the pleasantest and easiest way out, so he suggested waiting for someone to unlock it. And the one who had been drinking liquor said, "Oh hell, let's kick the damned thing down." Some say there is no harm in drinking if one will do it right. . . [but] so few are able to do it right.

Source: E. Guy Risien, *How to Run the Universe* (San Saba, TX, 1947), 8, 13, 23, 27.

with his missives appearing regularly in the *Dallas Morning News* and other newspapers. His words left no doubt about his distrust of government at all levels, his heartfelt convictions about the values of hard work and the business world, and his disappointment in the ability of religions to bring about world peace. In a letter to the *Morning News* in May 1968, at the height of US military action in Southeast Asia, he wrote:

> I have in my possession many color pictures in the *National Geographic, Life, Time, Newsweek,* and other magazines that were taken in communist countries which show the people to be good-looking, well dressed and apparently healthy and well fed. Many of the buildings are beautiful. If there are any ghettos or slums, the magazines I refer to never show them.
>
> In Russia and Siberia the winters are long and bitterly cold and the summers and growing seasons short, but the people are building factories, developing their water power, forests, mines and other natural resources. The countries seem to be booming much like Canada; all without any of the foreign aid, food or technical assistance we are sending to countries that have far better climate and soil.
>
> The point is that to save the South Vietnamese from communism we have wrecked and devastated their country far worse than any earthquake, cyclone flood or other natural disaster ever did.
>
> There is room to wonder if the war we meddled ourselves into is not adding far more to the sum of human misery than to the sum of human happiness.[12]

Risien certainly harbored no fondness for his fellow Central Texan, Lyndon B. Johnson. Writing of the president in 1964, he derisively declared: "The Russians have a 5-year plan, the Chinese a great leap forward. And now in order to provide everything for everybody, LBJ and Co. are going to give the American people a 'Great New Society.'"[13]

Regardless his fame and notoriety, Risien remained loyal to San Saba, not only giving of his time and talents to support a wide range of interests, including local history, but also reserving the right to admonish public officials when he thought they failed to serve in the best interests of the community. His 1975 obituary noted this trait: "He was critical of the City-County airport and the new County Rodeo Arena while on the other hand he made numerous donations which included the Golf Course and land on the San Saba River . . . now appropriately called Risien Park." Risien never married and so left a sizable and diverse estate divided among friends, family members, and charitable causes, such as the Methodist Home in Waco and the San Saba city park. Long interested in local history, he also provided a means for conveying parts of his business equipment and personal collections to the San Saba Historical Society, of which he was an active member. Years earlier he had conveyed ownership in other landholdings along the San Saba River that served as a city farm before their incorporation into the golf course and park.[14]

THE COURSE *IN* HISTORY

Intensive fundraising and planning for the San Saba Golf Course got underway in earnest in the summer of 1971, when the local newspaper included a proposed plan of the project and announced that

The pecan tree motif, shown here on a tee-box marker at the San Saba course, provides a visual reference to the site's history. Photograph by Stanley O. Graves.

supporters had raised $9,000 toward the projected goal of $31,000. At a public meeting in July, attendees heard from representatives of golf courses in the neighboring towns of Llano, Lampasas, and Brady, all of whom reported that their facilities were self-sustaining and generating considerable local interest in the sport. C. C. "Cotton" Baskin, Sorrell Smith, and Joe Ragsdale oversaw local planning for the San Saba course, which would include nine holes, a pro shop, and a parking area.[15]

Following the initial surge of interest, however, fundraising lagged behind projections, in part because of persistent speculation about the project's relevance to the community and of unfounded rumors that its completion might require tax resources. An editorial in the paper in October addressed such concerns through the lens of municipal "boosterism." Allaying the tax fears and decrying other unfounded rumors, the writer appealed to the community's collective pride and regional standing, calling on San Saba citizens to embrace progress, which in this particular case came in the form of a golf course.

> Have you noticed that San Saba is the last town in the area to get many things of progress? It takes the cooperation of all the people in the county to promote progress, whether it benefits them personally or not.
> Because we have not had a golf course, like most places, many persons do not play the game, have no interest in it and thus, don't believe it is necessary. But, on the other hand, anything that will help our town and county, will also benefit most all its residents in some way. The San Saba Municipal Golf Course will be another step in progress and we believe the time will come when most all county residents will be able to see that it will be an asset to the area.
> If we can't help in some manner to promote progress, let's not knock it![16]

Despite the persistence of such public concerns and the subsequent pleas for progressive pride, the course continued on schedule, although unexpected cost overruns placed the final price closer to $40,000. Regardless, the course formally opened on Sunday, August 27, 1972. A crowd of about 250 attended the ceremonies, which included the dedication of the Rader Dick Clubhouse, in whose name his family had made a large contribution to put the fundraising over the top. District attorney and former state senator Louis Crump served as master of ceremonies, and Johnny Watkins, the farm-and-ranch editor for Waco television station KWTX and recipient of an honorary lifetime pass to the club, provided the dedicatory comments. Although the local newspaper covered the event with laudatory detail, noting that "Jill Woodruff carried scissors for Watkins to cut the ribbon" and Methodist minister Lee Geldmeier delivered the invocation, no one apparently recorded the name of the first golfer to tee off on the new course. Actually, play had begun earlier that day, so when it came time for the afternoon dedication, officials had to scramble to clear the course. In all, eighty-nine golfers, more than half of whom were members of the newly formed San Saba Golf Association, signed up to play on the opening day.[17]

San Saba River Golf Course now includes eighteen holes, of which the back nine are the original holes. There is still a bottomland feel to much of the course, providing a sense of what Edmond E. Risien must have experienced when he began his horticultural work in the area as a young emigrant following the Civil War and Reconstruction. Even for those golfers who stay in the fairway and avoid the stands of massive pecan trees that guard the way, the site conveys a strong sense of both natural and cultural history. For those who know the story behind the course, it serves as an important visual reminder of agricultural industry, immigrant contributions, tree-bound harvesters, a rural philosopher, and a time when boosters viewed access to golf simply as a determinant of community pride and a symbol of municipal progress in a small Central Texas town.

13

A LINE THROUGH THE PINES

NECHES PINES GOLF COURSE, DIBOLL

SCORECARD FROM THE PAST

Recent Past: Neches Pines Golf Course

Historic Name: Texas Southeastern Railroad Company line

DETAILS: Eighteen-hole course; distance is 7,014 from the longest tees

Location: 900 East Lumberjack Road, Diboll

Historical Context: Texas Southeastern Railroad line between the vast Temple sawmill and its frontline camps

Historical Type: Sawmill railroad

Period of Significance: 1900–1908

Signature Hole of History: The par-five eighteenth hole (originally number one) plays uphill with a slight dogleg to the right that leads to a bunkered green. Leaving the green and heading to the clubhouse, golfers have a downhill view to what was the historic Texas Southeastern line at the turn of the twentieth century.

THE COURSE OF HISTORY

Moving westward into Texas, early settlers from the southern states first encountered a dense and, at places, seemingly impenetrable native stand of pines mixed with hardwoods. Residents would later refer to the area as "tight eye" country, denoting a natural landscape so thick it was a barrier to sunlight as well as travel. The deep woods of eastern Texas represented the western limits of the great southern forest that extended in an almost continual reach from the Atlantic seaboard, only to give way to the prairies

A bunker near the clubhouse at the Neches Pines course. Photograph by Dan K. Utley

and cross-timber regions west of the Trinity River. As William L. Bray noted in a 1904 survey of Texas forest resources, "Like a vast wave that has rolled in upon a level beach, the Atlantic forest breaks upon the dry plains—halting, creeping forward, thinning out, and finally disappearing, except where, along a river course, it pushes far inland."[1]

The vast Texas forest region, more commonly known as the Piney Woods, was equivalent in size to the state of Indiana, as forest historians Robert S. Maxwell and Robert D. Baker described, and "larger than twelve other states." From the Spanish colonial days through early statehood, the forests remained largely intact, a hindrance to those settlers intent on transplanting their historical cotton culture west of the Sabine River. Exploitation of the timberlands would have to wait until the requisite entrepreneurship, capital, market demands, and accessible transportation came together to make the resource a viable commodity. Those factors began to coalesce in the South in the decades following the Civil War, when unprecedented growth during the nation's Gilded Age spurred a broader reach for available timber stands. Stumpage soon turned to money—in a big way. In an era before conservation and scientific forestry, those who exploited the nation's timberlands practiced a "cut out and get out" approach to procurement that left depleted lands in their wake from the Northeast through the Midwest before reaching into the South. "From New England to New York and Pennsylvania, up through Michigan and across Wisconsin and Minnesota," environmental historian Curt Meine observed, "a trail of slash and ash had followed the lumber baron's exploitation. The bawl and din of emerging nationhood drummed out the isolated voices of protest." What occurred, then, was a bonanza era of timber production in the South, including Texas, from the 1880s to the 1920s. This part of the broader national story, however, played out amid some promise of change, with the emergence of new ideas like sustained yields and selective harvesting. There were signs that such conservation measures, considered radical but perhaps practical in the Progressive Era, might have a place in industrial development, not just along the timber fronts of the South. Change, though, was slow and paled in comparison with market demand.[2]

Rivers provided an early means of access from the East Texas timberlands to large mill operations along the coastal plains, but the streams were generally shallow and marginally practical for conveyance of logs only during seasonal floods. It was not until rail lines began piercing the forest core that the boom era began in earnest. With the railroad, there was not only better and more dependable access but also a means for the development of new mills and towns nearer the fronts. Spider-web networks of provisional trams and narrow-gauge lines reached into remote timber stands, connecting to regular lines and making relatively smaller milling operations possible. The advent of railroads also dramatically increased harvest rates, and by the early part of the twentieth century, most of the virgin stands in East Texas had been cut over, with cleared land going for good prices and some lumbermen beginning to invest those profits in new tracts in the western United States—soon to be the new bonanza land. So intense was the cutting that by the 1920s the boom era in Texas was rapidly waning. For those traversing the vast Piney Woods today, it is often difficult to comprehend that what surrounds them is largely a landscape of cultivated hybrid stock or, at best, managed woodlands.

It is within this context that lumberman Thomas Lewis Latané Temple sought his fortune in southern Angelina County amid the virgin pines of the Neches River valley. A native of Virginia, Temple made his way to southwestern Arkansas as a teenager and worked initially in farming before finding success in the lumber business in northeastern Texas, working in Bowie and Cass Counties. He incorporated his own operation under the name Southern Pine Lumber Company and in 1893 bought seven thousand acres of timberland from J. C. Diboll, for whom Temple's new sawmill settlement along the Houston East and West Texas (HE&WT) rail line was named. With prime market access via the railroad to the burgeoning commercial centers of Houston and Shreveport, Temple quickly built his milling operation into one of the most successful inland timber enterprises of the day, serving as the nexus for what became over time and generations the successful international corporation Temple Industries.

In the dense and abundant virgin timberlands of the Neches valley, Temple had a ready supply of marketable stock to grow his company. In contrast to other lumber barons of that era and region, he had a general appreciation for the principles of conservation measures represented by scientific forestry. Forgoing the standard practice of clearcutting that marked the mindset of others in the business, he relied on selective harvesting, sustained yields, and other measures to ensure longer-term productivity. Temple invested for the long haul, which gave his company both credibility and stature as a state leader in forestry for generations. In the forests of Angelina County in particular, there was some measure of woodland diversity, much of which the company utilized in its various operations. Pines predominated, the three common varieties being shortleaf (*Pinus echinata*), loblolly (*Pinus taeda*), and the giants of the forest, the longleaf (*Pinus palustris*), or marsh, pines. There were also marketable stands of hardwoods, including oak, gum, hickory, and in isolated locales cypress.[3]

A savvy businessman who valued centralized control of his operations, Temple quickly realized too the value of diversifying his rail options, which he deftly used to leverage his operational margins and to provide greater access to more rail cars. In addition to his use of the HE&WT main line, which converted from narrow gauge to standard gauge in 1894, Temple relied on railroad contractors to ship logs to his central mill. In 1898 he bought his own locomotives and other equipment to develop a frontline logging camp at Lindsey Springs, nine miles northeast of Diboll. Essentially an extension community of the sawmill town, such early logging camps took on the characteristics of small settlements despite their temporary, production-based underpinnings. Writing about Lindsey Springs, historian Jonathan K. Gerland noted that the 1900 census counted 110 people then living at the camp. "Of these persons," he wrote, "63 were males and 47 were females, representing 27 households. Household size ranged from one to seventeen persons." The age of workers ranged from fifteen to sixty-seven years old, a sizable majority of whom "were day laborers and teamsters, who worked with teams of oxen and mules to trans-port and load the cut logs." In addition, Gerland noted, "there was a railroad section foreman, a log contractor, a saw filer, and a general merchandise salesman, suggesting the possibility that the camp had a company store." Predominately southern in its makeup, the camp included only four individuals from outside the Southeast—one each from Pennsylvania, Illinois, Germany, and Norway. The camp was also largely white, with only seven residents identified as black. This racial makeup differed markedly from that of nearby Emporia Camp, an Angelina County frontline establishment of the Emporia Lumber Company, which showed a black population of 61 percent in that year's census.[4]

In 1900 Temple incorporated two lines—the Texas & Louisiana Railroad (T&L) and the Texas Southeastern Railroad (TSE)—to expand his logging operations. The former, which became part of the Cotton Belt line, extended eastward from Lufkin and in time reached into San Augustine County to a place called White City. The latter line, along which the Neches Pines Golf Course eventually developed, ran "12.7 miles northeastward from Diboll

A Southeastern Railroad crew poses with Engine No. 5 in front of a loaded hardwood-log train at the Diboll sawmills in Angelina County around 1910. Such scenes were common in East Texas during the state's bonanza era of timber production. Courtesy The History Center, Diboll, Texas.

to a connection with the T&L east of Lufkin at a point known as Diboll Junction," shown on some early maps as Frostville. "With the addition of logging spurs," Gerland wrote, "TSE operated more than 40 miles of standard gauge tracks east of Diboll in Angelina County by 1903 and began in 1906 constructing additional track mileage west of the mill town into Trinity and Houston counties." Although the TSE originally functioned as a private line exclusive to the Southern Pine Lumber Company (renamed Temple Lumber Company in 1906), the Texas Railroad Commission ruled in 1909 that as a common carrier the railway had to operate for the general public. While that served to diversify the cargo to a limited extent and enhance rail travel for individuals, it also marginalized the commercial advantages Temple had envisioned. Regardless, he had shut down the Lindsey Springs operation by 1906 and abandoned the eastward portion of his rail line soon after in favor of the new mainline to the west toward Trinity County. Renamed the Texas South-Eastern Railroad in 1931, the freighting venture remains in operation in the twenty-first century.[5]

Over time, Diboll outgrew its company-town origins, although the timber industry and related businesses have continued as its economic mainstay. With increased development on both sides of US 59, the main north–south transportation corridor, the town expanded well beyond its railroad configuration. The abandoned line, paved over and repurposed for automobile traffic, became Lumberjack Drive, so named for the mascot of the high school located along the route east of the city center. Where steam locomotives once hauled logs of Neches pines to the sawmill, sometimes around the clock, school buses now travel regularly along the former rail bed while golf carts scurry across from the front nine to the back nine of Neches Pines Golf Course, itself a vestige of the timber industry.

THE COURSE IN HISTORY

In the 1960s, in an effort to provide recreational facilities for his employees while also improving the quality of life for Diboll citizens, Arthur Temple Jr., T. L. L. Temple's grandson, spearheaded a plan to develop a city park that would include baseball fields, picnic areas, playground equipment, an equestrian area, and a nine-hole golf course. His company donated 173 acres of land known as the Pecan Orchard for the city to use as a match for US Department of the Interior and Texas Parks and Wildlife Department grants to fund the enterprise. In announcing the project's approval in October 1967, the local newspaper also recognized the political support of Congressman John Dowdy. The article went on to frame the proposed recreational center as an integral and logical next step in the progressive development of the city. Reflecting a sense of community pride reminiscent of earlier civic boosterism, an editorial piece noted, "in the past five years, Dibollians have seen the near total disappearance of slum housing; we have seen the emergence of an active city government; we have been blessed with new streets, new water system, and other needed city services; we have built one of the state's most widely recognized public libraries; we have upgraded our schools; and, we have seen new forest-based industries spring into operation almost every year." The following month the paper reported that the city had selected the Austin firm of Leon Howard and Associates to oversee the park's development, including the design of the new Diboll Municipal Golf Course.[6]

Leon Hugh Howard was one of the most prolific golf course architects in Texas during the latter twentieth century, designing an estimated 165 courses, many in partnership with his brother, Charles. A native of Graham in Young County, Leon Howard studied at Texas A&M University, where he attained a master's degree in soil physics through sponsorship by the US Golf Association. He designed courses throughout the United States, although the majority of his work was in Texas, primarily Central Texas. His work included the Babe Didrikson Zaharias Memorial Golf Course in Port Arthur, the Casa Blanca Golf Course in Laredo, the Lago Vista and Bar-K courses in Lago Vista, two courses at the Lakeway Resort outside Austin, and country clubs in Harlingen, Granbury, and Rockdale. Despite his firm's impressive record, the work at the Diboll course took longer than expected, in part due to water problems—an inadequate well and ironically too much rain—and Howard's illness during the later stages of construction, which delayed critical site inspections. Slated for completion in the fall of 1969, the course formally opened in September of the following year, with local resident and longtime avid golfer Ray Paulsey serving as the professional. Even as city officials planned for the big event, there was already preliminary talk of completing the

GHOST TRAPS

In 2009 Jonathan K. Gerland, executive director of The History Center at Diboll, conducted an oral history interview with Ray Paulsey, the first and longtime professional at Neches Pines. Among the topics discussed were the course bunkers, which were not part of the original design but added during the initial construction. The following is an excerpt from that interview.

In Leon Howard's design there was no sand traps involved, period. You have to remember, back then, East Texas golf courses didn't have sand traps, none of them. I mean, this was probably going to be the first golf course in East Texas with greens that were constructed the way greens should be constructed—elevated and not just cut out of the flat land that the golf course was built on. The older East Texas golf courses were just built on where they had cleared some land and, then put where they wanted greens and things like that. So, this was actually the first one that had tee boxes that were constructed with the proper material and also greens that were constructed with seed bed material and drainage, and things like that built into them.

So, no sand traps were involved in it, and there were several reasons for that. One was where you could get more play. It would keep players moving smoother and things like that, without sand traps and things. . . . When we decided that we were going to put in sand traps, we had to understand that the cost of maintaining [one] is almost the same as the cost of maintaining a green. It is a very expensive procedure. You have to build drains in them and you have to [lay] out where the drains are going to be. Then you have to have maintenance of the sand trap—that is even more so than the greens. It is more expensive to maintain a sand trap properly with the edging and keeping them raked, and things like that. So, the economics of it also contributed to the fact that we didn't have sand traps.

But, Mr. [Arthur] Temple [Jr.] decided we were going to have sand traps, so he brought down Jimmy Demaret from Champions Golf Course in Houston. They came out here, and Jimmy and myself and Mr. Temple, we went around with a can of spray paint and painted where the traps were going to be with white spray paint. So, we had all the traps laid out and Mr. Temple laid out a bunch of little what they call spot traps, just for decorative purposes, and you know, for no other reason than that. But, obviously I could see that it was going to be a real maintenance project, so a lot of those traps never got put in, and that did not make Mr. Temple very happy. The fact of the matter is, we had several meetings over that and I told him I had to maintain them, and economically I explained to him that I had to do away with several of his little spot traps that he had. Well, I never did convince him of that, but the course got built, the traps got put in without a lot of the spot traps.

Source: Ray Paulsey, oral history interview by Jonathan K. Gerland, Sept. 15, 2009. A transcript of the interview is available through The History Center, Diboll, Texas. The authors have made minor edits and formatting changes from the original.

course with an additional nine holes across the old railroad bed "when needed."[7]

Before that need could be determined or addressed, however, a more pressing concern occurred over the lack of bunkers in Howard's original design. Although rarely found in early East Texas woodland courses, where tight, tree-lined fairways; dense undergrowth; and numerous water features predominated as hazards, bunkers were considered a fundamental part of the game by the 1970s and thus were added to the Diboll course as an afterthought. Leon Howard did not oversee their placement, though. Instead, Arthur Temple hired family friend, pro golfer, and course designer Jimmy Demaret to make those decisions in 1973. A world-class golfer who claimed three Masters titles and numerous other notable tour victories during his distinguished career, Demaret was a colorful character who brought style and showmanship to what had been a rather staid and proper sport. Known as "The Wardrobe" for his flamboyant on-course apparel, he garnered widespread attention for his freewheeling lifestyle and raucous humor, but he also commanded respect as a serious golfer and later as a course designer and television sports commentator; the Champions Golf Club outside Houston was for many years his home course. Speaking to the visual flair he had on the game, the *New York Times* noted in his obituary: "Mr. Demaret often chose bright clothes during a period when everyone wore whites. His clothes were made to order—electric blue, bottle green, canary yellow, and vermillion were among his favorites. His hats were considered outlandish; a Swiss yodeler's hat was a staple for a while." Balancing the recognition of his showmanship, though, the article also mentioned that the Houston native had celebrated his first tour victory in 1934 with a win at the Texas PGA, for which he received twenty-five dollars. Playing in an era before the big purse, Demaret "was the leading money winner on the PGA tour in 1947 with $27,936 and achieved 31 career victories on the tour."[8]

Given its dramatic woodland backdrop, impressive Howard design, and challenging sand-trap placement by Demaret, the Diboll Municipal Golf Course drew a steady stream of visitors, both local and farther afield, as well as school clubs and teams. By the

"FORE! CITY TEED OFF AT GOLF COURSE COWS"

The Diboll golf course has been taken over by a small herd of wild cows.

Police Chief Dewey Wolf said this week that nine old cows have made the golf course a regular pasture ground and are doing considerable damage to greens and tee boxes.

Chief Wolf and his crew and Golf Pro Ray Paulsey have chased the cows time and again but have been unable to pen them.

"Those are the wildest danged cows I've ever seen," Wolf said. The cows retreat to nearby woods when chased. They usually return in the early morning.

Wednesday morning about half the city water and street crews joined police in a wild chase after the Naughty Nine. They finally corralled one of the cows, but the other eight escaped again.

Wolf said he plans to put out hay in the nearby baseball park and try to lure the cows in there. If that doesn't work, he says the problem probably will have to be resolved by the City Council.

Meanwhile, local golfers should be aware of additional hazards on the course. The cows don't exactly leave without leaving evidence behind.

Source: From *Diboll Free Press*, Jan. 29, 1976, 1.

1990s, though, the timing seemed right to add an additional nine holes, also designed by the Howard firm, on land across the historic rail line. In the new layout the original nine became the back nine, ending at the redesigned clubhouse. With such major changes came a new name as well. After debating a number of pine-related options, including Whispering Pine and Southern Pine, the Diboll Parks Board recommended, and the city council approved, the new name of Neches Pine (later pluralized). In addressing the change,

One of the original pin flags from the Neches Pine Course. The flag is now curated at The History Center in Diboll. Photograph by Dan K. Utley

board chair Harold Maxwell spoke of the historical significance of the local pines that initially attracted lumbermen like Temple to the area and became a standard of excellence in the industry worldwide. He spoke also to the decision to delete the town's name, noting, "golfers from Hudson, Corrigan, San Augustine, Rusk or even Lufkin might not wear golf caps or shirts with Diboll on them but would with Neches Pine Golf Course."[9]

14

LANDSCAPED BY MULES

OLD BRICKYARD GOLF COURSE, FERRIS

SCORECARD FROM THE PAST

Currently: Old Brickyard Golf Course

Historic Name: Ferris Brick Company

DETAILS: An eighteen-hole public course offering steep hills and drop-offs, large water features, and deep rough; distance is 6,486 yards

Location: 605 N. I-45, Ferris

Historical Context: Early brickmaking in Texas

Historical Type: Manufacturing site

Period of Significance: 1890s–1970s

Signature Hole of History: Number ten provides sweeping vistas of the old quarries and demands both power and accuracy. It is a par-five, 553-yard layout that requires golfers to carry the sizable quarry lake twice. As one golf-blog writer observed, "par this beauty and you deserve a margarita."[1]

THE COURSE OF HISTORY

Written in a somewhat exuberant and florid style seldom seen today in public history interpretation, the inscription for the Texas historical marker that honors the mule—appropriately in the Bailey County town of Muleshoe—begins thus: "Without ancestral pride or hope for offspring, the mule—along with buffalo, hound and longhorn—made Texas history." It goes on to highlight the animal's role in wartime, frontier settlement, and transportation, noting, "He went fast, endured much, ate sparingly." There is no mention in the marker of stubbornness, a general trait that has long frustrated those who have worked with such animals, regardless of the task. As cotton farmer Eddie Wegner of Burton in Washington County recalled, there were few viable remedies for outwitting a stubborn mule. The plight of his neighbor underscored the predicament when work was at hand. Faced with a balking mule in the field, the farmer first tried hitting the animal with a stick and putting sand in his mouth, even lighting small broomweed fires under its belly, but it moved only a few paces at most. Finally, as Wegner told, his neighbor "went to the house and got a good-sized fence post and a drop auger, dug a hole right beside the mule, put the post in, and tied the mule to that post—left that old balking mule stand there in the field all day." At the end of the day, the farmer came back, untied the mule, hitched him back up to the plow, and made him work a few rounds to let him reflect on the error of his ways. It is unlikely, however, that the exercise provided little animal memory in the long run.[2]

Despite the lead line in the state marker regarding ancestral pride, the mule enjoys an ancient lineage. A hybrid culturally bred, it is most often the result of matching a male donkey with a mare, resulting in a sterile offspring. The cultivation of mules dates back thousands of years, with ancient civilizations in Turkey, Egypt, Greece, and Africa prizing the animals as powerful beasts of burden with uncommon stamina. Introduced to the Americas via early explorers, in the United States George Washington was among the first serious breeders of the stock. The "Father of Our Country" is thus considered the "Father of the American Mule" as well. Favored over horses and oxen in many circumstances, mules proved invaluable to military field maneuvers, westward expansion, commercial viability, and agricultural development, especially in the South before tractors. While much has been written about mules in those historical aspects, relatively little is documented about their role in industry, though their contributions in that regard were equally significant.[3]

One enduring remnant of the industrial landscape shaped by mule power is the expansive site of a former brick-manufacturing operation at Ferris in northeastern Ellis County. The town, formed along the route of the Houston and Texas Central Railway in 1874 and named for the prominent Waxahachie attorney and jurist Justus W. Ferris, began as an agricultural settlement. The area's rich blackland soils, part of a dominant Houston black-clay belt running diagonally across the county from the northeast to the southwest and described as expansive, organic, and tenacious, proved ideal for the cultivation of cotton and corn. Underlying the surficial, tillable land, though, were deeply buried deposits of even denser clays suitable for the production of bricks. T. J. Hurst of Dallas was among the first to exploit this resource, establishing the Atlas Pressed Brick Company in 1895. Other manufacturers soon followed, and in a few years Ferris boasted such local pressed-brick operations as Globe, Lone Star, Diamond, Texas, Ferris, and others. By the early twentieth century, its booming brick business far outdistanced rivals elsewhere, and the town soon became known as the brick capital of the nation.[4]

Central to the successful yardwork of the brick plants were their teams of mules. Brick manufacturing was localized, with offices, crushers, extruders, dryers, and storage sheds located immediately adjacent to the clay quarries. Mules were the primary means of conveyance in the early days, moving sleds and slips between operations and dragging fresnos (Fresno scrapers)—large earth-moving pieces of equipment named for their first use in the Central Valley of California near Fresno to build irrigation systems. Before the advent of large traction engines that gave rise to steam shovels and bulldozers, fresnos were the mainstay of construction projects as well as large-scale mining and quarrying operations. At Ferris, each brick company had its own expansive quarries, and with land reclamation not yet a widespread environmental concern or governmental requirement, the operations reshaped the landscape, leaving steep-sided hills and cliffs, subject to erosion, and vast open pits, some of which partially filled with water to form ponds. All were subject to degradation over time, with the result being an abnormally undulating cultural landscape.

Among the mules that worked the brick plants, the most noted were those belonging to the Ferris Brick Company, which formed in 1923 as an amalgamation of several early companies. Even though machinery began replacing the animals in many plant opera-

How to Read a Brick

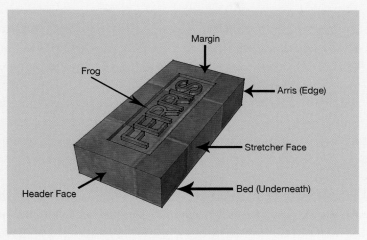

Computer-generated illustration by Owen Graves.

This illustration references the language of brick manufacturing. The frog or indented centerpiece of common pressed brick with a distinctive embossed name such as "FERRIS" provided company identity on a job site but more practically reduced the weight of the brick and served to improve the strength of the mortar joint, thereby enhancing the overall structural stability. Some bricks, such as those manufactured at Thurber in Erath County in the early twentieth century, often featured an indented triangle (sometimes with the letters "BTT") to signify the Brick, Tile and Terra Cotta Workers Alliance.

On July 31, 1975, staff of the Texas Historical Commission took this photograph of one of the former plants of the Ferris Brick Company as part of a historic-resources survey. The dramatic scene depicts the spur rail line and the vastness of the operation, only one of several plants that relied on local clays for bricks that supplied building projects around the state and far beyond. Courtesy Texas Historical Commission.

tions during the twentieth century, Ferris long continued to work teams of mules, and the sight of them contouring the company land became a draw—a reminder of the past—for highway travelers along the adjacent US 75. Overseeing the Ferris mule teams for many years was R. Troy Wilson, a native of the town and a long-time employee. Eventually named the director of the company, Wilson was also considered to be "the leading mule raiser in the Southwest." While he oversaw the operation, he relied on employees who worked daily as mule skinners, or handlers, directing the stock and keeping them in top shape. Most of the skinners—so-called because they could "skin," or outsmart, the mules—were African Americans. One of the best known was William "Cotch 'Em" Coleman, who worked the mule teams for more than forty years and gained considerable wisdom about their behavior in the

"IKE GETS PICTURE OF A FERRIS MULE"

A picture of an Ellis County mule named Lottie was mailed to President Eisenhower Thursday from Ferris, Texas. Lottie is gigantic—1,710 glossy pounds. She is beautiful and talented—she has been a blue ribbon hitching mule for five consecutive years at that world series for the equines, the American Royal Horse Show in Kansas City. Lottie is also one of the hard-working mules which the Ferris Brick Co. uses to pull fresnos and slip scrapers in its huge brickyard.

"We work our show mules and show our work mules," said Troy Wilson, general manager of Ferris Brick Co., who yields to no man on earth in his appreciation for fine mules.

Lottie and seven other handsome red sorrel animals, each over 1,400 pounds in heft, are used as a mule hitch which the brick company sends to celebrations, such as last week's 200th civic birthday party at Liberty, Texas. And Lottie and her seven pals have hauled celebrities from all over the hemisphere, not including that great admirer of mules, Dwight Eisenhower.

From Frank X. Tolbert, Tolbert's Texas (column), *Dallas Morning News*, Apr. 27, 1956. Tolbert concluded his column by referring to the Ferris mules as "the aristocracy of muledom."

process. "Never lodge no trust in a mule," he advised. "A mule is dangerous, live or dead. Never [abuse] a mule [except] with hard words. A mule won't pay no attention to a soft, little voice."[5]

Showing the company work mules in sanctioned competitions, Wilson and his skinners and herders built hitch teams that won the highest honors at such celebrated events as the Missouri State Fair in Sedalia, the Tennessee State Fair in Nashville, and the American Royal Horse Show in Kansas City. His teams also participated in Texas parades, rodeos, and livestock shows. The animals were not, however, Texas stock, coming primarily from Missouri, then the leading mule-producing state in the country. The Ferris

The work mules of Ferris ready for show. Courtesy Ellis County Historical Museum.

mules were large animals, generally weighing in the range of 1,400 pounds. For the most part, they were sorrels and iron grays, although there were a few strawberry roans as well. Wilson's prize-winning teams brought widespread attention to the town of Ferris as well as to the company, where he began working in 1919. A newspaper tribute to the "Texas Mule Man" following his death in 1956 noted that he "had the sharp eye and sound judgment that made his barnyard the home of champions and made his name respected wherever mules were raised." The phenomenon of the Ferris Mules—their show name—did not continue long after his passing, nor did the company he served most of his life. In 1969 the Ferris Brick Company sold out to the Acme Brick Company, head-quartered in Fort Worth with yards and plants in other locales. With time, operations at the old brickyard ceased, and the former plant succumbed to the elements. Although within the Dallas economic sphere of influence, the industrial site appeared to have limited potential for development until the latter part of the twentieth century, when a group of innovative investors began planning for a new use, one in which the property previously landscaped by mules could be viewed as both an asset and a personal liability to golfers challenged by history's imprint on the land.[6]

The Course *in* History

The Old Brickyard Golf Course is one of the newest facilities covered, completed in 2000. It reflects the styling of John Ponko, who worked with the noted course-design firm of Robert Trent Jones before striking out on his own. His vision for Old Brickyard was to create what he termed an inland links course evocative of Ireland. Working within a "shoestring budget" (about $100,000 a hole) on a unique and relatively small piece of property commanding sweeping vistas north to the Dallas skyline, Ponko came up with a layout that played to the existing terrain, formed by three brick quarries, and included "elevation changes, blind spots, lots of ups and downs, ravines and valleys, pinched fairways, and elevated greens." While he endeavored to avoid creating a monster of a course, Ponko nevertheless maintained a challenging core of holes—numbers eight through twelve—that one reviewer called the "quarry death march." The writer went on to acknowledge as the "heart and backbone of the course" a section that takes golfers down into the historic quarries and thus back in time. From the bottom along the quarry lake, players confront the enormity of the brick operation, although few realize that the clay deposits that once filled the space above them now reside elsewhere as essential elements of homes, commercial buildings, and other structures worldwide. Fewer still likely comprehend how mules contributed to the historical contexts of this course, from the rugged remains of industrial production to encroaching urban development and beyond to their time of recreation.[7]

15

RUMORS AT LAJITAS

BLACK JACK'S CROSSING GOLF COURSE, LAJITAS

SCORECARD FROM THE PAST

Currently: Black Jack's Crossing Golf Course

Historic Name: Lajitas

DETAILS: A public and membership facility; distance is 7,413 yards from the back tees

Location: Old Trading Post (pro shop) off Highway 170, Lajitas

Historical Context: Mexican Revolution, 1910–20

Historical Type: Military camp and intervention

Period of Significance: 1916–17

Signature Hole of History: Number eighteen is a par-five hole that provides players with a panoramic view of old Lajitas. It plays to the north, with the Rio Grande immediately to the left. There are bunkers along the right side of the fairway and around the green. North of the green is the Old Trading Post, which dates to the nineteenth century. To the northeast a couple of hundred yards and across Highway 170 is the general area where soldiers bivouacked during the Second Punitive Expedition. Part of their patrol regimen was to monitor areas up and down the river, so they would have traversed the area that is now the golf course on a regular basis.

THE COURSE OF HISTORY

The violent confrontations that occurred along the US-Mexico border in 1916 and 1917 stemmed from earlier events in Mexican history. While some historians have argued that the roots reached far back to the time of independence in 1821 or the US–Mexico War of the 1840s, the more immediate and direct cause was the Mexican Revolution, which military historian Thomas E. Alexander noted had a "long and fitfully sputtering fuse that ignited years before the shooting began." Emerging initially as a strong and stable leader in the 1870s amid the extended chaos of postwar Mexico, Pres. Porfirio Díaz set the country on an ambitious path to industrialization and modernization. While there were important gains during his rule, which reached from 1877 to 1910, there were also widespread economic inequities coupled with the rigidity of absolute power. As historians Charles H. Harris and Louis R. Sadler duly described, Díaz "constructed a dictatorship behind a constitutional façade." When the president chose to step down but then recanted, it became a trigger for an uncertain transition to the future. The main opposition came from Francisco I. Madero, who while exiled in San Antonio, Texas, devised the Plan de San Luis Potosí to consolidate the power of disparate groups in opposition to Diaz, with himself as the provisional successor. Through his actions, Madero helped unleash a revolutionary spirit in the land, especially among such "regional chieftains" as Francisco "Pancho" Villa in the north and Emiliano Zapata in the south. Furthering the immediate call for change through military power, Madero's forces seized the strategic metropolitan center of Ciudad Juárez, across the Rio Grande from El Paso, on May 11, 1911. The action so close to home—with stray bullets pelting the Texas side—caused grave concern in the United States, where officials remained uncertain of an official response to the revolt. Regardless, army leaders ramped up a contingency force at Fort Sam Houston in preparation for any defensive action that might be required.[1]

In relatively quick succession, the Díaz government collapsed and gave way to the Madero presidency, which ended in a fatal coup in Mexico City in 1913. An ill-fated leadership effort by Gen. Victoriana Huerta proved short lived as well, to be replaced by the rise of Venustiano Carranza, who proclaimed himself *premir jefe* (first chief) and focused power through his Constitutionalist Army. With the advent of Carranza, as Harris and Sadler observed, the Mexican Revolution "entered its bloodiest phase," one that ultimately drew the United States reluctantly into the fighting. Although Pres. Woodrow Wilson hoped to avoid military confrontation, the administration also lent important, albeit de facto, support to Carranza through select enforcement of neutrality laws, the lifting of an arms embargo, and limited access to US rail lines for the Constitutionalists. The latter in particular angered Villa, who had broken with Carranza and subsequently suffered an ignominious military defeat as a result of these US actions. Unable to sustain such losses, Villa boldly retaliated with a quick and deadly cross-border strike ultimately aimed at forcing action by the United States, thereby strengthening his own recruitment efforts in the north and embarrassing the Carranza regime at the same time. While such violent raids into the United States by Villistas and others were by no means uncommon at the time, the one focused on the tiny settlement of Columbus, New Mexico, proved particularly devastating and incendiary along an uneasy international boundary.[2]

Under the cover of darkness in the early morning of March 9, 1916, Villa led a sizable raiding party across the border west of Palomas, Mexico, in a two-pronged attack on the small village of Columbus and the inadequately manned army outpost at Fort Furlong. Catching the citizens and soldiers off guard, the Villistas swept through the town in a deadly two-hour fire fight before heading back across the border. Military historian Frank E. Vandiver eloquently described the aftermath: "Before that lurid night washed in a desert dawn, seventeen Americans, nine of them civilians, lay dead. In the smoulder of Columbus, a cause was ignited that burned wires and ears across the nation and exploded into the halls of a stunned Congress." While government leaders in Washington hastily met to consider a formal response, including the possibility of war, President Wilson authorized an immediate pursuit into Mexico in what would become the Punitive Expedition. The field command fell to Maj. Gen. John J. "Black Jack" Pershing, then stationed at Fort Bliss in El Paso, whose orders were "to capture Villa and his bandits." The initial plan was for a quick and decisive strike from New Mexico, with the implied understanding that the US Army would at some point withdraw, following their successful mission, to be replaced by Carranza's Constitutional Army. Pershing's challenges were considerable; pursuing a fast-moving, elusive enemy through desolate land with primitive roads that slowed mechanized armaments and transports, he also had to keep Mexican forces from retaliating against the invasion.[3]

As Pershing led more than four thousand troops deep into the state of Chihuahua, intensified attacks by pro-Villa forces broke out hundreds of miles to the east along the Big Bend region of Texas, an area already the scene of countless raids. Too far east of US forces to be afforded adequate military protection, the Rio Grande settlements in Texas were particularly isolated, exposed, and vulnerable. Pervasive rumors of violence became reality on the morning of May 5—Cinco de Mayo—when Villistas launched deadly attacks on Glenn Springs, the site of a large candelilla-wax processing plant, and a few miles farther east at Boquillas, where fighting focused on Jesse Deemer's store. The attacks came at a time when military officials of the United States and Mexico began deliberations to bring about an end to the fighting. Despite the timing and a paucity of available soldiers and materiel, given the ongoing action in Chihuahua, the US Army acted swiftly with what it had

This 1917 photograph of the Glenn Springs wax factory shows the boiler building, with its tall smokestacks and a sophisticated hoisting system over the extracting vats. Courtesy Texas Historical Commission.

to address the raids along the Texas border. The first to respond were cavalry units transferred from Fort Clark, headed by Col. Frederick W. Sibley, and Fort Bliss, led by Maj. George T. Langhorne, to command headquarters at Marathon. Quickly assessing the situation and the need for additional reinforcements, army officials petitioned for a massive call up of National Guard units to back up the limited number of regulars. Responding immediately on May 9, Wilson ordered the activation of guard units in Arizona, New Mexico, and Texas; of the total number of more than four thousand troops, Texas supplied approximately 60 percent. Soon these units would be joined by guardsmen from other states, including Michigan, Pennsylvania, and Rhode Island.[4]

The US military response, known as the Second Punitive, or Sibley-Langhorne, Expedition, got underway quickly, with Langhorne, in his Cadillac touring car, personally leading troops across the river from Boquillas on the evening of May 11. With great conviction and purpose, the expedition made swift progress, not only dispersing rogue bands of Villistas but also adding to mounting pressure for massive retaliation by elements of the Constitutional Army, which were under orders to expel the US forces at all costs. Despite tense moments amid various engagements, the expedition prevailed, recovering stolen items and freeing captives, including Deemer himself, while suffering no casualties. Following the sixteen-day mission that stretched approximately 140 miles into the interior of Mexico, the soldiers returned to the United States and conducted regular patrols along the river to guard against further attacks. While the raids diminished markedly, rumors of incursions nevertheless persisted.[5]

Along the still-uneasy border, few settlements were as vulnerable as Lajitas in the remote reaches of southwestern Brewster County. In late April 1916, only a few days prior to the Glenn Springs and Boquillas raids, it appeared that the town might be the focus of a pending raid. The rumors at that time, however, proved unfounded. *The Washington Times* reported: "It appears the rumor originated from the fact that a number of peons became desperate for food and crossed the Rio Grande at Lajitas with a view to working and obtaining supplies to sustain life. Loafing in the town, their number gave rise to the tale of many bandits overrunning the stick and mud village." Rumors following the Second Punitive Expedition, however, often included more specific details that served to intensify the public alarm because of their perceived legitimacy. Reports in late July, for example, of two hundred Villistas gathering downriver from Lajitas in anticipation of a raid into the United States referenced the probable objective of securing wheat at "Clyde Buttrill's irrigated farm." Another warning of a pending massive invasion by "several hundred Mexican bandits" came in September of the same year. Although no major raids occurred at the community, there were isolated incidents of snipers and return fire. As a result, a small detachment of troops remained in the region.[6]

Daily life for soldiers stationed at Lajitas brought mixed reactions from the men. Although their isolated outpost was far from ideal, the locale afforded a ready supply of water and generally cooler temperatures. In a newspaper report from the border town, John H. Regan provided a description of the military installation. "Our quarters consisted of two adobe shacks, while built all around and between are shadings of dried branches. We sleep under the dead branches," he added, and "eat and cook in one of the shacks, while Lieut. [W. E.] Elliott and the orderly occupy the other structure." Probably lacking a vision of a future golf course, but with a clear eye for his natural surroundings, Regan provided a description similar to those later used by marketers and promoters. "All about these environs are mountains. Those to the northeast are great reddish mounds, tinged with splotches of stubby green, while here and there are great daubs of white stone formation, the variety of tones being almost exaggerative if by chance they should be transferred to canvas."[7]

Although failing to capture the elusive Villa, Pershing and his fellow army leaders deemed that the greater contextual achievement of the Punitive Expeditions—the restoration of the status quo antebellum along the border—had been achieved by the end of December 1916. The general later recalled, "we had broken up and scattered his band, which was our original mission." Withdrawal of US forces from Mexico began the following month and concluded

HIZZONER CLAY HENRY

*Clay Henry, the beer-drinking goat of Lajitas. Courtesy Karl Schatz/
Aurora Photos.*

One of the most noteworthy historical residents of Lajitas,
which has seen its share of colorful characters through the
years, was a billy goat named Clay Henry. To be accurate, there
have been several incarnations of Clay Henry, the first a beer-
drinking, hircine drifter that frequented the historic Ivey Store
grounds. In the 1984 Lajitas mayoral election, he was even
a candidate, "along with a dog named Spot, a mule named
Clyde Festus, and Kaw-Liga, the wooden Indian on the board-
walk." Although Clay Henry lost that race, his son, who like-
wise enjoyed hoppy beverages, eventually achieved the office
through appointment in 1992 and served until his demise
seven years later. His successor, originally called Billy the Kid
but renamed Clay Henry III for the sake of tradition, suffered
a life-threatening assault that resulted in castration and a subsequent 2002 jury trial in the Brewster County seat of Alpine.

After much serious testimony and deliberation, the trial ended in a deadlocked decision, causing one resident to suggest as a possible newspaper headline, "Jury Hung, Clay Henry Not."

Source: Kendra K. DeHart, "Jury Hung, Clay Henry Not: Scandal and Judicial Intrigue in Lajitas, Texas," *Sound Historian* 15 (2013): 9–26.

when the last of the soldiers crossed the border toward Columbus at three o'clock on the afternoon of February 5, 1917. Pershing's short-lived expedition, along with Sibley and Langhorne's lesser-known but perhaps more successful column to the east, brought changes far beyond what the leaders intended. The nation's attention turned immediately to involvement in the Great War overseas in part because of the infamous Zimmermann Telegram from German to Mexican officials, which as the expedition evacuation came to an end threatened to reopen old sores in US-Mexico relations. When hostilities came with the formal declaration of war against Germany on April 4, many in the US Army and National Guard were already trained and ready for action, given their service along the Mexican border. Ready too was the seasoned "Black Jack" Pershing, who would lead the American Expeditionary Force in that greater mission in Europe.[8]

THE COURSE *IN* HISTORY

The Mexican Revolution essentially ended in 1920, when Carranza and Villa found common ground for brokering peace. Both, however, would soon die from assassins' bullets—Carranza in 1920 and Villa three years later. With its bloody revolution finally over after a decade of fighting, Mexico moved forward on a somewhat steadier path to peace. Its vast northern border, however, remained an uneasy line where rumors still circulated. Lajitas survived in the postrevolutionary era as the center of a widely dispersed agricultural and mining area marked by a strong sense of community. There were outside influences as well, most notably from Houston businessman Walter M. Mischer, who beginning in the 1970s, developed Lajitas as a popular "Wild West" resort town and tourist attraction adjacent to Big Bend National Park. Amenities in his resort included a nine-hole golf course, but the modern era of golf at Lajitas began in 2002, shortly after Austin communications magnate Steven R. Smith acquired the operation. That year the Ambush Golf Course, designed by the Austin team of Roy Bechtol and Ray Russell, formally opened. Known widely for its high risk-reward challenges and an oasis-like setting amid rugged mountains adjacent to the Rio Grande, it featured a unique hole—designated 11-A—that afforded golfers an opportunity to hit a nonretrievable ball to a green on the Mexico side of the border. There were also holes located on a riverine island. Despite its promise, the Ambush course proved to be short lived; in 2008 a tropical storm drove inland and inundated the lower portions of the course, including the back nine and the island green. The damage was extensive and devastating, but Smith chose to rebuild, albeit with an eye to an elevated layout that proved both more secure and more dramatic.[9]

For the redesign, he turned to the firm of former professional golfer Lanny Wadkins, winner of twenty-one PGA tour championships and an inductee of the World Golf Hall of Fame—an honor he first learned about while on the job at Lajitas. Granted the innovative design freedom necessary to build a destination course, Wadkins incorporated "huge elevation changes, forced carries, strategically placed bunkers, narrow fairways and uneven lies, tough approach shots, doglegs and blind shots." The course opened in 2012 as Black Jack's Crossing and has, in its relatively short existence to date, garnered a host of design awards. The course name is evocative of an earlier historical period of significance for Lajitas and plays against age-old rumors of revolution, brinksmanship, and international intrigue.[10]

16

HELL IN THE SHADOWS

MEMORIAL PARK GOLF COURSE, HOUSTON

SCORECARD FROM THE PAST

Currently: Memorial Park Golf Course

Historic Name: Camp Logan

DETAILS: An eighteen-hole layout; distance is 7,164 yards from the longest tees

Location: 1001 E. Memorial Loop, Houston

Historical Context: World War I; civil rights

Historical Type: Military training camp

Period of Significance: 1917–18

Signature Hole of History: Numbers ten and thirteen provide strong historic senses of place for the course as they roughly outline the north and northwest perimeters of the Camp Logan parade ground, which is to the left of each fairway. According to a detailed map drawn by soldier Paul Hendrickson in 1918, the area to the right of the thirteenth hole housed the 370th Infantry (denoted as "colored"), the 130th Infantry, the 129th Infantry, and nearest the green, a machine-gun battalion.

THE COURSE OF HISTORY

Memorial Park Golf Course overlays the primary historic footprint of Camp Logan, a World War I training installation in operation from July 1917 until shortly after the end of the conflict in 1918. Despite its short existence, the camp served a vital mission in war preparedness and reflected with distinction the vital role Texas played in meeting unprecedented demands for the rapid deployment of soldiers to European battlefronts. Troops trained

One of two signature holes of history at Memorial Park Golf Course, number ten is in the vicinity of what would have been the Camp Logan parade ground. Photo by Anne C. Vance, with thanks to Julie Blum, General Manager, Memorial Park Golf Course.

at Camp Logan served primarily along the Western Front in key strategic efforts, including the massive Meuse-Argonne Offensive in 1918. As a reminder of the vital US involvement in the Allied victory, the site of Camp Logan is historically significant, even though extensive changes to the cultural landscape in the century since its existence have obscured much of the original integrity. Nevertheless, vestiges remain, principally as archeological deposits but also through related archival resources. If the camp were remembered today only for its wartime training mission, it would nevertheless be worthy of protection, commemoration, and interpretation. There is a far different aspect of Camp Logan's history, however, that dramatically overshadows its training role, giving it a tragic place in the nation's history. This involves an incident that occurred on the evening of August 23, 1917, which paradoxically occurred prior to the formal opening of the camp and outside its historical perimeters. Regardless, it is an incident that continues to define the enduring public memory of the place as well as the name.

The entangling alliances, rising nationalism, and regional disputes that sparked and fanned the flames of what came to be known as the Great War, later World War I, eventually reached the United States as well, when Congress formally issued a declaration of war against Germany on April 6, 1917. By that time, the war had raged overseas almost three years, with little hope for a viable termination, and Allied forces desperately needed US intervention to turn the tide in their favor. War preparedness thus took on the mantle of a national emergency, with plans quickly implemented for the development of new training installations to move available regular troops and reserves, as well as raw recruits, to combat-ready status without delay. Across the nation, as states and communities competed for due consideration of new facilities, business and civic leaders provided integral support for what they viewed as not only their responses to patriotic pride but also important catalysts for economic stimulation. Houston, an economically progressive, burgeoning town of about 130,000 at the time, offered a number of features that made it an ideal candidate for consideration. Among these were its modern transportation systems, a warm-weather climate, and the availability of relatively flat terrain ideal for the quick construction of sprawling camps. Houston also had dynamic business leaders who worked as a team for the city's common good. These men included real-estate magnate Charles J. Kirk, timber baron John Henry Kirby, pioneering oilman Joseph S. Cullinan, and many others who were instrumental in developing an environment of almost unrivaled economic progress in Texas and the South. Consequently, the city received formal notice on June 11, 1917, that it would be the home for a temporary camp that one historian described as "designed for sharpening up National Guard units before they were shipped overseas." To that end, news followed soon about the development schedule for Camp Logan, named for Illinoisan John A. "Black Jack" Logan, a prominent Union general during the Civil War and later an influential congressman and US senator. Influenced early on by the antiabolition environment that pervaded his home area of southern Illinois, Logan remained loyal to the Union and eventually became a staunch Republican supporting early civil rights measures. Additionally, he is credited with being the founder of Memorial Day.[1]

Houstonians soon tempered their pride and enthusiasm for the new camp, which would serve primarily the Thirty-Third Illinois Infantry Division of the National Guard, with grave concerns about the concurrent announcement that an African American army unit—the Third Battalion of the Twenty-Fourth Infantry—would arrive first to guard the construction site. To avoid interference with those building the camp, soldiers of the Twenty-Fourth provided regular guard posts from a separate tent camp about a mile to the east. Despite a distinguished history that had recently involved service in the Philippines during the Spanish-American War and in Mexico as part of the Punitive Expedition (see chapter 15), a black unit stationed in the Jim Crow South at the turn of the twentieth century put undue pressure on the troops. Unfamiliar with and appalled by the cultural customs of the time and place, the soldiers—most from the North—were rightfully fearful of how their brief (six to seven weeks) assignment at Houston would play out. Their fears were quickly confirmed upon arrival. A July 29 newspaper article headlined "Melons Make Happy the Negro Guards" expressed appreciation for the unit's history but noted too that their officers were white, "of course." It also cautiously sought to allay underlying concern among white residents. "Discipline among the negro regiments is almost perfect," the writer reassured such readers, "and they are among the most efficient troops the army has." Two days later, under the heading "A Need for Caution," the same paper, responding to reports of a recent racial clash at the site of Camp MacArthur in Waco, admonished readers, "It is an unfortunate fact that negro soldiers, wherever they may be stationed, almost invariably get into trouble with white people, and it is not necessary to say that it would be exceedingly embarrassing to Houston if such trouble should occur here." Presciently and with naked disregard for the moral course of action, the paper left no doubt about the more devastating repercussions: "Therefore, so long as the colored soldiers are in Houston all citizens must be careful to see that clashes between the soldiers and citizens are avoided. This is important because it is within the power of an idle and none too lawabiding [sic] white element here to lose Camp Logan for us."[2]

In hindsight the story that unfolded around Camp Logan less than a month later seemed predestined and unavoidable. What took place was complex and multilayered, with myriad nuances that have confounded historians and others for a century, with new interpretations continually emerging in reasoned efforts to somehow make sense of what seems to have been a senseless incident. The magnitude of the tragedy only serves to add to the frustration felt by those who encounter the story decades later from a different frame of cultural reference.

Within the pervasive pressure-cooker environment of the Jim Crow South, with all the far-reaching complications it engendered, what became known as the "Camp Logan Riot" began away from the installation and without the involvement of its soldiers. The triggering event centered on two over-zealous Houston mounted policemen, Lee Sparks and Rufus Daniels. On their beat along San Felipe Street on the morning of August 23, the two men broke up a game of craps and fired shots at the fleeing youths. In hot pursuit of one of the miscreants, Sparks entered the home of Sara Travers, a black housewife and the mother of five children, and his bigoted and physically abusive manner toward her exacerbated the situation and resulted in her arrest for disorderly conduct. In the ensuing chaos that spilled out into the neighborhood, Pvt. Alonzo Edwards, a Camp Logan soldier, attempted to intercede and quell the situation but was pistol-whipped in the process. As Sparks later testified, "I hit him until he got his heart right." The policeman subsequently released Travers but booked Edwards. That afternoon Cpl. Charles W. Baltimore, "a senior member of the provost guard and a model soldier," learned of the arrest and, while duly inquiring of Sparks about the soldier's situation, received a beating as well and ended up in jail along with Edwards. Fueled by outrage and rumor, including speculation that Baltimore had been wounded or killed, the situation quickly edged beyond a point of no return.[3]

Subsequent events that day are clouded by differing accounts, but at some point following a break-in at the ammunition-storage area, rumors of an approaching white mob, a brief round of sporadic gunfire, and an ineffectual attempt by commander Maj. Kneeland S. Snow to suppress the growing disturbance, a group of about one hundred troops left the guard camp and made its way back to the neighborhood to exact retribution. Whether their actions were spontaneous or premeditated remains open to speculation, but the magnitude of their actions are known with grim certainty—hell broke loose in Houston for several long hours. Nineteen individuals died in the killing spree that evening, including four policemen (among them Rufus Daniels), eight white citizens, two soldiers of the Twenty-Fourth, and two National Guard soldiers involved in trying to end the violence. One of the dead African American soldiers, whose body was recovered the next day, was Sgt. Vida Henry, who many believed led the assault at some point. According to testimony not corroborated by the autopsy report, once the troops decided to return to camp, Henry committed suicide.[4]

Reaction to the riot—some labeled it a mutiny since it involved army regulars—was swift and certain by state and city political leaders as well as the military command. Emergency decrees of martial law and curfews addressed immediate concerns, with Brig. Gen. John A. Hulen ordering the mobilization of units from Galveston and San Antonio for support. Complementing the military call-up was a posse of citizen-deputies quickly organized by Harris County sheriff Frank Hammond. Despite disagreements on jurisdictional matters, the army proceeded with plans to ship the black unit out of the city as soon as possible. On the morning of August 25, two trainloads of soldiers from the Twenty-Fourth left Houston under military escort bound for their former station at Columbus, New Mexico. Their relocation served to solidify the army's plan to try the accused men in military court. Investigations, allegations, emergency planning, and speculation ensued. Meanwhile, work continued at Camp Logan, Houston landed a second military installation with Ellington Field, and a grand jury moved to indict Officer Sparks, although he was never

CELESTE BEDFORD WALKER'S CAMP LOGAN

Celeste Bedford Walker's riveting 1987 play *Camp Logan* engenders praise and shapes important discussions wherever it is performed across the nation, helping ensure the enduring viability of the story within the broader contexts of World War I and civil rights. It is a production that changes lives, something the NAACP recognized when it honored the Houston playwright with its prestigious Image Award for the positive portrayal of African Americans in the media. Told through the lives of characters based closely on the soldiers involved in the 1917 incident, the play ends in a uniquely engaging manner that audiences find both compelling and personal. The setting is a Houston auditorium in 1919, where Walker's 2nd Lt. Charles W. Hardin speaks poignantly of his experiences of both war and resistance amid the vividly portrayed memories that immediately surround him:

HARDIN: (*Crisply.*) After the war, I returned to the States and resumed my education. For I strongly believe that the only way for me, as a colored man, to deal with the wall of prejudice that surrounds this country, is to take advantage of any opportunity that allows me to open a door that was once closed to my race. And I still remain confident that if the colored man continues to chip away at that wall whenever, wherever, and in whatever form he can, one day that wall must crumble to the ground. For if France can honor the colored soldier, can America, the greatest country on earth, do less?

(HARDIN steps to the side of the lectern and puts on his hat. We observe for the first time that he has lost an arm.)

HARDIN: (Continued.) And now to the men of the 24th, and for all the soldiers of every race, who have given their

blood, sweat, and tears for this country—I, Second Lieutenant Charles W. Hardin, salute you!

(HARDIN salutes the audience, turns sharply, and
marches up through the barracks and into the future.
Operating cadence begins.)

VOICES OF THE MEN: (Off Stage.) Oh here we go, oh here
we go, we're at it again, we're at it again, we're movin'
out, we're movin' out, we're movin' in! Your left, your left,
right, left!

(At this point, an announcement is made.)

ANNOUNCER: Out of respect for the tragedy that happened in Camp Logan, there will not be a curtain, but the
men will meet the audience in the lobby.

(The men, still in uniform, form a reception line in
the lobby to greet the audience.)

THE END

Source: Celeste Bedford Walker, *Camp Logan, in Acting Up and Getting Down:
Plays by African American Texans*, ed. Sandra Mayo and Elvin Holt, Southwestern Writers Collection Series (Austin: University of Texas Press, 2014),
92. Permission for the excerpted passage granted by the playwright, Celeste
Bedford Walker.

convicted for his incendiary role in the riot. Between November
1917 and March 1918, the army conducted three separate courts-
martial in the Gift Chapel at Fort Sam Houston in San Antonio. As
historian Robert V. Haynes concluded, the monumental case provided verdicts that, in effect, exonerated the army command but
extracted a heavy toll on the enlisted men.

Out of the 118 men charged with mutiny, rioting, and murder,
110 were found guilty of at least one charge and only seven
were acquitted. In the case of one soldier who was judged
incompetent to stand trial because of mental deficiencies, the
charges were dropped. Eighty-two men were declared guilty

Courtroom scene, Gift Chapel, Fort Sam Houston, San Antonio. As the provenance on the picture notes, this was the largest murder trial ever held in the United States to that point in late 1917. Sixty-four individuals were tried "for mutiny and murder" in association with the Camp Logan riot several months earlier. Photo NAID 533485, RG 165, Records of the War Department General and Special Staffs, 1860–1952, National Archives and Records Administration, Washington, DC.

of all charges, and twenty-nine of these were given the death sentence although only thirteen had been hanged by April of 1918. Fifty-three men were sentenced to prison for life while the remaining twenty-eight men received prison sentences ranging in length between fifteen and two years.[5]

The courts-martial did little to repair strained racial tensions in Houston, however, and what followed was an extended period of accusations, suppositions, and heightened fear and tension. The number of groups blamed for the riot, including the police, the business community, the local military command, the white community and its Jim Crow customs, and the soldiers themselves, points to the complex layering of the incident. It also serves to explain the wide-ranging diversity of accounts left for future historians to explore and analyze. One of the most detailed and insightful independent investigations of the time came from activist, journalist,

Hangings in an Arroyo

At 7:17 A.M. on the morning of Tuesday, December 11, 1917, on a scaffold constructed in an arroyo along Salado Creek two miles east of Camp Travis, San Antonio, the US Army carried out the executions of thirteen African American soldiers convicted in the Houston Riot. According to a press report, the condemned men were escorted to the gallows by "a column of one hundred and twenty-five cavalrymen and one hundred infantrymen" along with an unspecified number of officers. The only civilian witness that day was the Bexar County sheriff, John Wallace Tobin, later the mayor of San Antonio. "Without a tremor the negroes stepped out with soldierly tread," the article noted, "and singing a hymn they walked to their places on the scaffold." Following prayers by a black minister and two army chaplains, special "trigger" mechanisms engaged on command, dropping the soldiers to their deaths. "Eleven died almost instantly," the press reported, with "the other two quivering a moment or two after the rope became taut." Those executed that day were Sgt. William Nesbit; Cpls. Larmon J. Brown, Charles Baltimore, James Wheatley, and Jesse Moore; and Pvts. William Breckenridge, Thomas C. Hawkins, Carlos Snodgrass, Ira B. Davis, James Divins, Frank Johnson, Risley W. Young, and Pat McWhorter. Afterward, at around 9:00 A.M., the press and the public first learned of the hangings through a statement by US Army general John Ruckman.

Sources: Associated Press, "Negroes Were Hanged Today: Thirteen Pay Death Penalty for Being in the Houston Riot," *Corsicana (TX) Daily Sun*, Dec. 11, 1917, 1; Robert V. Haynes, *A Night of Violence: The Houston Riot of 1917* (Baton Rouge: Louisiana State University Press, 1976), 271–73.

educator, and lawyer Martha Gruening, who published the findings of her NAACP report in *The Crisis* in November 1917, just as the first of the courts-martial got underway. Placing the primary blame on police brutality and poor military discipline, she noted, "It was not a cold-blooded slaughter of innocents but the work of angry men whose endurance of wrong and injustice had been strained to the breaking point, and who in their turn committed injustices." Then in concluding her report, she added in the most positive and uplifting manner possible: "However much the riot is to be condemned from the standpoint of justice, humanity, and military discipline, however badly it may be held to have stained the long and honorable record of Negro soldiers, however necessary it may be that the soldiers should be severely punished, it seems to me an undeniable fact that one of its results will be a new respect and consideration for the Negro in the South."[6]

The Course *in* History

Little is known of the original golf course on the former grounds of Camp Logan, but there are general references to a nine-hole layout with sand greens. It was likely built after the formal closing of the camp and was reportedly located near the Public Health Hospital, which remained on the site through the early 1920s convalescing veterans of the war. Planning for a municipal park there began in earnest in 1924. Houston resident Ilona Benda, a native of Hungary who had long advocated for community memorials to the war's veterans, is credited with the initial concept, with Catherine Mary Emmot and other Houstonians working diligently on behalf of the effort as well. The original tract of 1,503 acres came from holdings of the Hogg family and the Reinerman Land Company and at the time was one of the largest municipal parks in the nation— even larger than Central Park in New York City. *The Houston Post* reported in November: "No name for the park has been selected by the council, but the one eventually chosen will express the memorial idea. In presenting their offer two weeks ago, the owners of the site suggested that it be called Memorial Park."[7]

Looking southeast across a berm and bunker along the number ten fairway, a location that in the days of Camp Logan would have been just south of the officers quarters row. Photo by Anne C. Vance, with thanks to Julie Blum, General Manager, Memorial Park Golf Course.

The overall design of Memorial Park reflected the vision of the prestigious landscape-architectural firm of Hare and Hare of Kansas City, Missouri, in keeping with the City Beautiful movement of the era. Designers Sidney J. Hare and his son, S. Herbert Hare, were early twentieth-century pioneers in the landscapes of public places that sought to work with natural environments within urban settings to promote ideals of civic pride, harmony with nature, and an overall quality of life. As part of their master plan for what became Memorial Park, they called for the development of a public golf course, which eventually moved ahead in 1934 through funding by the Works Progress Administration (WPA) and a voter-approved match from the City of Houston. Although overtaken by Dallas that September as the official Texas Centennial Celebration host city, Houston stayed the course with its progressive nature, which included the full development of Memorial Park as a key component of its own commemoration.[8]

Memorial Park Golf Course reflects the design work of the noted golf architect John Bredemus (see chapter 2). Considered the "Father of Texas Golf," Bredemus drew up plans for courses in Dallas, Victoria, Fort Worth, Houston, Corpus Christi, and Beaumont, among other Texas cities. Combining his training as an engineer with his intense interest in golf (albeit without noteworthy ability as a player) and his innate appreciation for the natural landscape, he was the state's most prolific course designer during the sport's early growth in Texas. He also figured prominently in the founding of the Texas Professional Golfers Association and was instrumental in securing the PGA Championship—the first major tournament in the Southwest—for Dallas in 1927. Commissioned to oversee the design work at Memorial even while he worked to develop Colonial Country Club in Fort Worth, which many consider his masterpiece, Bredemus followed a practical approach dictated by a limited budget. As golf historian Art Stricklin observed, the designer began with his largely unskilled WPA crews early in 1935, "building the first holes with one tractor and 20 teams of mules." The course opened in the summer of 1936 as the largest in the state in terms of area. Although Bredemus is perhaps best remembered as the designer of Colonial, a premier course in the state, he often cited Memorial as his best work. It remained a popular course as Houston eventually enveloped it, but time took its toll on the grounds, necessitating a significant rehabilitation in the 1990s. The drought of 2011 proved even more debilitating to the course and its surroundings, but ongoing efforts seek to revitalize the landscaping and to bring more recognition to its original design as a significant element of the memorial at Memorial. In 2017 heavy rains and floodwaters generated by Hurricane Harvey affected the park, once again demonstrating its vulnerability, and assessments of damages and necessary repairs continue as of this writing.[9]

17

THE BOYS OF LOCKHART

LOCKHART STATE PARK GOLF COURSE, LOCKHART

SCORECARD FROM THE PAST

Recent Past: Lockhart State Park Golf Course

Historic Name: Lockhart State Park

DETAILS: Nine-hole course; distance is 2,989 yards from the longest tees

Location: 4179 State Park Road (Highway 20), southwest of Lockhart

Historical Context: Near the Battle of Plum Creek, 1840; along the Chisholm Trail, late 1860s to mid-1880s; German farmstead, early twentieth century; state park developed by the Civilian Conservation Corps and the Works Progress Administration, 1935–39

Historical Type: State recreational park

Period of Significance: 1840–1939

Signature Hole of History: The par-three number six was originally number one, a par-five hole with the tee box located near the CCC refectory at the top of the park's highest promontory. Remains of the steep and often treacherous cart path are still evident in the woods north of the modern tee.

THE COURSE *OF* HISTORY

Located along a rocky woodland ridge that breaks steeply in uneven cliff faces to open prairies below dotted with motts of small trees, the natural landscape of Lockhart State Park is predominated by ash, oak, elm, bois d'arc, pecan, and other native hardwoods. The Clear Fork of Plum Creek cuts through the area and eventually merges with the main channel several miles southeast of Lockhart. Historically, the presence of water and the relatively open prairies of the area made it a preferred route for both Native Americans and later settlers wishing to avoid the rougher terrain nearby. The grasslands provided a relatively open route running approximately from the northwest to the southeast.

The general area has a stratified cultural past marked early on by significant associations with two distinct and seminal events in Texas history. The first occurred during the republic era, largely the result of oppressive governmental policies against Native Americans during the presidency of Mirabeau B. Lamar. In contrast to his predecessor, Sam Houston, Lamar adopted a program much more focused on expulsion or reservations than on peaceful coexistence through controlled trade and verifiable treaties. Although not opposed completely to conciliation, at least initially, Lamar eventually pursued a more strident policy designed to provide frontier security in order to open new areas to settlement. The flash point for the seminal event that played out on the prairies near present Lockhart in August 1840 had occurred in March at San Antonio. There a failed round of peace negotiations with Comanche tribal leaders resulted in the Council House Fight, in which numerous chiefs and warriors were killed. Enraged by the attack and spurred on by Mexican agents intent on destabilizing the new republic, the Comanches launched a massive retaliatory raid against settlements southeast of San Antonio, striking first at Victoria and then at the coastal town of Linnville in Calhoun County on August 8. News of the barbarous attacks spread quickly, and militia groups that formed in response moved from several points to head off the war party as it retired westward toward its own settlements on the upper Colorado River. The militia leaders knew they had to act decisively and with all haste to prevent the raiders from reaching the Hill Country above present San Marcos, where chances of gaining in pursuit would be severely limited by the rocky terrain. The point of confrontation, the Texans realized, had to be on the open prairies to the east, their focus soon coalescing on Plum Creek. There men under the command of Maj. Gen. Felix Huston, joined by a small number of Tonkawa warriors with their leader, Placido, laid in wait for the war party, headed by Chief Buffalo Hump. In all, the Texan force numbered around two hundred men, while estimates for the Comanches put their number at considerably more. Regardless of the disadvantages, the Texans enjoyed the strategic upper hand and thus initiated the confrontation on August 12. As historian and Lockhart resident Donaly Brice described the moment the war party came into view, the "entire cavalcade, stretching for several miles across the prairie, posed an awesome spectacle at it moved over the open country." An oft-quoted firsthand account of the encounter by John Holland Jenkins bears out Brice's claim: "There was a huge warrior, who wore a stovepipe hat, and another who wore a fine pigeon-tailed cloth coat, buttoned up *behind*. They seemed to have a talent for finding and blending the strangest, most unheard-of ornaments. Some wore on their heads immense buck and buffalo horns. One headdress struck me particularly. It consisted of a large white crane with red eyes."[1]

Caught off guard by the well-concealed militia forces, the Comanche main body quickly dispersed into smaller parties in the general vicinity of the present park, a few hundred yards north from the entrance and along the east side of Clear Fork Creek. Continuing to fight while in general retreat, many of the warriors bogged down their pack animals in a swampy branch (now Boggy Creek) and were either killed or gave up their plunder as they fled on foot. The Texans pressed their advantage and pursued the scattered parties, some as far as the vicinity of the San Marcos River between the present towns of San Marcos and Kyle. Later, other forces would pick up the trail and follow the Comanches to the upper reaches of the Colorado, where another encounter occurred, but for all intents and purposes, the Battle of Plum Creek culminated with a Comanche rout, effectively ending their presence in south-central Texas. As a result, Anglo-American settlers began moving into the area, and within a few years there were sufficient numbers to warrant the establishment of a county. Named for Mathew Caldwell, who was in the Texan command structure during the battle, Caldwell County became a reality in 1848, with the town of Lockhart as the seat of government.[2]

Even as the county began the business of organization in the years after Texas joined the United States, national and regional events ultimately led to the Civil War in 1861. With the conflict's end four years later, Texas faced an uncertain future, both politically and economically, as it worked through Reconstruction on the path to renewed statehood. While its economy fared better than others of the late Confederacy, given its distance from the most intense fighting of the war and its relatively strong agricultural base, Texas had another commodity advantage waiting to be fully exploited. Longhorn cattle, introduced to the region by the Spaniards during the colonial era, had roamed South Texas without much control during the US–Mexico War and subsequent Civil War. The semiferal cattle thus numbered in the millions by the late 1860s and provided an abundant resource for a war-ravaged nation eager to find new supplies of beef to replace its depleted stock. As no viable rail lines reached that deep into Texas at the time, it became necessary to develop a system to round up the wild herds and drive them overland north to the nearest railhead, which thanks to the direction of Illinois businessman Joseph G. McCoy was Abilene, Kansas. Thus was born the celebrated open-range route that in time became known as the Chisholm Trail, although it extended much farther south than the original trace Jesse Chisholm blazed from the Canadian River up to Kansas.[3]

The short-lived Chisholm Trail, which followed in part the earlier Shawnee Trail, eventually became the primary trunk line, particularly between San Antonio and Abilene, for moving millions of head of cattle north for expedient rail shipment to midwestern slaughterhouses. As the noted trail historian Wayne Gard wrote: "Some of the herds came from ranges along, or even beyond, the Rio Grande. Drovers bought or stole cattle from Mexico and swam them across the border stream. They trailed them northward through the brush country, either following the old Beef Trail past Beeville, Gonzales, and Lockhart to Austin or bending westward to San Antonio." In one of his studies of the trail, Gard quoted T. C. Richardson of Dallas, who spoke to the complex nature of the route, particularly the lower portion along points of acquisition: "We shall get rid of a good deal of geographical difficulty at once by recalling that the [feeder] trails originated wherever a herd was shaped up and ended wherever a market was found. A thousand minor trails fed the main routes, and many an old-timer who as a boy saw a herd of stately longhorns, piloted by bandanaed, booted, and spurred men, lived with the firm conviction that the Dodge or Chisholm Trail passed right over yonder." The relatively new town of Lockhart, located along several of these feeder routes, thus developed a strong historical connection to the primary era of cattle drives, which lasted from the initial promotional enterprises of McCoy in 1867 until the development of barbed wire and the subsequent closing of the open range in the mid-1880s. No doubt longhorn herds passed through Caldwell County in the vicinity of Lockhart State Park, taking advantage of seasonal grasses, reliable water sources, and the same prairie terrain settlers and Native Americans had found conducive to travel years earlier.[4]

Despite the gravity of the Plum Creek battle and the enormous environmental and economic effects of the cattle drives, neither event left significant changes on the cultural landscape, except perhaps archeologically. More-distinct changes occurred as farmers and ranchers fenced off tracts for improved agricultural development, as petroleum companies explored for oil and gas, or as rail lines and highways crossed the land, leading to the establishment of towns and rural communities that have grown substantially over time. Such changes are evident in all regions of the state. Less common, though, in the contexts of community planning and quality-of-life considerations is the development of a small recreational area evocative of a time of hope and promise during an era of unprecedented economic uncertainty.

When Franklin D. Roosevelt became president in March 1933, the Great Depression, coupled with the critical environmental devastation centered in the Dust Bowl states, was in full force, with no sustainable plan for recovery in place. Both the nation's soil and work force faced depletion. In response Roosevelt embarked on a multifaceted New Deal program focused on recovery, relief, and reform. Central to his early efforts was a response to the emergency status of conservation needs across the nation, not just in the Dust Bowl region. There were precedents, both foreign and domestic, for the programs he proffered and widespread support from those who laid the groundwork in the Progressive Era, including former chief forester Gifford Pinchot, who FDR's distant cousin Teddy Roosevelt had entrusted with the new US Forest Service in 1905, during his own presidency. In setting up his emergency plan for conservation, though, FDR envisioned a way to tie it together with his long-held support of public parks and outdoor recreational facilities; such places had been an integral part of his formative years. As historian Douglas Brinkley noted, "It was his dream to initiate meaningful state park systems throughout America."[5]

Within days of his inauguration, Roosevelt sent his plan for an Emergency Conservation Work Act to Congress, which approved it in late March 1933. Central to the proposal was an interdepartmental program that came to be known officially as the Civilian Conservation Corps (CCC), with participants colloquially referred to as Roosevelt's "Tree Army," "Soil Soldiers," or simply as the "CCC boys." The program called for a joint-oversight partnership with the Departments of War, Agriculture, Interior, and Labor. The primary worker targets for the corps were young unmarried men, initially ages eighteen to twenty-three (later increased to age twenty-eight and expanded to include World War I veterans), who could work in reforestation, soil reclamation, and recreational development, with a substantial part of their meager pay (generally a dollar a day) going back home to their families for needed assistance. Directing the new agency under the supervision of Interior Secretary Harold Ickes was Tennessee-born and Boston-based Robert Fechner, a prominent leader in the American Federation of Labor. Fechner's appointment, in part, served to assuage critics in Congress and the unions who were concerned that the CCC might undermine labor programs and rights gains.[6]

Initially, the Department of Labor set the criteria for the enrollees while the War Department handled the induction at the various work sites, known as camps. The Departments of Interior and Agriculture selected the project sites and set the agendas for the scope of work. Camp numbers designated organizational purpose—for example, SCS-1 for a Soil Conservation Service project, F-2 for the US Forest Service, S-16 for a state forest. In the case of

Lockhart State Park, SP-51 denoted its association with the Texas State Parks Board in a joint association with the National Park Service. Other CCC ventures emphasized wildlife management, fire control, historic preservation, or range management, among other things. The focus was always on conservation in its broadest sense, which held true for recreational parks as well. This meant that, as in the case of Lockhart and other parks, the CCC could not build golf courses or swimming pools, although they could handle the requisite land preparation and contouring. The completion of such features, though, fell under the domain of another New Deal agency, the Works Progress Administration (WPA).[7]

The basic administrative structure of each CCC camp was a shared responsibility between the War Department and the specific federal agency sponsoring the work project. Because there was a strong military component to the logistical setup and daily operations, many believed that the CCC represented a military-training effort. While that was not the intended object, familiarity with regimented structure and discipline, even in a peacetime setting, prepared the enrollees for the eventuality of service, which became a greater possibility as the nation dealt with possible involvement in crises then developing in Europe and Asia. Each camp had a commander, normally some captains and first lieutenants, and support officers drawn from the ranks of the Regular Army as well as the reserves. The army established the camps, ordered supplies, oversaw discipline, and provided the basic support for a timely accomplishment of the mission. Although there were considerations for local needs, a typical schedule, such as the following one from a camp in the Northwest, showed the influence of the military regimen:

6:00 A.M.	Rising bugle
6:15–7:00	Breakfast, followed by sick call
7:15	Police camp and draw tools
11:15	Return from work
12:00	Dinner
1:00	Sick call
1:15	Police camp

1:30	Draw tools
1:45	Go to work
4:45	Return from work
6:00	Supper followed by the study program[8]

Education was a key component of the CCC experience. On-the-job training at the sites came from what the corps referred to as "locally experienced men" (LEMs), and local teachers or CCC educational advisors offered classes in the evenings on a wide range of topics and interests, such as metalwork, social etiquette, basic educational skills, bookkeeping, leather craft, mechanics, and radio operations. In the park projects the LEMs generally were previously unemployed, or underemployed, professionals with specific experience in such relevant skills as masonry, carpentry, landscaping, surveying, architecture, plumbing, and electrical. Balancing the regular schedule were sports activities, social gatherings with women from local communities, a camp library, and worship services. During the day, typical work clothes included cotton tee shirts, dungarees, and caps, but in the evenings army-like uniforms, referred to as ODs (olive drabs), were the norm. Meals came largely from local sources, thus the CCC provided needed financial support for nearby farms and ranches, while the enrollees—many for the first time—enjoyed three full meals a day.[9]

Lockhart community leaders acted quickly to secure a CCC camp for the area by purchasing 265 acres from the Henry Masur family in 1934 as enticement for federal recognition. Official word of the camp approval, however, did not come until the summer of 1935, given the intense competition from locales across the nation. On July 28 Capt. Owen E. Jensen, acting on behalf of the CCC through assignment from the US Marine Corps Reserve, brought twelve CCC leaders with him to establish Company 3803 at Lockhart. The initial group transferred from the camp at Ottine, south of Lockhart in Gonzales County, where they and others had worked on what would become Palmetto State Park. By the time of their arrival in Caldwell County, the temporary barracks that constituted the camp were already in place on private land immediately northeast and across the main road from the present entrance. Such a setup allowed a separation of the living area from the work area, minimizing the disruption to the land and preventing undue logistical and safety concerns.[10]

Despite some initial delays in procuring supplies, work began in earnest by late 1935, with eventually a couple of hundred CCC boys enrolled. The membership changed with time, but one roster showed most were from the south-central Texas area. There were workers from as near as Lockhart, Seguin, Gonzales, Wimberley, San Antonio, and San Marcos as well as more distant places like Pearsall, Houston, Harper, and Bay City. From the beginning, the support of the Lockhart community was evident, and reports on the progress at the park site regularly appeared in the local newspaper. A banner headline article in the *Lockhart Post-Register* in August reported on the formal dedication ceremony planned for later that month:

> Citizens of the community will learn from addresses [speeches] how they can cooperate to secure the most benefit from the location of the CCC camp here; what they can do to show their appreciation and what means can be employed to make the stay of officers and men in this community pleasant.
>
> Not only should the camp and the officers in charge know that this community appreciates them and their work but means to convey this information to those higher up the line.[11]

The CCC boys named their new work home Camp Colp in honor of David Edward Colp, the head of the Texas State Parks Board, who had lived in Lockhart as a young man, an association that could only have served to help the town in its quest to secure a state park. Colp, who made an address to the crowd assembled at the opening of the camp, was perhaps the state's strongest advocate for parks and tourism at the time. A native of the Paris area in East Texas, he worked as an automobile dealer in San Antonio and eventually a leader of the Texas Good Roads Association, which figured prominently in Gov. Pat Neff's interest in developing a statewide system

A Tale of Two Clubhouses

The year 1925 must have seemed like the best of times to young architect George Louis Walling, landing his first major commission after having only recently opened his office in Austin upon his return from studies abroad. He had been enrolled at the University of Texas for three years, then studied in France at the Acadamie American at Fontainebleau, Atelier Pontremoli, École des Beaux Arts, and finally by special invitation at the French Acadamie, Villa Medici in Rome. Walling's Austin client, Judge James David McClendon, was a man of considerable education and accomplishment as well. A member of the first graduating class of the University of Texas Law School in 1897, he practiced law locally, served as a judge, and eventually became the chief justice of the Texas Court of Civil Appeals. It was in this role that McClendon presided over the landmark *Sweatt v. Painter* case. In 1950 the US Supreme Court overturned McClendon's Texas court verdict in the civil-rights case, forcing the University of Texas to admit African Americans to graduate-level courses of study, presaging the 1954 *Brown v. Board of Education* decision declaring racial segregation in American public schools unconstitutional.

Judge McClendon retained Walling to design his family's new home on the outskirts of Austin. The property would eventually become the Westwood Country Club, with the house serving as the clubhouse. The structure's design, apparently overseen by McClendon's wife, Mary Anne, was to be in a Normandy French château style. Walling prepared plans for the main house, a guesthouse, a bridge, and entrance-gate pillars, all constructed of limestone collected on the eleven-acre site.

The mansion featured a slate roof, Mexican-tile floors, and two towers connected by a bridge, which formed an enclosed porte-cochere. Famed local ironworker Andrew Weigel provided wrought-iron door hardware, bar fireplace sets, and the railings for the circular staircase. Another noted Texas craftsman, Peter Mansbendel, provided woodcarvings, while Alison Mason Kingsbury of New York painted frescoes on various interior and exterior walls.

The impressive complex served as the McClendon's home until purchased by the Westwood Country Club in 1955. Although substantially enlarged over the years, with dining and party rooms, a large swimming pool, marina, tennis courts, and other outbuildings and facilities, Walling's French-inspired château remains the centerpiece of the country club.

Around the same time, Walling designed other prominent structures in Central Texas, including the LaSalle Hotel in Bryan and the Kyle Hotel in Temple, both multistory complexes completed in 1928. But times and fortunes were changing for Texas and the nation, for soon afterward the Roaring Twenties ended with the Great Depression. Facing his own financial crisis by that time, Walling resigned from the American Institute of Architects, to which he had been elected in 1924, being unable to afford the annual dues of fifteen dollars.

At the height of the Great Depression in 1935, Walling (with partners Kirk Scott, R. J. Hammond, and George T. Patrick) received a commission from the National Park Service and the Texas State Parks Board to design the "keeper's house" for the new Lockhart State Park. The structure provided limited clubhouse and office space for the adjacent golf course while serving as the superintendent's home; it later returned to strictly residential use.

Walling's style eventually moved away from the exotic and romantic European influences used in the elaborate McClendon house and based his park design on German immigrant architecture once common in Central Texas. The sturdy, simple, and organic building tradition best exemplified by the pioneer buildings of German Americans who settled Hill Country towns such as nearby Fredericksburg featured unadorned masonry and half-timbering with stone, brick, or adobe infill covered with plaster in a method known as fachwerk. The keeper's house he built has walls of stucco and stone with some fachwerk sections as well as a characteristic outside stairway leading to an attic door. The multiple internal chimneys, plank doors, and flat-arched openings for casement windows, coupled with the absence of a central hall, contribute to the rustic vernacular impression.

Walling would go on to have a long and productive architectural career, working in both the public and private sectors but never regaining the prominence reflected by his late-1920s high rises. He would even eventually regain admission to the American Institute of Architects, but the striking contrast between his McClendon and Lockhart commissions, only ten years apart, served to bookend his early career.

Sources: David R. Williams, "Toward a Southwestern Architecture," *Southwest Review* 16, no. 3 (Apr. 1931): 301–13; "History," Lockhart State Park, http://tpwd.texas.gov/state-parks/lockhart/park_history; "Texas Parks Civilian Conservation Corps Drawings Database," Texas State Library and Archives Commission, https://www.tsl.texas.gov/apps/arc/CCCDrawings/; Norfleet Bone Collection, Texas Parks and Wildlife Department; Kenneth Hafertepe, *A Guide to the Historic Buildings of Fredericksburg and Gillespie County* (College Station: Texas A&M University Press, 2016).

of parks to serve the burgeoning traveling public. Giving his all in his zeal for new state parks, Colp collapsed during a visit to Bastrop State Park only a few months after his Lockhart remarks and died soon after.[12]

As reported in a subsequent issue of the local paper, Camp Colp consisted initially of twelve main buildings and various ancillary structures. In addition to the five dormitory barracks that held forty enrollees each, there was a headquarters building, an infirmary, officer quarters, mess hall, and bathhouses "complete with hot

and cold running water." A key structure for camp life was the recreation hall, which included a "post exchange where enrollees may
buy such articles which supply their daily needs including tobacco,
candy, cigarettes, soft drinks and toilet articles." The recreation
hall also included a library, an important part of the educational
programs headed by former public teacher and principal Finley
E. Milstead, a graduate of Southwest Texas State Teachers College
in nearby San Marcos. Other LEMs at Lockhart included Austin
architect George Louis Walling, who had a distinguished career in
residential and commercial design, and landscape designer Kirk
Hamilton Scott, a former nurseryman from Edinburg who would
later supervise work at Big Bend National Park for the CCC. As with
many of the camp leaders, Walling, Scott, and Milstead, in addition
to the military personnel, later served in the armed forces during
World War II.[13]

A review of the 1930s issues of the Lockhart paper indicated
that the close association between the town and the camp never
wavered. Articles reflected optimism for the finished product, with
a bit of hometown "boosterism" thrown in as well to promote what
the editors and citizenry felt would be "one of the most attractive
picnic spots in Texas." Local women's groups reportedly worked
to acquire additional acreage for the park, although those efforts
failed to materialize, as did a short-lived and perhaps tongue-
in-cheek suggestion to name the site in memory of nearby "dirt
farmer" Alexander D. Mebane—actually a well-known hybridizer
of cottonseed. Numerous reports mentioned community activities
specifically for the CCC boys and their leaders, including a special
showing hosted by town merchants at the Baker Theater of the
movie *Murder in the Clouds*, an action-packed film featuring stunt
flyers. No news of the camp life seemed too mundane or insignificant to include. The paper reported on the addition of game tables
in the recreation hall and the hanging of new curtains under the
supervision of the commander's wife, Joyce Jensen. Even the addition of a picture of FDR in the hall caught the press's attention.
Sadly, some items spoke to the drama and the danger inherent in
such a massive construction project. A front-page article on July
30, 1936, reported on the death of Walter W. Bowles, an eighteen-

NPS Rustic

As designed by architect George Louis Walling, the Lockhart State Park residence, which also once housed the course pro shop, is a good example of the NPS Rustic style. References to Texas German architecture include the outside staircase, gable-end chimney, and rusticated stonework. Courtesy Historic Sites & Structures Program, Texas Parks and Wildlife Department.

In designing the structures at Lockhart State Park, George Walling and Kirk Scott utilized a National Park Service design idiom known as "NPS Rustic," but including localized vernacular references. As NPS architect Albert H. Good outlined in the 1935 book *Park Structures and Facilities*: "Successfully handled, it is a style which, through the use of native materials in proper scale, and through the avoidance of rigid, straight lines, and over sophistication, gives the feeling of having been executed by pioneer craftsmen with limited tools. It thus achieved sympathy with natural surroundings and with the past." Herbert Maier, the NPS regional architect who oversaw all design work in Texas parks through the CCC, echoed

Good's fundamental tenets in his own architectural philosophy of NPS Rustic:

> Since the primary purpose in setting aside semi-wilderness areas is to conserve them in as nearly a primitive state as possible it follows that every structure, no matter how necessary, must be regarded as an intruder and should be designed with an eye toward making it inconspicuous. These primitive areas are most beautiful in their native condition, and introducing man-made structures cannot improve the beauty of the whole but tends to rather rob the picture which nature has painted of much of its wholesome effect on the visitor, no matter how pleasingly such buildings may have been designed. This may be theory, but it is good theory.

Source: Quoted in Dan K. Utley and James W. Steely, *Guided with a Steady Hand: The Cultural Landscape of a Rural Texas Park* (Waco: Baylor University Press, 1998), 48–49.

year-old enrollee from Creedmoor, who was killed in a gravel pit cave-in by having "suffered internal hurts for which little relief could be given." The accident occurred at a quarry site on property owned by the Rev. J. M. Purcell four miles east of town.[14]

In 1936 came a report that the main CCC company at Ottine had transferred to Arizona, leaving some of the park work in Gonzales County incomplete. This was not uncommon within the CCC, as officials often had to consider a broader scope of work commitments that sometimes reflected political pressures or intense community action. Because of the transfer, though, the CCC maintained a small contingent of workers at Ottine for a time as a side camp responsible to Company 3803. The summer of 1936 also brought a major change in the leadership at Lockhart when its popular superintendent, Maj. E. A. Kingsley, who had previously served at Palo Duro, transferred to the state-park operations at

Bastrop. His replacement was Mr. V. R. Eclekamp, who moved east from his work at the park in Big Spring.[15]

Despite the often dangerous and tedious work, the changes in leadership and enrollee personnel, various reconsiderations in park design, and other complicating factors, work on the state project progressed at a steady pace and came to a close late in 1939. In all, the Lockhart CCC boys cleared large tracts of land and planted new trees and shrubbery, building the park roads, a stone bridge, the refectory, the superintendent's residence, furniture, a dam, a storage tank, culverts, and trails as well. They also handled the initial work on the golf course through a partnership of local and federal assistance. As reported years later, "CCC workers cleared the site of the park's golf course. The Lockhart Business Men's Club cooperating with the Works Progress Administration, completed it."[16]

On January 5, 1940, the last of Company 3803 left Caldwell County and headed west for work at Fort Griffin State Park (now Fort Griffin State Historic Site). While they left behind a small but impressive state park that fully opened later in the 1940s, their former campsite across the way returned to farmland. Currently, only the wellhead, located on private land, serves as a visible landmark of their multiyear work home, only a few hundred yards east of the core of the Plum Creek battlefield.[17]

Just over a decade after the CCC boys left Lockhart, their park became the focus of a broader debate over equal access to state recreational facilities, which remained primarily segregated in an era when the rule of "separate but equal" prevailed. Even the CCC itself was subject to such controversy. Despite some exceptions to the rule nationally, the camps themselves, especially in the South, remained segregated, with separate projects for Anglo-Americans and African Americans. There were also companies composed almost exclusively of Hispanic or Native American members. As CCC director Fechner believed, separation of the races did not constitute discrimination, and his rule generally prevailed. Lockhart was something of an exception, however, in that there was a balanced mixture of English, German, and Spanish surnames represented in the roster of enrollees.[18]

Historian Donaly Brice (left) and assistant park superintendent Chris Dooley survey the view from the original number-one tee box at the Lockhart State Park course as laid out by the WPA. Photograph by Dan K. Utley

The matter of segregation at parks—at the local, state, and national levels—remained a matter of social concern until the advent of civil rights legislation in the 1960s. Before that, there were a number of steps taken to address the matter, including separate days for specific races. In 1951, though, grassroots action at several parks, particularly in East Texas, brought renewed attention to the issue. In an effort to address the growing concerns, Texas senator Warren McDonald of Tyler introduced a bill that would effectively legitimize the separate-but-equal doctrine. It called for the creation of new "Negro parks" at the Lavon Reservoir near Copeville in Collin County and at Lake Whitney in Hill County. As reported in the press, the bill also called for

> conversion of all or part of five parks now used by whites to Negro use.
>
> Portions of Lockhart state park [sic], Tyler state park, and the Possum Kingdom dam recreation area would be converted.

Teeing area sign, Lockhart State Park Golf Course. Photograph by Dan K. Utley.

A reminder of the steep side trail that once led caddies to the first hole at the Lockhart course. Photograph by Dan K. Utley.

All of Caddo Lake state park would be devoted to Negro recreation.

The only area at Lockhart specifically excluded from the provisions of the bill was the golf course. The legislation eventually gave way to a court order that ended the segregation plan.[19]

The Course *in* History

CCC landscape architect Kirk Scott, a native of Floydada and a graduate of Texas A&M, designed the nine-hole course at Lockhart State Park. As constructed by the CCC boys and the WPA workers, the site is a relatively open prairie course. Scott's signature first hole, shortened and reworked in the 1950s to become number six, originally featured an elevated tee box atop the park's highest point, and the tight fairway dropped dramatically to the flats below, where the other holes are located. A 1957 newspaper column described it: "The first tee, originally, was on the hill top and was said to have the greatest drop of any golf course. Its novelty was offset by the difficulty to climb, and the present course is all on lower ground. Extensive work has been done in the last year improving both fairways and greens."

Evidence of the original tee box is still visible through brush to the west of the hilltop combination building and water tank. While a steep cart path once provided access to the tee, an alternate route for those walking the course was via a woodland path known as Caddy's Trail, which is still marked and used for hiking. For reasons not noted in available records, the course initially opened as the Lockhart Country Club under lease to a local association. It remained a private venture until 1948, when it again became part of the state park.[20]

18

A PEACEFUL VILLAGE SMALL

HONDO GOLF COURSE, HONDO

SCORECARD FROM THE PAST

Currently: Hondo Golf Course

Historic Name: Hondo Army Air Field; Hondo Air Force Base

DETAILS: Nine-hole public golf course; distance is 5,964 yards from the longest tees when played as eighteen holes

Location: 702 Disoway Road, Hondo

Historical Context: World's largest air-navigation school during World War II; USAF base during Korean Conflict and early Cold War years

Historical Type: Military training base for aviation navigators and engineers

Period of Significance: 1942–58

Signature Hole of History: While all the holes on the course were once associated with the base, the tee box for number one—a 392-yard, left-dogleg hole—is in the general vicinity of the original base headquarters.

THE COURSE OF HISTORY

Early in the 1940s, as the United States prepared for the inevitability of another global war, military and government leaders began systematically putting programs in place that would, when needed, quickly accelerate the requisite call for training and the procurement of materiel. In the summer of 1940, Pres. Franklin Roosevelt requested a dramatic increase in the production of military planes, resulting in a call for seven thousand fully trained

Early morning birds at the Hondo Golf Course. Courtesy Jerry Busby, Hondo Golf Course.

and combat-ready pilots. But they were only part of the training equation, and programs soon developed to provide the requisite number of support personnel, including navigators and bombardiers. The closer the nation came to entering the war, the more those numbers increased; by 1941 the strains on existing flight and navigation schools, both public and private, were extraordinary. US Army Air Corps officials at Kelly Field, San Antonio, considered options for relocating navigation-training programs to an auxiliary site in order to maximize the base's potential for ever-increasing flight-training demands. One location they examined was about thirty miles west of the city near the small agricultural settlement of Hondo in Medina County. An unincorporated village of approximately 2,500 residents at the time, Hondo was centered within a rural landscape that afforded relatively flat and open terrain that, when coupled with the region's relatively dry climate, proved ideal for an air-support training facility.[1]

Preliminary plans moved quickly to the forefront with the Japanese attack on Pearl Harbor on December 7, 1941, and the citizens of Hondo responded with a formal request for a training base in their vicinity. Despite best efforts to maintain security and secrecy until a formal announcement by the government, the *Hondo Anvil Herald* reported in early February 1942: "A U.S. Army blimp was seen over Hondo Tuesday, and especially in the vicinity of the proposed location for the air field. It was surmised by County officials that the blimp was being put to use while army officials were taking pictures of the land under consideration and for other tests." Two weeks later, under the front-page headline "Hondo in Earnest about the Air Field," the paper reported, "In order to meet the army's demands for housing in the event the air field is located in Hondo, a body of forward looking citizens met Wednesday night and entered into the tentative organization of a $15,000 corporation, to be known as The Victory Homes, Inc." The purpose was to sell stock in the local venture to secure a Federal Housing Administration project in support of the base, for the small town then had little available housing stock for rent. Later, as plans for base construction got underway and workers began flooding into the area, residents answered the immediate call by renting rooms, garages, and animal pens for temporary housing. They also repurposed barns and warehouses as makeshift worker dormitories.[2]

Army engineers soon signed off on a site west of town that represented a complex of multiple tracts and owners, and in March 1942 the official announcement of the new base came via Sen. W. Lee O'Daniel's office in Washington. Civilian construction of the field fell to H. B. "Pat" Zachry, a successful contractor in San Antonio who had only a hundred days to complete the project, including the entire runway system, streets, hangars, support buildings, and utilities. Driven by the urgency of war, the process of evictions began immediately, with some families in the project area receiving only a few days' notice before having to leave their longtime homes during the first weeks of April. Among them was the family of Robert and Nettie Koch, who had lived on their 300-acre farm for twenty-five years. As Nettie Koch described: "They cut our fences and let our sheep out, and then told us we had to move. We were not notified ahead of time. . . . We got up one morn-

ing, and the sheep were everywhere, and the milk cows were out."
In a scene played out at other locations in quick succession across
the new airfield, as Robert D. Thompson noted in his history of the
base, construction crews bulldozed the Koch family's "home, barn,
windmill, water tank, and smokehouse to the ground." They then
filled in the well and leveled the land; by mid-April, "concrete for
a runway covered part of their old homestead." Where fence lines
once denoted ownership and provided a measure of containment
for livestock, armed guards took positions to secure the developing
base and prevent former owners from returning to their farms.[3]

Although most of the initial base buildings were of minimalist
construction, essentially frame barracks covered in tar paper, they
still had to conform to army regulations. Zachry, however, pressed
for and received dispensations for such considerations as revised
heavy snow-load limits, unnecessary in the South Texas environment, and thus moved even more rapidly toward project completion. In this and other actions, Thompson noted, "the workers
learned that the trick was to convince army inspectors they were
doing things the army way, while in fact they were doing things the
Zachry way—fast." The contractor prevailed and met his assigned
deadline ahead of schedule, and with sufficient infrastructure in
place, the army formally activated the field on the Fourth of July
1942. With no time to lose in preparing for war, as military historian Thomas E. Alexander noted, the Kelly Field Navigation School
packed up soon after and headed west to Hondo along US 90.
"Classes that were already in session at the old school," he wrote,
"made the transition in such an efficient manner that reportedly
not one hour of scheduled training time was lost in the move."[4]

Amid the flurry of construction on the new base, residents of
Hondo and Medina County also worked tirelessly to meet their
obligations to the project. The town of Hondo incorporated in May,
giving residents greater input on related infrastructure, such as
the realignment of roads and rail lines. As the local newspaper
reported just prior to this, several political entities were already
working together on plans for the primary entry route to the base
from US 90. "The county, we understand, is to furnish the 150-foot
right-of-way, and the State and Federal highway departments to

An aerial view of Hondo Army Air Field as it appeared shortly after it opened for training programs in 1942. The speed with which the base was completed reflected the urgency of the wartime situation, the commitment of the contractors, and the support, pride, and patriotism of the community. "Hondo Army Airfield, Texas, Station Area, 1942," Wikimedia Commons, last edited Jan. 24, 2017, https://commons.wikimedia.org/wiki/File:Hondo_Army_Airfield_-_station_-_2.jpg.

build the road. By proposing an alternate road, and if accepted by Army officials, a large number of Mexican homes will not have to be moved and the County will be saved several thousands of dollars, we were informed." As promised, there was new housing in the vicinity of the base, including more than three hundred units in Navigation Village along the southeast section of the field. Despite the frenetic and unrelenting activity, and the dramatic and game-changing effects on Hondo and the surrounding area, the town remained resolute in its support of the war effort and all it represented. A celebratory front-page poem in the *Hondo Anvil Herald* read, in part:

> We welcome the soldiers to our town,
> And trust they will never meet with a frown,

Just cheery smiles and a helping hand
While they train here to defend our land.

We are just a peaceful village small,
With nothing much to offer at all!
Just friendship true, good water and air,
And we trust that you will treat us fair.

The same issue of the paper reported on the ongoing training at the Navigation School. In providing an overview of daily activities, the article noted that the training, while rigorous and time consuming, nevertheless allowed for recreational activities, with intrasquadron leagues for softball, football, volleyball, and basketball. Further, the paper reported, "post tournaments will offer boxing, tennis, badminton, horseshoes and ping pong." There was no mention of golf, however, which would not make its imprint on the grounds until much later.[5]

The first class of cadets (42-11), which transferred to Hondo from Kelly Field in August, completed its training that same month. Others soon replaced them as programs became operational, and by year's end there were almost continuous flights in the air as the new field grew to become the largest Army Air Forces navigational school in the world. At its peak, operations included more than five thousand military personnel. The base provided training on a wide range of aircraft, including bombers, fighters, and cargo planes, as well as basic training for glider pilots. The standard workhorse of the training efforts, however, was the Beechcraft AT-7, a twin-engine classroom in the sky for cadet navigators. Other planes based at Hondo Army Air Field during the war included B-34s, B-18s, AT-11s, C-60s, and later B-29s.[6]

While women constituted a portion of civilian personnel at the airfield soon after it opened, it was not until 1943 that the army based a number of women's units there as well. The first was the 743rd Women's Army Auxiliary Corps (WAAC) Post Headquarters Company, which at first primarily provided administrative assistance. Following new army policies later that year, the auxiliary

WARTIME SHADOWS OVER HONDO

Military aircraft utilized in training programs at Hondo included the following, among others.

T-6 North American Aviation Texan: single-engine advanced trainer used to train pilots from World War II until the 1970s; more than fifteen thousand in production; some still fly in air shows, including the Reno National Air Races in Nevada.

T-28 North American Aviation Trojan: single-engine military trainer used by the US Air Force and Navy beginning in the 1950s; designed as a replacement for the T-6 and eventually replaced by the T-34C. In 1962 a T-28 was the first US combat aircraft lost during the Vietnam War.

T-34 Beechcraft Mentor: introduced in the late 1940s as a military trainer; with numerous upgrades it remains in limited service, although superseded by the T-6 Texan II as the primary training craft of the US military.

B-34 Lockheed Ventura (known as the Humming Bird at Hondo Army Air Field): twin-engine bomber developed in 1941, with some early models sent to the Royal Air Force at the beginning of World War II.

B-18 Douglas Bolo: medium bomber in service during the late 1930s and early 1940s; based on the DC-2 airliner, it was underpowered, inadequately armored, and unable to carry an adequate bomb load.

B-25 North American Aviation Mitchell: twin-engine medium bomber named in honor of Maj. Gen. William "Billy" Mitchell, a pioneer of US military aviation; served in every theater of World War II and remained in service afterward; more than ten thousand produced with several variants.

AT-7 Beechcraft Navigator: based on the Beechcraft Model 18 and used as a navigation-training aircraft in World War II; more than 90 percent of US navigators and bombardiers trained in the AT-7 and similar AT-11.

AT-11 Beechcraft Kansan: US Army Air Forces trainer used for bombing and gunnery training; equipped with a bomb bay, a transparent nose for bombardier trainees, and .30-caliber machine guns.

B-24 Consolidated Liberator: four-engine heavy bomber introduced in 1941; more than nineteen thousand manufactured; served in all theaters during World War II; faster, longer range, and greater bomb capacity than the B-17.

A-28 Lockheed Hudson: twin-engine light bomber and reconnaissance aircraft originally built for the Royal Air Force; used for antisubmarine warfare during World War II.

C-60 Lockheed Lodestar: military transport used during World War II and based on the Lockheed Model 18 Super Electra.

C-47 Douglas Skytrain: military transport based on the civilian DC-3 airliner; extensively used during World War II, from flying the Hump, ferrying supplies from India to China, to deploying paratroopers on D-Day; thirteen thousand produced; more than three hundred remain in active service.

T-41 Cessna Mescalero: militarized version of the company's 172 model; used for pilot training beginning in the 1960s; phased out early in the twenty-first century.

reactivated as part of the Women's Army Corps (WAC) at a base ceremony in August and thereafter enjoyed full military status. Increased duties under the new command structure included aircraft and equipment inspections, flight-instrumentation calibration, and photography. In November two members of the Women Airforce Service Pilots (WASP) group—Betty Heinrich and Mary Wiggins—joined the operations at Hondo. Both were recent graduates of the advanced flight-training school at Avenger Field near Sweetwater, Texas, who went on to distinguished careers in aviation. Later joined by other WASP personnel, the women served first as copilots, then lead pilots, and finally as test pilots, performing

Members of the Women Airforce Service Pilots (WASP) at Hondo Army Air Field, c. 1943 (L–R, with class designation in parentheses): Mary Wiggins (43-W-4), Kathryn Stamps (43-W-8), Maxine Edmondson (43-W-8), Emeral Drummond (43-W-7), Mary Burke (43-W-7), Mary Canavan (43-W-7), Ann Brennan (43-W-4), and Mary Beritich (43-W-3). Courtesy The WASP Archive, Texas Woman's University, Denton.

vital services like ferrying military aircraft to Hondo from various locales.[7]

Although segregated accommodations prevailed at training bases during the war, there were a number of African American soldiers assigned to Hondo Army Air Field beginning in 1942. They first served with a quartermaster company and worked primarily as part of the base motor pool, but others served in the short-lived Crop Harvesting Program and provided a wide range of manual labor. As pressure mounted to open its training opportunities, the army began offering additional flight training, and an all-black class of cadets (44-3N) started at Hondo in the fall of 1943. Despite such progress in military service, the men remained relegated to separate barracks, with a separate base exchange and service club as well, and often traveled to nearby San Antonio for everything from entertainment to haircuts. In all, five classes of back cadets trained at Hondo, with the last (44-12N) receiving its wings toward the end of fighting in the European theater in 1945.[8]

A Last Scene Alone

Hollywood stuntwoman Mary Wiggins joined the WASP during World War II and was one of the first two women of that division to serve at Hondo Army Air Field. An accomplished aviator by the 1930s, she ferried aircraft and served as a flight instructor during World War II. Leaving the WASP in 1944, she returned to her work in films, which included serving as a double for such noted actresses as Barbara Stanwyck, Ann Sothern, Dorothy Lamour, and Claudette Colbert. Tragically in December 1945, for reasons known only to her, Wiggins committed suicide by shooting herself in the backyard of her California home. She was only thirty-five years old. The *Los Angeles Times* reported: "There was no gallery such as had gasped in the days when she made high dives while her clothes were aflame and plunged into a pool of flame. There was no spectacle of a balloon ascension, of driving a motorcycle through a burning building, of being locked in a mail sack and thrown into a swimming pool." She had, as the paper darkly noted, "played her last scene alone."

Source: *Los Angeles Times*, Dec. 21, 1945, 13.

In the summer of 1945, as other bases faced cutbacks and program curtailments, Hondo Army Air Field became the new home of the B-29 Flight Engineer School as operations moved to Texas from Colorado. With the change in mission, the army began phasing out the navigational school at Hondo. The Boeing B-29 Superfortress, a heavy bomber powered by four propeller engines, represented a new phase of advanced military technology, and Hondo benefited greatly from its developmental role in training flight engineers for the aircraft. Although the bombers required longer runways—longer than those at Hondo—there were none to spare for training anyway and no forthcoming funding for new purchases; classes took place utilizing B-24 Liberators modified with space for eight cadets and an instructor in addition to the regular flight crew. Even with the new mission, though, the need for continued training declined dramatically as the war drew to a close, and it soon became apparent that field operations at Hondo would cease. Such realizations, however, had little effect on the associated dangers of training missions, which continued. Early on the morning of September 1, 1945, the day before the signing of the Japanese instrument of surrender, a B-24 crashed on takeoff at the north end of the field, killing eleven crewmembers, including one WAC private. The following month another B-24 crashed, this time three miles north of the field, killing all thirteen aboard. It was the last aircraft accident at the base during the world-war era.[9]

By November, efforts to close the airfield accelerated as units moved on, workers shuttered buildings, and pilots ferried remaining planes to Aloe Field in Victoria. In his summation of the World War II years at Hondo, Thompson noted that in its brief two-and-half-year existence, the base had produced more than fourteen thousand navigators and almost three thousand flight engineers and served as home to ten thousand additional personnel. It provided civilian jobs for six thousand workers and increased the size of the town, temporarily it turned out, almost six fold. Deactivated on the last day of 1945, the base became government surplus property in 1946, with buildings sold and moved offsite for other purposes. It was not to be the end of the airfield, though, as the nation soon turned its attention to a new type of war in search of a sustainable peace.[10]

Military flight training through a private aviation school continued at the site after the war, but with the advent of the Korean Conflict in 1950, the US Air Force formally reactivated it as Hondo Air Force Base in 1951. Operations continued until June 1958. By the early 1960s, advertisements in numerous South Texas newspapers touted the government sale of surplus housing. With a deal of no money down and a payout cash price of less than $2,500 over five or six years, "plus $2 per mile delivered anywhere," the ads noted that the surplus structures were two-bedroom frame houses complete with plumbing fixtures, oak floors, evaporative coolers, steel-casement windows, "nice kitchen sinks," and other amenities. Although stating that the houses, once moved off the base, were ready for residential occupancy, they also described them as suitable for motels, lake cottages, or farm use. Management of the former base property eventually conveyed to the City of Hondo, which used the land largely for industrial purposes and as the city airport. The site saw a brief return of military activity in the 1970s and 1980s involving flight screening for the Cessna T-41 Mescalero, but new businesses eventually moved to what became an industrial park. One of the few remaining vestiges of the military past is the Hondo Golf Course, which dates from the base operations of the 1950s.[11]

THE COURSE *IN* HISTORY

The Hondo Golf Course dates to the second phase of the air base and its utilization during the Cold War. A newspaper report in 1954 announced that members of the fledgling Hondo Golfers Association—apparently composed of base personnel and town residents—would start work on the new golf course on Saturday, August 28. "The nine-hole layout-to-be is scheduled to be built with $4,200 gleaned through the offices of Col. Earl V. Riley, post commander at Hondo Air Base," the article noted. Additional funding came from a "special grant" as well as a sizeable donation from the "3304 Pilot Training Squadron Unit Fund," with dirt donated by Texas Aviation Industries. The site the members selected was in the southeast corner of the base on land previously leased to rancher Jim Anderson. Once completed, the newspaper observed, primary access would be to base personnel, although in acknowledgement of the financial support of Hondo residents, there would be provisions for the general community as well. After the base closed and the property transferred to the city, the facility formally became a public course by the 1960s.[12]

Credit for construction of the course generally goes to the base commander, who made the project viable. A native of Belton, Texas, Lt. Col. Earl Vaughan Riley began collegiate studies at Southwest

Texas State Teachers College in San Marcos but interrupted his education in 1940 to pursue flight training in California. Initially a P-51 Mustang fighter pilot, he eventually flew more than two hundred combat missions, earning an impressive number of medals, including the Distinguished Flying Cross with one oak leaf cluster and the Special Breast Award of the Cloud and Banner. Following the war, he served at Kelly Air Force Base in San Antonio and at other bases, including those in Amarillo and Laredo, before taking command at Hondo in January 1954. The air force transferred him to the Northeast in 1955, and after other tours of duty, he retired to San Antonio in 1964. In appreciation of his passion for golf and his leadership in establishing the Hondo course, a longstanding annual tournament dating to 1956 bore his name. For many years, Riley returned to Hondo to attend the event and to present trophies to the winners. While he no doubt deserved overall credit for the course, another name perhaps bears remembering as well. Joe Mitchell, who lettered as an athlete and served as captain of the golf team at Sam Houston State University in Huntsville, Texas, later served as an early instructor at the Hondo course. A 1959 newspaper article in Las Vegas, New Mexico, where he then served as the new pro, noted that Mitchell "built the golf course at Hondo Air Force Base." (Efforts to confirm that distinction through available records and other sources, though, proved inconclusive.)[13]

The Hondo Golf Course remains essentially the same as originally designed, although as with many courses of that era, there have been some changes. At Hondo these include the removal of base structures and impediments, construction of a new clubhouse, the renumbering of some holes, and the addition of an irrigation system. While much has also changed in the surrounding cultural landscape since the 1940s when Hondo Army Air Field reigned as the nation's largest air-navigation training facility and planes flew above the former farm fields day and night, there are still vestiges of that era for those who look carefully. Current aerial maps, for example, clearly show the ghost marks of former street alignments.

EPILOGUE

FROM THE
NINETEENTH HOLE

In the golf tradition, the so-called nineteenth hole is a place of rest and reflection where one follows up a round of play with good food and maybe a round or two of drinks. It is also a place to wind down and to revisit the game with friends and competitors and reminisce about the great and near-great shots of the day. Following in that storied analytical tradition—albeit without the food and drink—this is the appropriate point to ponder the eighteen stories that have led readers to this epilogue. The chapters, as noted in the introduction, represent a commonality of place in that all played out on Texas cultural landscapes that are now active golf courses. Some vestiges of the past remain readily discernible in terms of names or ruins, but for the most part the landscapes reflect dramatic changes over time, from places of historical significance to current landmarks of recreation. Change underpins history, which when properly nurtured, preserved, and interpreted, can continue on despite the loss of a physical place. The *sense* of place, however, often endures, especially for those who cherish the past and seek out connections in situ.

In addition to the sense of place that interlaces the stories in this book—despite the obvious diversity of time, events, people, and geography—there are a number of shared similarities that speak more directly to the need for preservation. In general, the historical details of sites that predate current golf courses are often fragmented and dispersed, awaiting the work of historians, archivists, and others to bring together the disparate pieces and perspectives. This is understandable, in part, because of the nature of community development. As towns and counties grow and sprawl across the landscape, even historical sites—and particularly those marginalized over time—are subject to a variety of lost and compromised resources, from artifacts and buried features to historical documents, period photographs, and oral histories. Federal and state efforts to mitigate the effect of public-sector growth through mandated cultural resource management procedures have worked in some important respects, but in many cases the weight of greater social and economic considerations can be overwhelming. Even golf courses themselves have limited lives in that regard, and a number of courses originally slated for this book closed before research even got underway. One tenet of preservation is that it is not permanent. At its best it can be trans-generational; that is, one generation decides to preserve a site and then eventually passes it along in trust to another, which in turn has to evaluate that shared commitment through its own value systems and available resources. At any point along the timeline, one generation can make decisions that break that chain of inheritance.

While the historical resources for precourse uses can often be difficult to recover or reconstruct, the histories of these emerging recreational sites can be even more problematic and subject to loss. Even the best-maintained and revered courses have been altered considerably from their original designs due to changes in game technology, environmental considerations, or societal preferences. More importantly for sports historians, though, is the lack of accessible archival resources. Golf professionals are not historians, and their files are not considered archival collections, although they may hold important historical resources. In general, though, the records are largely related to the operation of a business, which can present many gaps. There are few photos of site development, for example, and even fewer records of archeological investigations, especially for private courses. Where photos are available, most are posed shots of tournament winners or distant shots of players in action. Surprisingly, there are also few records on the course designers themselves beyond their names and lists of other projects. In some cases, particularly with older, rural courses, even that scant information has been lost or forgotten. Research on one site noted in this book never yielded precise information on its designer, developers, or date of construction, leaving a gap that could only be narrowed, though not closed, by limited related sources. The authors hope that this book may spur further investigations at the local level that will eventually tell the complete story of that course and others.

Even when basic course-development information is available and accessible, though, it can sometimes be confusing and contradictory. There are myriad discrepancies even with biographical information on some of the better-known designers, such as Tilly Tillinghast and John Bredemus. Incorrect or misleading information can then be picked up and distributed widely through promotional materials and social media, making it difficult to track information back to a reasonably reliable source. Newspapers generally serve as worthy complements to sketchy developmental records, as do focused interviews by journalists and sportswriters. While limited in scope, they nevertheless often serve in lieu of professional oral history interviews, which are preferred by historians but rare. Perhaps through this call for preservation, those trained in oral history methodologies will seek to record the memories of landscape architects, golf pros, maintenance professionals, board members, and others associated with how the game works at the course level. The memories of players are important and encouraged, but so too are first-person insights into the design principles that challenge the players and lend credence to their legends.

The analytical perspective from this particular nineteenth hole is that history is all around us, and much of it is worthy of preservation and recognition. That can be addressed through easements and covenants, avoidance, designations, promotional materials, and other means of historical and archeological awareness. Where preservation is no longer a viable option, though, interpretation is vital to keeping the stories moving from one generation to another. Such measures as historical markers and signage, oral histories, and records donations to local archives can help in that process.

There is in all of this what educators call a transference of learning. That transference may come through the recognition that all sites have inherent history and that some of those aspects of the past may be worth preserving or interpreting to share with future generations. It may come through the realization that history can be fun or that education and recreation are not mutually exclusive. It may also serve to remind golfers, in particular, that there are even more layers to the game than they previously realized. It is just one more thing for them to remember when they stride across historic grounds to address the ball or gather at the nineteenth to reminisce.

NOTES

CHAPTER 1

1. Wann Langston Jr., *The Onion Creek Mosasaur*, Museum Notes 10 (Austin: Texas Memorial Museum, 1966), 10.

2. Ibid., 14.

3. Stephen E. Clabaugh and Angel D. Leshikar, eds., "The Onion Creek Mosasaur," *The University of Texas Department of Geology Newsletter* 15 (Sept. 1966): 1, 4–5; Matthew A. Brown, director of vertebrate paleontology, Jackson School Museum of Earth History, University of Texas at Austin, email message to Dan K. Utley, Oct. 19, 2016.

4. "Fierce Mosasaur Reptile Uncovered by 2 Students of University of Texas," *Longview (TX) Daily News*, June 7, 1936, 18; "At Museum: Big Lizard to be Seen," *Austin Statesman*, Apr. 13, 1965, 25.

5. National Park Service, US Department of the Interior, *El Camino Real de los Tejas National Historic Trail: Comprehensive Management Plan/Environmental Assessment* (Santa Fe, NM: National Trails Intermountain Region, NPS, 2011), 7, 21–23.

6. Wayne Gard, "The Shawnee Trail," *Southwestern Historical Quarterly* 56, no. 3 (Jan. 1953): 363.

7. T. R. Havins, "Texas Fever," *Southwestern Historical Quarterly* 52, no. 1 (July 1948): 147; Wayne Gard, "Retracing the Chisholm Trail," *Southwestern Historical Quarterly* 60, no. 1 (July 1956): 57–58.

8. Gard, "Retracing the Chisholm Trail," 67.

9. Robert Baeumel, *The Legends of Onion Creek* (Austin: K & C Publishing, 2012), 50–52; "Legends of Golf Tournament," 1978 tournament program in possession of Dan K. Utley, unnumbered page.

10. Baeumel, *Legends of Onion Creek*, 101–8; list of participants, "Legends of Golf Tournament," n.p.; Chuck Clark, "New Course Opens," *Austin American Statesman*, May 26, 1974, C7; "Onion Creek Club Opening: Show Biz Celebrities Due Here," ibid., Apr. 21, 1974, B1; Bill Kennedy, "For $100,000: Snead, Dickinson Take Legends' Top Prize," *Taylor (TX) Daily Press*, May 1, 1978, 6.

Chapter 2

1. Gary L. Pinkerton, *Trammel's Trace: The First Road to Texas from the North* (College Station: Texas A&M University Press, 2016), 1; personal recollection of Dan K. Utley, based on a presentation by Bruce Nightengale, archeologist with the Lower Colorado River Authority, ca. 1996.

2. Gunnar Brune, *Springs of Texas*, vol. 1 (Fort Worth: Branch-Smith, 1981), 449–52.

3. Douglas K. Boyd, "What Do Golf and Archeology Have in Common?" *Heritage 4* (2007): 10–13.

4. Ibid., 10–11.

5. Douglas K. Boyd and Karl W. Kibler, "Geoarcheological Investigations at the San Felipe Springs Site, 41VV444," in *"Val Verde on the Sunny Rio Grande": Geoarcheological and Historical Investigations at San Felipe Springs, Val Verde County, Texas,* ed. Gemma Mehalchick et al., Reports of Investigations 122 (Austin: Prewitt and Associates, 1999), 93, 133; ibid., xi; "Toyah Horizon," Texas beyond History, accessed Apr. 16, 2017, https://www.texasbeyondhistory.net/st-plains/prehistory/images/toyah.html.

6. Doug Braudaway, "Camp Michie: A World War One Era Training Camp in Del Rio," 2006, Val Verde County Marker Files, Texas Historical Commission, Austin; Terri Myers, "Historic Overview of San Felipe Springs, Del Rio, and Val Verde County, Texas," in Mehalchick et al., *"Val Verde on the Sunny Rio Grande,"* 42.

7. "Regimental Notes," *Cavalry Journal* 30, no. 122 (Jan. 1921): 329; Nathan C. Shiverick, "The Twelfth Cavalry on the Road," *Cavalry Journal* 31, no. 126 (Jan. 1922): 60–61.

8. Myers, "Historic Overview of San Felipe Springs," 52–53.

9. "Thorpe Rolls Up a Record Score: Breaks the Record in the All-Around A.A.U. Championship, Scoring 7,476 Points," *Brooklyn (NY) Daily Eagle*, Sept. 3, 1912, 22; "Bredemus, Thorpe's Successor, Made No Records in College," *Huntington (IN) Herald*, Feb. 8, 1913, 6; "Thorpe Victim of Circumstances Says Friedman," *Harrisburg (PA) Telegraph*, Jan. 28, 1913, 1; Terri Myers, "Descriptions and Assessments of Historic Properties," in Mehalchick et al., *"Val Verde on the Sunny Rio Grande,"* 53–54; Harvey Penick with Bud Shrake, *Harvey Penick's Little Red Book: Lessons and Teachings From a Lifetime of Golf* (New York: Simon and Schuster, 1992), 142–47; Art Stricklin, *Links, Lore, & Legends: The Story of Texas Golf* (Lanham, MD: First Taylor, 2005), LOC 188–256, Kindle ed. Some sources indicate that Bredemus was Irish, but the 1900 Federal Census, taken when he was a sixteen-year-old student, shows that both of his parents listed Germany as their birthplaces. Such a notation is understandable,

given the complexities of historical associations between Luxembourg and Germany. Extrapolating from the dates of the children's birth years, it appears that the family emigrated to the United States around 1882. The 1900 census also lists Adam Bredemus, his father, as a saloon keeper.

10. Penick, *Harvey Penick's Little Red Book*, 145.

11. Ibid., 145–47; "Inductees," Texas Golf Hall of Fame, accessed Apr. 16, 2017, http://texasgolfhof.org/inductees.

CHAPTER 3

1. William Edward Dunn, "The Apache Mission on the San Sabá River: Its Founding and Failure," *Southwestern Historical Quarterly* 17, no. 4 (Apr. 1914): 379–414; Kathleen Kirk Gilmore, "San Luis de las Amarillas Presidio," June 15, 2010, *Handbook of Texas Online*, accessed Dec. 21, 2016, http:// tshaonline.org/handbook/online/articles/uqs28; Robert S. Weddle, "Santa Cruz de San Sabá Mission," June 15, 2010, ibid., accessed Dec. 21, 2016, http://www.tshaonline.org/handbook/online/articles/uqs36.

2. Robert S. Weddle, *The San Sabá Mission: Spanish Pivot in Texas* (Austin: University of Texas Press, 1964), 53, 75.

3. Ibid., 78.

4. Ibid., 212; Lauren Whitman, "Ceramic Analysis and Interpretation from Presidio San Saba (41MN1), Menard, Texas" (MA thesis, Texas Tech University, 2009), 14–15; David Stanley Weir, "Ruin of Ruins: (Re) Building Myth and Memory in Menard, Tx." (MA thesis, Texas Tech University, 2004), 30–46; James Ivey et al., "A Reexamination of the Site of Presidio San Sabá," *La Tierra: Journal of the Southern Texas Archeological Association* 8, no. 4 (1981): 3–8; Tamra L Walter, "The Archeology of Presidio San Sabá: A Preliminary Report," *Historical Archaeology* 38, no. 3 (2004): 94–105.

5. Jesse Milligan, "A Man and a Mission," *Fort Worth Star-Telegram*, Oct. 22, 2003, 1F, Newspapers.com; John Reynolds, "Archaeologists on Historical Mission," *Lubbock (TX) Avalanche-Journal*, Nov. 2, 2003, Newspapers.com.

6. Harold Schoen, comp., *Monuments Erected by the State of Texas to Commemorate the Centenary of Texas Independence: The Report of the Commission of Control for Texas Centennial Celebrations* (Austin: Commission of Control for Texas Centennial Celebrations, 1938), 45; "Contract Is Let by State for Reconstructing Old Landmark," *Lubbock (TX) Morning Avalanche*, Dec. 11, 1936, 13.

7. Rhonda Lashley, "Christopher Reeve Has Old Ties to Hill Country Theater," *Kerrville (TX) Times*, June 11, 1995, 1.

8. Official dedication program, "The Fall of the Mission San Saba," May 8, 1937, copy in author's possession.

9. J. Marvin Hunter, "The Restoration of Mission San Saba," *Frontier Times* 14, no. 9 (July 1937): 406.

10. "Centuries-Old Spanish Fort May Rise Again at Menard," *Abilene Reporter-News*, Apr. 9, 1959, 9.

11. "Menard Airport," *Denton (TX) Record-Chronicle*, Sept. 25, 1929, 18; Dissamae Lorrain, site analysis for Texas Parks and Wildlife Department, Apr. 14, 1972, copy in State Archeological Landmark Files, Texas Historical Commission, Austin.

12. Menard County Historical Society, *Menard County History: An Anthology* (San Angelo, TX: Anchor, 1982), 99–100.

13. Jason Stone, "Archeology and Golf Seek Harmony in Menard, Texas," Nov. 4, 2003, Texas Golf Courses Golfnow, accessed Dec. 27, 2016, www.golftexas.com/departments/features/menard-texas-golf.htm.

CHAPTER 4

1. David B. Gracy II, *Moses Austin: His Life* (San Antonio: Trinity University Press, 1987), 4–5, 201–2; Eugene C. Barker, *The Life of Stephen F. Austin, Founder of Texas, 1793–1836* (Austin: Texas State Historical Association, 1949), 25.

2. Charles A. Bacarisse, "Baron de Bastrop," *Southwestern Historical Quarterly* 58, no. 3 (Jan. 1955): 319–26.

3. Gregg Cantrell, *Stephen F. Austin: Empresario of Texas* (New Haven, CT: Yale University Press, 1999), 97; Noah Smithwick, *The Evolution of a State, or Recollections of Old Texas Days* (Austin: Gammel, 1900), 55.

4. Smithwick, *Evolution of a State*, 59–61; Barker, *Life of Stephen F. Austin*, 78; Richard W. Moore, "Bastrop, Baron de," last modified May 9, 2016, *Handbook of Texas Online*, accessed Mar. 5, 2017, http://www.tshaonline.org/handbook/online/articles/fbaae; Michael R. Moore, "Regulation Double Log Cabins—The Built Environment of Colonial San Felipe de Austin," report prepared for the Texas Historical Commission, 2014, unpublished manuscript, excerpted copy provided by Site Manager Bryan McAuley, in author's possession.

5. Bryan McAuley, oral history interview by Dan K. Utley, San Felipe de Austin State Historic Site, Mar. 8, 2017; Charles Christopher Jackson, "San Felipe de Austin, TX," last modified May 9, 2016, *Handbook of Texas Online*, accessed Mar. 12, 2017, http://www.tshaonline.org/handbook/online/articles/hls10.

6. Jackson, "San Felipe de Austin, TX."

7. McAuley, interview.

8. "SFA Golf Course Planned," *Brookshire (TX) Times*, Nov. 13, 1952, 1; "Golf Course Due for State Park," *Corsicana (TX) Daily Sun*, May 8, 1952, 13; *Lubbock (TX) Morning Avalanche*, Feb. 12, 1953, 16; "Senate Hears Plan to Give Negroes Equal Park Rights," *Abilene (TX) Reporter-News*, Feb. 9, 1951, 3; Ricky F. Dobbs, *Yellow Dogs and Democrats: Allan Shivers and Texas Two-Party Politics* (College Station: Texas A&M University Press, 2005), 55–56; "Stephen F. Austin Golf Association Plans Opening Sunday, July 18," *Brookshire (TX) Times*, July 15, 1964, 1.

9. "SFAGA Lady Golfers Organize; Have Play Day Thursdays," *Brookshire (TX) Times*, Sept. 16, 1954, 1; "Humble Announces Katy District Management Changes," *Brookshire (TX) Times*, Dec. 29, 1966, 1; Tom Davison, "Old Stephen Would Have Been Proud of the New Generation," Golfing Corner, *Houston Chronicle*, undated photocopy, Historical Files, Stephen F. Austin Golf Course.

10. "Nine Holes to Be Added at S.F.A. Golf Course," *Brookshire (TX) Times*, Aug. 5, 1971, 13; copy of kiosk text, provided by Bryan McAuley, site manager, Stephen F. Austin State Historic Site; Dan K. Utley, personal inspection of golf course, Mar. 9, 2017.

CHAPTER 5

1. "Butterfield Stage Moves Mail along Trail to San Francisco," *El Paso Herald-Post*, Oct. 1, 1958, 7; "'Boom!' Stagecoach Rolls into E.P. and Happy Folks Turn Out Big Welcome," *El Paso Herald-Post*, Sept. 30, 1958, 1.

2. Ben F. Dixon, "Butterfield Mail Centennial," *History News*, Sept. 1958, 86–88.

3. Devin Leonard, *Neither Snow nor Rain: A History of the United States Postal Service* (New York: Grove, 2016), 853/6973, Kindle ed.

4. Roscoe Conkling and Margaret B. Conkling, *The Butterfield Overland Mail, 1857–1869: Its Organization and Operation over the Southern Route to 1861; Subsequently over the Central Route to 1866; and under Wells, Fargo and Company in 1869*, vol. 1 (Glendale, CA: Arthur H. Clark, 1947), 30–36.

5. Glen Sample Ely, *The Texas Frontier and the Butterfield Overland Mail, 1858–1861* (Norman: University of Oklahoma Press, 2016), 13–14.

6. Ibid.

7. Ibid., 16.

8. Ibid.

9. Ibid., 220–46; J. W. Williams, "The Butterfield Overland Mail Road across Texas," *Southwestern Historical Quarterly* 61, no. 1 (July 1957): 1–19.

10. Ely, *Texas Frontier and the Butterfield Overland Mail*, 351–53.

11. FAZIO Design, accessed July 2, 2016, www.faziodesign.com; Edward

Kiersh, "A Master by Design: Tom Fazio," Oct. 1, 1999, *Cigar Aficionado*, accessed June 28, 2016, cigaraficionado.com.

CHAPTER 6

1. Brenda B. Whorton and S. Alan Skinner, "Application for Official Texas Historical Marker, Subject: Coho Smith Site (41PR27)," 1–22, Parker County Marker Files, Texas Historical Commission, Austin.

2. Ibid., 1.

3. Coho Smith, "Dallas County Long Ago: Reminiscences of Pioneer Life by Coho Smith of Azle," letter to *Dallas Morning News*, July 30, 1903, Newspapers.com.

4. Whorton and Skinner, "Application," 5–11; William S. Warren, "Smith, John Jeremiah [Coho]," July 24, 2014, *Handbook of Texas Online*, accessed July 10, 2016, http://www.tshaonline.org/handbook/online/articles/fsmco; Iva Roe Logan, ed., *Cohographs by Coho* (Fort Worth: Branch-Smith, 976), i–xiv.

5. Whorton and Skinner, "Application," 11–12.

6. Ibid., 13; marker inscription for Coho and Nancy Jane Smith Farmstead Site, Parker County Marker Files.

7. "Feature Interview with Jeff Brauer," May 2011, Golf Club Atlas, accessed July 7, 2016, golfclubatlas.com/feature-interview/jeffrey-brauer-may-2011.

8. Ibid.

CHAPTER 7

1. Henry C. Dethloff, *A Centennial History of Texas A&M University, 1876–1976*, 2 vols. (College Station: Texas A&M University Press, 1975), 1:5; Clarence Ousley, *History of the Agricultural and Mechanical College of Texas*, Bulletin of the Agricultural and Mechanical College of Texas, 4th ser., vol. 6, no. 8 (College Station: Agricultural and Mechanical College of Texas, 1935), 39.

2. Dethloff, *Centennial History*, 1:5, 9–11, 14–16.

3. Ibid., 18–20.

4. Ibid., 18–20; Ousley, *History of the Agricultural and Mechanical College of Texas*, 40–42.

5. Ousley, *History of the Agricultural and Mechanical College of Texas*, 43.

6. Ibid., 46.

7. Dethloff, *Centennial History*, 2:534.

8. David L. Chapman, "Fore! Fifty-Five Years of the Texas A&M Golf Course," *Texas Aggie*, Jan.–Feb. 2006, 30; original course scorecard, Texas

A&M Rec Sports Files, Private Collection of Mark J. Haven.

9. Lou Duran and Jeff Brauer, "Ralph Plummer: Golf Course Architect," Aug. 2006, Golf Club Atlas, accessed Jan. 27, 2017, golfclubatlas.com/in-my-opinion/ lou-duran-jeff-brauer-ralph-plummer-golf-course-architect/.

10. "A. O. Nicholson to Be Present for Dedication of Aggie Golf Course," *The Eagle (Bryan, TX)*, Dec. 5, 1950, 7; "Bauer Sisters to Be on Hand for Opening of Aggie Golf Course," ibid., Nov. 30, 1950, 6.

11. Original course scorecard; Dethloff, *Centennial History*, 2:533.

12. "Ground Broken for Clubhouse," *Bryan (TX) Daily Eagle*, Apr. 10, 1969, 5; Chapman, "Fore!"

13. Richard Croome, "The Campus Course at Texas A&M Readies for Its First Game," Oct. 20, 2013, *The Eagle (Bryan, TX)*, http://www.theeagle. com/news/local/the-campus-course-at-texas-a-m-readies-for-its/ article_0aaae5f8-d519-57a5-a1a7-a5e6edc3ad75.html.

CHAPTER 8

1. Charles G. Davis, "Yellow House Draw," June 15, 2010, *Handbook of Texas Online*, accessed Feb. 22, 2017, http://www.tshaonline.org/hand-book/online/articles/rky01; William C. Griggs, "The Battle of Yellowhouse Canyon in 1877," *West Texas Historical Association Year Book* 51 (1975): 38.

2. John R. Cook, *The Border and the Buffalo: An Untold Story of the Southwest Plains* (repr., Buffalo Gap, TX: State House, 2009), 197; Griggs, "Battle of Yellowhouse Canyon," 38.

3. Cook, *Border and the Buffalo*, 194; A. C. Greene, *The Last Captive: The Lives of Herman Lehmann, Who Was Taken by the Indians as a Boy From His Texas Home & Adopted by Them. . . .* (Austin: Encino, 1972), 114.

4. Greene, *Last Captive*, 114–15; Griggs, "Battle of Yellowhouse Canyon," 42–48.

5. Griggs, "Battle of Yellowhouse Canyon," 48–50; Ray Westbrook, "In 1877, Mackenzie Park Was Site of Deadly Battle," *Lubbock (TX) Avalanche-Journal*, Nov. 27, 2007, Newspapers.com; Sharon Cunningham, "Yellow House Canyon Fight," *Wild West* 16, no. 1 (June 2003), online version.

6. "New Municipal Golf Course Will Be Built for Followers of Sport," *Lubbock (TX) Morning Avalanche*, Sept. 13, 1928, 4; "Arthur Allen Bonebrake," death certificate and various records, accessed Feb. 17, 2017, Ancestry.com.

7. "New Municipal Golf Course North of City Opened to Public Today: Public Links to Furnish Need of Lubbock Section," *Lubbock (TX) Morning Avalanche*, Apr. 12, 1929, 6; advertisement, "Golfers, Here's Good News," ibid., Sept. 14, 1929, 6.

8. "State Park, CCC Camp Seem Near," *Lubbock (TX) Morning Avalanche*, Jan. 10, 1935, 6, 10; James Wright Steely, *Parks for Texas: Enduring Landscapes of the New Deal* (Austin: University of Texas Press, 1999), 217.

9. Collier Parris, "A Golf Course for 'Fun,'" Sportometer, *Lubbock (TX) Evening Journal*, June 2, 1939, 4.

10. "Recalls Career's Thrills: New President Warren Cantrell Plans to Restore PGA Prestige," *Lubbock (TX) Morning Avalanche*, Aug. 22, 1957, 6, 8, Newspapers.com (shown as 18, 20); Ray Westbrook, "Warren Cantrell Inducted into Golf Hall of Fame," *Lubbock (TX) Avalanche-Journal*, Nov. 6, 2010, Newspapers.com.

CHAPTER 9

1. Reid E. Meyers, *The Ghosts of Old Brack: A Pictorial History of the Brackenridge Park Golf Course* (Anacortes, WA: Mira Digital Publishing, 2010), 7–8; Marilyn McAdams Sibley, *George W. Brackenridge: Maverick Philanthropist* (Austin: University of Texas Press, 1973), LOC 2475–2537, e-book version; Joe Stubblefield, Steven Land Tillotson, and Daniel Hardy, preparers, "National Register of Historic Places Nomination for San Antonio Water Works Pump Station No. 2," 1981, sec. 8, Texas Historical Commission, Austin; "Brackenridge, George Washington," last modified Aug. 19, 2016, *Handbook of Texas Online*, accessed Nov. 25, 2016, http://www.tshaonline.org/handbook/online/articles/fbr02.

2. "Brackenridge, George Washington"; Meyers, *Ghosts of Old Brack*, 7–8. The Brackenridge Hall known as B Hall no longer exists. It is not to be confused with the present Brackenridge Hall, a dormitory on the University of Texas campus a few blocks south of the earlier structure.

3. Meyers, *Ghosts of Old Brack*, 7–8; Sibley, *George W. Brackenridge*, LOC 2690–2697.

4. Gilbert C. Fite, "Gutzon Borglum: Mercurial Master of Colossal Art," *Montana: The Magazine of Western History* 25, no. 2 (Spring 1975): 4, 6; "Warrant to Arrest Sculptor Is Issued," *Galveston Daily News*, Feb. 26, 1925, 1; "Gutzon Borglum, Famous Sculptor, Died in Chicago," *Corsicana (TX) Semi-Weekly Light*, Mar. 7, 1941, 11; "Gutzon Borglum Deposed Sculptor to Carve in Texas," *The Eagle (Bryan, TX)*, Aug. 5, 1925, 1.

5. Stubblefield et al., "National Register of Historic Places Nomination for San Antonio Water Works Pump Station No. 2"; Caroline Remy, "Borglum, John Gutzon de la Mothe," last modified Aug. 19, 2014, *Handbook of Texas Online*, accessed Nov. 17, 2016, http://tshaonline.org/handbook/online/articles/fbo31.

6. Carol Morris Little, *A Comprehensive Guide to Outdoor Sculpture*

in Texas (Austin: University of Texas Press, 1996), 401–2; Gutzon Borglum to Charles Gibson, Sept. 5, 1934, Robin Borglum Kennedy Papers, quoted in Norman C. Delaney, "Gutzon Borglum's Vision for Corpus Christi's Bayfront," part of Official Texas Historical Marker Application for John Gutzon de la Mothe Borglum, Nueces County Marker Files, Texas Historical Commission, Austin.

7. "Henry Lee McFee, 67, Southland Artist, Dies," *Los Angeles Times,* Mar. 21, 1953, 13.

8. Meyers, *Ghosts of Old Brack*, 22; "Employ Golf Expert," *San Antonio Light*, Sept. 21, 1915, 3; "Golf Expert on Way," ibid., Sept. 29, 1915, 1; "City Workmen Clear Ground with Dispatch," ibid., Oct. 6, 1915, 3.

9. Maria Watson Pfeiffer and Steve A. Tomka, preparers, "National Register of Historic Places Registration for Brackenridge Park," 2008, secs. 7, 8, Texas Historical Commission.

10. Ibid.

11. Meyers, *Ghosts of Old Brack*, 32–44, 86.

12. Ibid., 80–85.

CHAPTER 10

1. "San Francisco Xavier de Náxara Mission," in *The New Handbook of Texas*, ed. Ron Tyler et al., 6 vols. (Austin: Texas State Historical Association, 1996), 5:849–50; San Francisco Xavier de Nájara, Bexar County, Official Texas Historical Marker Files, Texas Historical Commission, Austin; Thomas E. Alexander and Dan K. Utley, *Faded Glory: A Century of Forgotten Texas Military Sites, Then and Now* (Texas A&M University Press, 2012), 87–89.

2. Alexander and Utley, *Faded Glory*, 87–89; Dale L. Walker, *The Boys of '98: Theodore Roosevelt and the Rough Riders* (New York: Tom Doherty Associates, 1998), 48–58; Joseph G. Dawson III, "William T. Sampson and Santiago: Blockade, Victory, and Controversy," in *Crucible of Empire: The Spanish-American War & Its Aftermath*, ed. James C. Bradford (Annapolis, MD: Naval Institute Press, 1993), 48–50.

3. Carmelita Funk Faught, "Theodore Roosevelt's Rough Riders in San Antonio, Texas" (MA thesis, University of Texas at Austin, 1950), 9–14; "Warren, Francis Emroy (1844–1929)," *Biographical Directory of the United States Congress, 1774–Present*, accessed Mar. 30, 2016, bioguide.congress. gov/scripts/biodisplay.pl?index=w000164.

4. Faught, "Roosevelt's Rough Riders," 22–25; John C. Rayburn, "The Rough Riders in San Antonio, 1898," *Arizona and the West* 3, no. 2 (Summer 1961): 115; San Antonio International Fair advertisements, 1906, University of Texas at San Antonio Libraries Special Collections (online version).

5. Nathan Miller, *Theodore Roosevelt: A Life* (New York: William Morrow, 1992), 277.

6. Ibid.; "Aristocrats and Cowboys: Odd Mixture in Teddy Roosevelt's Regiment of Rough Riders," *Salt Lake Herald* (Salt Lake City, UT), May 12, 1898, 3.

7. Theodore Roosevelt, *The Rough Riders* (New York: P. F. Collier & Son, 1899), 27 Kindle ed.; Rayburn, "Rough Riders in San Antonio," 117.

8. Walker, *Boys of '98*, 123, 125.

9. Ibid., 122–23; Tom Hall, *The Fun and Fighting of the Rough Riders* (New York: Frederick A. Stokes, 1899), 47–50.

10. "Shot Lights: Rough Riders Made Good Their Name by Causing Terror in San Antonio," *Guthrie (OK) Daily Leader*, May 28, 1898, 4.

11. Walker, *Boys of '98*, 133.

12. Miller, *Theodore Roosevelt*, 309–11.

13. Roosevelt, *Rough Riders*, 47–48; Richard A. Marini, "Remembering Teddy's Three Trips to S.A.," *San Antonio Express-News*, Jan. 26, 2015, Newspapers.com.

14. "Ascarate Municipal Golf Course," Texas Golf Courses Golfnow, accessed Apr. 1, 2016, www.golftexas.com/golf-courses/west/el-paso/ascarate.htm; George Adolph Hoffman, US draft registration card, 1942, accessed Apr. 1, 2016, Ancestry.com; "Olmos Basin Golf Course," Alamo City Golf Trail, accessed Apr. 1, 2016, http://alamocitygolftrail.com/san-antonio-golf-courses/olmos-basin-golf-course/.

15. A. W. Tillinghast Association, accessed Apr. 1, 2016, www.tillinghast.net; Dave Clark, "George Jacobus, Ridgewood's Head Golf Professional for More Than Half a Century," Ridgewood Country Club, accessed Mar. 30, 2016, www.rcc1890.com/files/GeorgeJacobus_Jan2014.pdf.

16. Harold Henk, phone conversation with Stanley O. Graves, Mar. 30, 2016.

Chapter 11

1. Charlene Nash, *Lampasas County: Its History and Its People* (Maceline, MO: Walsworth, 1991), 5.

2. Janet Mace Valenza, *Taking the Waters in Texas: Springs, Spas, and Fountains of Youth* (Austin: University of Texas Press, 2000), 1328, Kindle ed.

3. Gunnar Brune, *Springs of Texas*, vol. 1 (Fort Worth: Branch-Smith, 1981), 286–87.

4. Glynda Carson Carpenter, *The History of Hancock Springs, 1852–1992* (Lampasas: Oran Milo Roberts Chapter of the Daughters of the Republic of Texas, 1992), 17–18.

5. Ibid., 25–33; "To Buy Hancock Park: Baptists of Texas Are Discussing Plans for Future," *Dallas Morning News*, June 28, 1907, 3.

6. Carpenter, *History of Hancock Springs*, 38–41; Nash, *Lampasas County*, 63; Camp Marlamont advertisement, *Houston Post*, May 14, 1922, 2; Camp Marlamont advertisement, *Waco News-Tribune*, May 29, 1921, 12.

7. Carpenter, *History of Hancock Springs*, 42; Glynda Carpenter, "Hancock Springs Swimming Pool Celebrating 100 Years, 1911–2011," *Lampasas (TX) Dispatch Record*, June 7, 2011, Newspapers.com.

8. Van Berry and Harold Harton, conversations with Dan K. Utley and Stanley O. Graves, Hancock Park Municipal Golf Course, Lampasas, Jan. 3, 2017; Van Berry, subsequent email correspondence with Dan K. Utley, Jan. 5, 2017; Nash, *Lampasas County*, 87, 224.

CHAPTER 12

1. James McWilliams, *The Pecan: America's Favorite Nut* (Austin: University of Texas Press, 2013), 2.

2. Ibid., 3.

3. Ibid.

4. Jane Manaster, *Pecans: The Story in a Nutshell* (Lubbock: Texas Tech University Press, 2008), 14; McWilliams, *Pecan*, 7.

5. McWilliams, *Pecan*, 43–44.

6. Ibid., 54–55.

7. Bonnye Stuart, *It Happened in Louisiana: Remarkable Events That Shaped History* (Guilford, CT: Globe Pequot, 2015), 18–20.

8. "Pecan Breeder Who Gave Texas Start in Improved Kinds Dies after Poet's Wish Is Fulfilled," *Dallas Morning News*, Sept. 24, 1940, 9; San Saba County Deed Records, 1:437, San Saba County Clerk's Office.

9. Lester Bowles and Izola Crumley Bowles, oral history interview by Dan K. Utley, June 30, 1995; Dan K. Utley, *Through Boundary Waters: Continuing Historical Investigations along the Colorado River in Burnet and Travis Counties, Texas*, Cultural Resource Report 5 (Austin: Lower Colorado River Authority, 1996), 46–47.

10. L. J. Grauke and Tommy M. Thompson, "Pecans and Hickories," in *Fruit Breeding: Nuts*, ed. Jules Janick and James N. Moore, vol. 3 (New York: John Wiley and Sons, 1996), 198–200.

11. Nancy Richey Ranson, "San Saban Sends Gift of Pecans to Britain's Princess Elizabeth," Dallas Morning News, Nov. 29, 1947, 11.

12. "Letters from Readers," ibid., May 14, 1968, 2.

13. Ibid., Sept. 9, 1964, 2.

14. "Life Ends for E. Guy Risien," *San Saba News and Star*, Aug. 7, 1975, 1–2; "E. Guy Risien," Probate Records, San Saba County Clerk's Office.

15. "Proposed Golf Course Estimated at $31,000," *San Saba News and Star*, July 8, 1971, 1, 10, 12.

16. "The Round-Up," ibid., Oct. 21, 1971, 4.

17. "Local Golf Course Opening Draws Large Crowd Sunday," ibid., Aug. 31, 1972, 1, 10.

Chapter 13

1. Quoted in Robert S. Maxwell and Robert D. Baker, *Sawdust Empire: The Texas Lumber Industry, 1830–1940* (College Station: Texas A&M University Press, 1983), 3.

2. Ibid.; Curt Meine, *Aldo Leopold: His Life and Work* (Madison: University of Wisconsin Press, 1988), 75.

3. Bob Bowman, "Temple, Thomas Lewis Latané," in *The New Handbook of Texas*, ed. Ron Tyler et al., 6 vols. (Austin: Texas State Historical Association, 1996), 6:249; Laurence C. Walker, *Axes, Oxen and Men: A Pictorial History of the Southern Pine Lumber Company* (Diboll, TX: Angelina Free Press, 1975), 3–13.

4. Maxwell and Baker, *Sawdust Empire*, 45; Jonathan Gerland, "A Look at Two Early Angelina County Logging Camps through the U.S. Census of 1900," *The Pine Bough* (Diboll, TX), Dec. 1999, 27–29.

5. Jonathan Gerland, "A Brief Chronicle of Texas South-Eastern Railroad," *The Pine Bough* (Diboll, TX), Sept. 2000, 2–3; St. Clair Griffin Reed, *A History of the Texas Railroads; and of Transportation Conditions under Spain and Mexico and the Republic and the State* (Houston: St. Clair, 1941), 477–78; Charles P. Zlatkovich, *Texas Railroads: A Record of Construction and Abandonment* (Austin: Bureau of Business Research, University of Texas, and Texas State Historical Association, 1981), 92; "'Tap Line Case' Summary of Texas South-Eastern Railroad," Texas Transportation Archive, accessed June 2, 2016, www.ttarchive.com/ Library/Articles/Texas-South-Eastern_ICC-Tap-Line.html.

6. "$173,000 Park Grant Approved This Week," *Free Press* (Diboll, TX), Oct. 12, 1967, 1; "Our New City Park," ibid.; "Austin Firm Selected as Architect for City Park: Firm Said Top Notch on Parks," ibid., Nov. 23, 1967, 1.

7. Kevin Newberry, *Texas Golf: The Best of the Lone Star State* (Houston: Gulf Publishing, 1988), 459, 507; "Leon Howard, Courses Built," WorldGolf, accessed June 4, 2016, www.worldgolf.com/golf-architects/ leon-howard.html; "Leon Hugh Howard," obituary, *Austin American-Statesman*, Feb. 11, 2015, Newspapers.com; "Golf Course Delayed," *Free Press (Diboll, TX)*, June 18, 1970, 1; "Golf Course Officially Opens up This Weekend," ibid., Sept. 3, 1970, 8.

8. Stephen R. Lowe, "Demaret, Jimmy," Feb. 2000, *American National Biography Online*, accessed June 3, 2016, www.anb.org/articles/19/19-00351.html; untitled but captioned photograph, *Free Press* (Diboll, TX), Sept. 20, 1973, 3; James A. Wilson, "Demaret, Jimmie Newton," in Tyler et al., *New Handbook of Texas*, 2:584; "Jimmy Demaret, First Golfer to Win 3 Masters, Dies at 73," *New York Times*, Dec. 29, 1973, Newspapers. com.

9. Ernie Murray, "Neches Pine Gets Nod for Golf Course," *Free Press* (Diboll, TX), Aug. 1, 1991, 1.

CHAPTER 14

1. "Old Brickyard Review," [Aug. 14, 2011], TexasOutside.com, accessed Mar. 26, 2017, http://www.texasoutside.com/golf-courses/old-brickyard-in-ferris.

2. Edward F. Wegner, oral history interview by Dan K. Utley, Sept. 9, 1994, quoted in Thad Sitton and Dan K. Utley, *From Can See to Can't: Texas Cotton Farmers on the Southern Prairies* (Austin: University of Texas Press, 1997), 114; "The Mule," Bailey County Marker Files, Texas Historical Commission, Austin; Dan K. Utley and Cynthia J. Beeman, *History along the Way: Stories beyond the Texas Roadside Markers* (College Station: Texas A&M University Press, 2013), 29–30.

3. Dave Babb, "History of the Mule," American Mule Museum, accessed Mar. 21, 2017, http://www.mulemuseum.org/history-of-the-mule.html.

4. David Minor, "Ferris, Justus Wesley," June 12, 2010, *Handbook of Texas Online*, accessed Mar. 25, 2017, http://www.tshaonline.org/handbook/online/articles/ffe09; Brian Hart, "Ferris, TX," June 12, 2010, ibid., accessed Mar. 18, 2017, http://www.tshaonline.org/handbook/online/articles/hjf03; "Ferris Holds Title as 'Brick Capital," *Dallas Morning News*, Oct. 2, 1960, 4; Frank Bennett, R. T. Avon Burke, and Clarence Lounsburg, *Soil Survey of Ellis County, Texas* (Washington, DC: Government Printing Office, 1911), 23–24; "Brick Manufacturing in Ellis County," *Ellis County History*, Ellis County Museum, accessed Mar. 26, 2017, http://www.rootsweb.ancestry.com/~txecm/ellis.htm#Brick Industry.

5. "Brick Manufacturing in Ellis County"; "Texas Mule Man," *Dallas Morning News*, Aug. 7, 1956, 2; "Mule Train: Show Hitch Will Parade in Paris," *Paris (TX) News*, July 15, 1951, 2; "Ferris' Fame for Its Mules Travels Afar," *Waxahachie (TX) Daily Light*, Sept. 29, 1947, 4; Frank X. Tolbert, "Tolbert's Texas: Cotch 'Em Speaks on Mule-skinning," *Dallas Morning News*, Apr. 11, 1957, 1.

6. "Brick Manufacturing in Ellis County"; "Texas Mule Man"; Tolbert, "Cotch 'Em Speaks on Mule-skinning."

7. *Insperity Golf Bible to Dallas–Fort Worth*, 2013–2014 ([Mesquite, TX]: TexasGolfOn.com, n.d.), 122–25; "Old Brickyard Review."

CHAPTER 15

1. Thomas E. Alexander and Dan K. Utley, *Faded Glory: A Century of Forgotten Texas Military Sites, Then and Now* (Texas A&M University Press, 2012), 106; Charles H. Harris III and Louis R. Sadler, *The Great Call-Up: The Guard, the Border and the Mexican Revolution* (Norman: University of Oklahoma Press, 2015), 11–14, Kindle ed.

2. Harris and Sadler, *Great Call-Up*, 11–16.

3. Frank E. Vandiver, *Black Jack: The Life and Times of John J. Pershing*, vol. 2 (College Station: Texas A&M University Press, 1977), 604–6.

4. Alexander and Utley, *Faded Glory*, 117–18; Harris and Sadler, *Great Call-Up*, 19–21; Joseph A. Stout Jr., *Border Conflict: Villistas, Carrancistas and the Punitive Expedition, 1915–1920* (Fort Worth: Texas Christian University Press, 1999), 76–79.

5. Ronnie C. Tyler, "The Little Punitive Expedition in the Big Bend," *Southwestern Historical Quarterly* 78, no. 3 (Jan. 1975): 276–85; Alexander and Utley, *Faded Glory*, 117–18.

6. "Peons Mistaken for Villa Bandits: Alarm over Presence of 600 Hungry Mexicans in Lajitas Subsides," *Washington Times*, Apr. 30, 1916, 1; "200 Villistas Are Ready to Raid: Camped near Lajitas and Threaten to Cross Border and Raid Wheat Ranches," *El Paso Herald*, July 25, 1916, 4; "Bandits Head for the Line: Reported That Large Number Are Nearing La Jitas on Texas Border," *El Paso Herald*, Sept. 13, 1916, 4.

7. John H. Regan, "El Paso Boys Hike to Lajitas: None Drops Out on 17 Mile March under Pack; Face to Face with Mexico," *El Paso Herald*, July 12, 1916, 2.

8. Quoted in Vandiver, *Black Jack*, 668.

9. Clifford B. Casey, *Mirages, Mysteries and Reality: Brewster County, Texas, the Big Bend of the Rio Grande* (Seagraves, TX: Pioneer, 1972), 135–41; "Black Jack's Crossing That Was Once Home to Ambush Golf Course," Mar. 25, 2012, XtremeSport, accessed Apr. 3, 2017, http://xtremesport4u.com/extreme-land-sports/extreme-golf/is-this-golf-or-snooker/.

10. Steve Habel, "Excellence and Luxury in Stark Isolation," *Texas Golf Insider*, Summer/Fall 2015, 8–12.

Chapter 16

1. Robert V. Haynes, *A Night of Violence: The Houston Riot of 1917* (Baton Rouge: Louisiana State University Press, 1976), 49; "General John A. Logan, Memorial Day Founder," Jan. 21, 2015, Historical Army Foundation, accessed Apr. 30, 2017, https://armyhistory.org/general-john-a-logan-memorial-day-founder; General John A. Logan Museum, accessed Apr. 30, 2017, www.loganmuseum.org; Louis F. Aulbach, Linda C. Gorski, and Robbie Morin, *Camp Logan: Houston, Texas, 1917–1919* (Houston: Louis F. Aulbach, 2014), 11–14.

2. "Melons Make Happy the Negro Guards," *Houston Post*, July 29, 1917, 11; "A Need for Caution," ibid., July 31, 1917, 6.

3. Haynes, *Night of Violence*, 95–96; C. Calvin Smith, "The Houston Riot of 1917, Revisited," *Houston Review* 13, no. 2 (1991): 85–102; Robert V. Haynes, "The Houston Mutiny and Riot of 1917," *Southwestern Historical Quarterly* 76, no. 4 (Apr. 1973): 418–39; Edgar A. Schuler, "The Houston Race Riot, 1917," *Journal of Negro History* 29, no. 3 (July 1944): 314–32; Garna L. Christian, *Black Soldiers in Jim Crow Texas, 1899–1917* (College Station: Texas A&M University Press, 1995), 150–55.

4. Smith, "Houston Riot of 1917," 97; Haynes, "Houston Mutiny and Riot," 430fn.

5. Haynes, *Night of Violence*, 296.

6. Martha Gruening, "National Association for the Advancement of Colored People: Houston," *The Crisis*, Nov. 1917, 18–19.

7. "City Buys Logan Land for Park," *Houston Post*, May 4, 1924, 12; Roger G. Moore, William E. Moore, and David S. Pettus, *An Archeological Survey of Nine Land Units within Memorial Park in Houston (Harris County), Texas*, April 1989, Texas Antiquities Permit report, 11–17, Texas Historical Commission, Austin (access restrictions may apply).

8. Art Stricklin, *Links, Lore, and Legends: The Story of Texas Golf* (Lanham, MD: Taylor Trade Publishing, 2013), LOC 1138–1158/3679, Kindle ed.; Kevin Newberry, *Texas Golf: The Best of the Lone Star State* (Houston: Gulf Publishing, 1998), 213; "Hare & Hare," Cultural Landscape Foundation, accessed Apr. 30, 2017, https://tclf.org/pioneer/hare-hare.

9. Newberry, *Texas Golf*, 22; Stricklin, *Links, Lore, and Legends*, LOC 1153/3679.

Chapter 17

1. Donaly E. Brice, *The Great Comanche Raid: Boldest Indian Attack of the Texas Republic* (Austin: Eakin, 1989), 40; John Holland Jenkins III, ed., *Recollections of Early Texas: The Memoirs of John Holland Jenkins* (Austin: University of Texas Press, 1958), 65.

2. Brice, *Great Comanche Raid*, 38–48; Vivian Elizabeth Smyrl, "Caldwell County," in *The New Handbook of Texas*, ed. Ron Tyler et al., 6 vols. (Austin: Texas State Historical Association, 1996), 1:896–99.

3. Wayne Gard, "Retracing the Chisholm Trail," *Southwestern Historical Quarterly* 60, no. 1 (July 1956): 53–68.

4. Ibid., 57, 55.

5. Douglas Brinkley, *Rightful Heritage: Franklin D. Roosevelt and the Land of America* (New York: HarperCollins, 2016), 162.

6. Ibid., 173–75.

7. James Wright Steely, *Parks for Texas: Enduring Landscapes of the New Deal* (Austin: University of Texas Press, 1999), 104–5.

8. Leslie Alexander Lacy, *The Soil Soldiers: The Civilian Conservation Corps in the Great Depression* (Radnor, PA: Chilton, 1976), 101–2.

9. Dan K. Utley and James W. Steely, *Guided with a Steady Hand: The Cultural Landscape of a Rural Texas Park* (Waco: Baylor University Press, 1998), 36–44.

10. *Civilian Conservation Corps Official Annual*, n.d., 55–56, photocopied pages in the possession of Donaly Brice, Lockhart.

11. Ibid.

12. "Biographical Sketch," *A Guide to the David E. Colp Papers, 1917–1936*, Dolph Briscoe Center for American History, University of Texas at Austin, http://www.lib.utexas.edu/taro/utcah/01496/cah-01496.html.

13. CCC Camp Welcoming Edition, *Lockhart (TX) Post-Register*, Aug. 22, 1935, n.p.; "CCC Camp Gets Educational Advisor," ibid., Sept. 12, 1935, n.p. The article incorrectly gives the spelling of the adviser's name as "Milstedt" instead of "Milstead."

14. "Home Atmosphere Feature of Lockhart Recreation Hall," *Lockhart (TX) Post-Register*, Oct. 31, 1935, 2; "Lockhart Gets New Pictures," ibid., Oct. 10, 1935, 8; "Under the Court House Clock," ibid., n.d.; "CCC to be Guests Baker Show and Lockhart Merch'ts," ibid., Aug. 22, 1935, n.p.; "CCC Worker Crushed to Death in Gravel Pit Cave-In," ibid., July 30, 1936, 1.

15. "Co. 873 Transferred to Arizona," ibid., Oct. 31, 1935, 4, 5.

16. "Lockhart State Park Has Natural Setting," *Taylor (TX) Daily Press*, June 24, 1957, 5.

17. Steely, *Parks for Texas*, 216.

18. Ibid., 95; *Civilian Conservation Corps Official Annual*.

19. "Park Segregation Plan Is Offered to Legislature," *Corsicana (TX) Daily Sun*, Feb. 18, 1951; "Parks for Negroes Provided in Bill," *Valley Morning Star* (Harlingen, TX), Apr. 6, 1951, 11.

20. "Lockhart State Park Has Natural Setting," *Taylor (TX) Daily Press*, June 24, 1957, 5.

CHAPTER 18

1. Robert D. Thompson, *We'll Find the Way: The History of Hondo Army Air Field during World War II* (Austin: Eakin, 1992), 10–11.

2. "Hondo in Earnest about the Air Field," *Hondo (TX) Anvil Herald*, Feb. 20, 1942, 1; Thomas E. Alexander, *The Wings of Change: The Army Air Force Experience in Texas during World War II* (Abilene, TX: McWhiney Foundation Press, 2003), 47; untitled article, *Hondo (TX) Anvil Herald*, Feb. 6, 1942, 5; "Hondo in Earnest about the Air Field," ibid., Feb. 20, 1942, 1.

3. Thompson, *We'll Find the Way*, 12–15; Alexander, *Wings of Change*, 48.

4. Thompson, *We'll Find the Way*, 13, 19; Alexander, *Wings of Change*, 49.

5. "Work on Navigation School Progressing," *Hondo (TX) Anvil Herald*, Apr. 17, 1942, 1; "Welcome Soldiers," *Hondo (TX) Anvil Herald*, Aug. 14, 1942, 1; "Hondo Navigation School Is Activated," ibid.

6. Thompson, *We'll Find the Way*, 30, 138–46; Ruben E. Ochoa, "Hondo Army Airfield," in *The New Handbook of Texas*, ed. Ron Tyler et al., 6 vols. (Austin: Texas State Historical Association, 1996), 3:681–82.

7. Thompson, *We'll Find the Way*, 47–52.

8. Ibid., 55–60.

9. Ibid., 128–32; "Air Crash Claims Eleven," *Hondo (TX) Anvil Herald*, Sept. 7, 1945, 1; "Two Iowans Killed in Plane Crash," *Mount Pleasant (IA) News*, Oct. 19, 1945, 1.

10. Thompson, *We'll Find the Way*, 156–61; Alexander, *Wings of Change*, 50.

11. Advertisement, *San Antonio (TX) Express and News*, Feb. 18, 1962, 39; "Hondo Closing Final," *Corsicana (TX) Daily Sun*, Feb. 10, 1945, 10; Ochoa, "Hondo Army Airfield," 682.

12. "Volunteers Start Labor on Golf Course, Aug. 28," *Hondo (TX) Anvil Herald*, Aug. 27, 1954, 8.

13. "Native Texan Lt. Col. Riley Served Country in Hot and Cold Climates," *Hondo (TX) Anvil Herald*, July 23, 1954, 3A; "Riley Is Transferred; AB Commander Due," ibid., Sept. 16, 1955, 1; "Neel Dwyer Wins 1st in Riley Invitational," ibid., June 1, 1956, 12.

INDEX

Page numbers in *italic* refer to illustrations.

Wood, Leonard, 120–22
Woods, Tiger, 40
Woodruff, Jill, 160
Woodul, Walter, 34–35
Works Progress Administration (WPA), 202, 210, 219, 222
World Golf Hall of Fame, 190
World War I, 23, 97, 191–201, 209
World War II, 62, 67, 83, 140, 223–33

Yellow House Canyon, 91–92, 96; battle of, 94–95

yellow press journalism, 119
Young, Risley W., 200

Zachry, H. B. "Pat," 225–26
Zaharias, Mildred Ella "Babe" Didrickson, 85, 88
Zapata, Emiliano, 183
Zimmermann Telegram, 189